THE
ANGEL
Almanac

THE
A N G E L
Almanac

An inspirational guide for healing & harmony

Angela McGerr

Illustrations by Richard Rockwood

Quadrille

The pure energy of angels is woven with unconditional Love out of Light.
It descends in spirals from Above to mankind Below; these may be
accessed at any time through the heart and ascended through the soul.
Will you choose to follow the angels' spirals all the way to Sun, Moon,
Stars and beyond?

Look, how the floor of heaven
Is thick inlaid with patines of bright gold;
There's not the smallest orb which thou behold'st
But in his motion like an angel sings,
Still quiring to the young-eyed cherubins;
Such harmony is in immortal souls;
But, whilst this muddy vesture of decay
Doth grossly close it in, we cannot hear it.
– William Shakespeare, *Merchant of Venice*, Act V Scene 1

OTHER BOOKS BY ANGELA MCGERR

A Harmony of Angels

Harmony Angel Cards

Angelic Abundance

Gold & Silver Guardian Angels

An Angel for Every Day

Heart & Soul Angel Cards

The Angel Quest of the Heart

Love & Light Angel Cards

All published by Quadrille

VISIT THE AUTHOR'S WEBSITE:
www.angelamcgerr.com

Introducing The Angel Almanac

The Angel Almanac is a book about life transformation and healing with the wisdom of angels (also known as angelology). To travel the Way of Love and Light is a quest through this and many other lifetimes; this quest contains two aspects: heart and soul. The objective of this almanac is to aid you to travel further on the Way of Love and Light by pursuing your personal Heart Quest (self-healing and opening higher heart); this is linked to your Soul Quest (finding true physical and spiritual harmony: Oneness with All). The book is intended to be inspirational and instructional, as well as providing a practical reference guide to angelology for all those wishing to work daily with angels. The Angel Almanac is in three parts as follows.

PART ONE: THE ANGELIC YEAR is filled with topical channellings containing advice from a host of angels, combined with angelology instruction. This is designed to inspire you to set one or more true heart's desire or life change that you want to accomplish during the year, and actually work towards achieving it. Angels are always around us, but most of us cannot see them as their vibration is so much higher than our own. As you deepen your angelic connection you will increasingly sense their energy in your heart, hands and atmosphere around you. When angels leave our presence a kind of 'wing print' remains, an essence of Love and Light. If you act on the angels' advice, your heart will be lifted, your spirit healed, by this essence.

The Angelic Year traces the ancient symbol of the Wheel of Life. As it travels through Raphael's eight solar festivals of the year you can work with angels every day, including the rulers of elemental alchemy, to self-heal physically (Heart Quest) and spiritually (Soul Quest).

You can address key issues with Ophaniel and Gabriel by exploring the potential of the 28 Mansions of the Moon. By year's end you will have gradually become a true conduit for angelic energy as you link to All Above (Heaven) and All Below (Earth). The Angelic Year is undated, so it can be used year after year. This will continuously deepen your understanding and levels of working with angels.

PART TWO: WORKING WITH YOUR GUARDIAN ANGELS enables you to gain and build the necessary knowledge to be able to invite your relevant guardian angels – day of birth, zodiac, elemental, Quinary Star angel and personal guardian angel (on the CD) – into daily life: a truly life-transforming step.

PART THREE: ANGELIC HEALING FOR HEART AND SOUL is for self-healing and helping to heal others. Here, you will find information on colour and chakra healing, Ascension, an introduction to sacred geometry, the Cabbala Tree of Life, the Malachim angel alphabet as well as an A-Z of angels and their guardianships.

CD: Working daily with the angels is the key to deepening your personal angelic connection and the three meditations I voice on the CD in this book will also assist with this. Accompanied by Chas Cronk's lovely music, the first (with Cassiel) helps you find your personal guardian angel and begin to experience Oneness with All. The second meditation (with Melchisadec and Ithuriel) is about healing and balance, moving you towards true self in the etheric Crystal Temple. Then there is guidance on Sacred Breathing to enhance energy work (see also page 36) before the third meditation in which Pistis Sophia and other angels offer an angelic route to Oneness within heart (Unity Consciousness) and universal harmony.

ABOUT ANGELS AND ANGELOLOGY

As those of you who have read my other works will know, the philosophy of angelology contained in them is drawn from ancient wisdom, combined with modern information with which the angels have favoured me. Depictions of winged messengers are as ancient as the oldest of glyphs (Sumerian clay cylinder seals over 7,000 years old). The philosophy of angelology is c2,000 years old and linked to the Essenes, who believed that to work with angels every day was to find spiritual and physical harmony. So, angelology is the study of angels and harmony, but what exactly are angels? My own view is that angels can manifest in any form, from humanoid to geometric shapes or twinkling clouds of energy. In the early days, they did appear to me in meditation in humanoid form. I feel this is because they knew that at this time I would not otherwise recognise them. But in reality I believe they are *Spiritus Dei* – the Love and Light breath of the Creator. Light is of course also connected with colour and shades of colour; the higher the vibration the paler the colour, with the Seraphim (highest group of angels) at the pure, clear diamond vibration.

We need to raise (and keep raising) our own vibration to sense angels more easily. In this book we do that by self-healing, clearing blocks and gradually increasing our sophistication in how we connect with the angels. The first real connection (Heart Quest) is through healing and opening the higher heart with Love; this is the Love Factor. On the Soul Quest, as our vibration rises further, we can work with higher and higher groups of angels, until finally we can hold Angelic Light within our own higher heart. This, the Light Factor, means we can reach through the 44:44 Angel Star Gate to connect with the highest angelic realms of all: Seraphim, Star Angels of Creation, aiding our Personal and Planetary Ascension.

Why not start right now? Let the angels become your friends. Work with them every day and you will find yourself moving further on the Way of Love and Light. The choice is yours; Love is the Key.

Angelic wisdom for the spiritual journey, inspired by Essene angelology

THIS IS WHAT I TEACH MY STUDENTS:

Your spirit is eternal, for it is pure energy; energy can never die, only change form through transmutation.

All that happens in your life is in Divine Order and in accord with Divine Timing.

At every healing level you will face karmic challenges. Each challenge you face and surmount offers an opportunity to:
* demonstrate that you trust and surrender in your unfolding life path
* gain certain wisdom that enables spiritual development
* reach the next level of self-mastery.

There is a single source of All, also called The One. The quest is to reunite with All, finding Oneness, or Unity Consciousness.

This quest is in two parts:
* The Heart Quest resolves duality. It starts self-healing and finding masculine/feminine and physical/spiritual balance to third-eye level, culminating in opening the higher heart flower, an inner 'knowing'.

* The Soul Quest moves to crown, linked to the higher heart. Here there is no more duality – only Oneness, for you have moved into Unity Consciousness, and the role then is to aid others to find the Way of Love and Light.

Part One: The Angelic Year

The Wheel of Life is as old as time itself, and turns in accordance with the yearly cycle of eight solar festivals. In this book I name them as Raphael's festivals (see page 41 for more on Raphael, ruler of the Sun) although they have many names in other belief systems, being also known as the Wheel of Karma, Medicine Wheel, Celtic Wheel of Fire, or even Wheel of Fortune.

Each of the eight solar festivals is complete in itself, and so forms a Microcosm of the Macrocosm – All That Exists. Over the year the wheel covers the four seasons: Nature's cycle of preparation and seeding, birth, growth, flowering and re-seeding – in other words, life, death and re-birth. We, ourselves, can mirror this age-old miracle with death and re-birth as our transfiguration – a chance to change ourselves. As Raphael rules the sun and its healing and colour influence, if we are willing to put in the effort, the solstices of winter, spring, summer and autumn and their angels will aid us. Each festival offers its individual promise, while overall the eight festivals are a time to self-heal as well as birth, grow, enjoy and conclude something brand new in life, like a quest to achieve a heart's desire: the Heart Quest.

The alternate festivals during the year are heavenly keys traditionally linked with Elemental Alchemy Angels, respectively earth, water, air and fire. We must also take into account that Raphael's solar rays concern masculine balance, while Gabriel, ruler of the moon's lunar rays are feminine. Whatever gender you are born in, your personality will have a mix of masculine and feminine attributes. Masculine aspects (solar chakra) are logical thought processes, decision-making ability, and taking appropriate and timely action. Feminine aspects (heart chakra) are intuition, feelings, emotions and hunches. It is the balance between the two that is vital. During the alternative festivals the Alchemy Angels ask us to focus on our Soul Quest, as the two quests underpin each other. Through heeding the angelic words and wisdom we can first work to heal and balance our solar and lunar aspects to third-eye level, then,if ready, progress to crown chakra with Metatron and Shekinah. These mighty beings, the guardian angels of the Tree of Life (also known as the Sacred Eden Tree) gradually aid us to make and deepen our links to All.

At the end of the section covering the eight solar festivals we turn our attention to the thirteen lunar cycles in any year, each containing 28 Mansions (days), each with its own angel. For the reasons explained above, the lunar influence in our life is extremely important for balance. But in addition to this the angel Ophaniel oversees the full 28-day lunar cycle. This cycle can be utilised in a completely different way: by working with the Mansions of the Moon angels you can undertake specific activities according to what is actually happening or needs to be addressed in your life.

EARTH: Conceiving and birthing a quest for a more
fulfilled life

Farlas, Guardian Angel of Winter says:

*My festival is a time of muted colours: of brown, purple and
grey – an apparent absence of Light. While frost embroiders
the earth, I enfold sleeping nature with my strong wings,
protecting her secrets from the elements, knowing the darkest
time is turning, making way for Light to return. But although
all seems lifeless, nothing is further from the truth. Even now
new buds are forming and as the sun returns, Mother Earth
awakens. This is merely her time of conserving strength and
biding time; coming soon is the promise of birth or re-birth.*

*This is also your chance to conceive something new: a quest
towards true heart's desires in line with your soul journey. On
dark days I urge you to shine your own Light within to
illuminate where your heart wishes to be at the end of the
coming year, for as acorn leads to oak and back to acorn, all
is in cycles and cannot remain the same.*

*As winter draws towards its close, little by little I open my
wings to embrace the sun. My subtle monochromes acquire
brighter hues as I allow nature to begin her age-old, magical
transformation once more. Your own desire for change can
start this same moment and, if you harmonise with all solar
festivals, your quest will lead you to greater balance at year's
end, when I gladly extend my wings towards you once again.*

Commencing your quest

The angels advise how to start a quest to change self or life this year. Choose which of these messages resonates most in your heart, and work with this angel to conceive your change. To invoke the angel you chose, see page 16 or 36.

Dokiel, Guardian Angel of Balance:

It is time to consider whether or not you are happy. Do you love your work, your life and, more importantly, yourself unequivocally? I am called the weighing angel, who holds all aspects of you in the balance. If you feel all is not completely well in this respect then I give you this opportunity to correct the situation. First, determine your priority. Then you may call on me to support you in bringing unconditional love into the equation, to effect a truer balance for your future.

Isiael, Guardian Angel of the Future:

The future is not fixed and immutable – you can influence it if you try. Like time, it is fluid, with certain points at which your decisions are made, and these will change both the flow of time and future outcomes irrevocably. So, if your future seems uncertain, work with me: apply positive thought and energy to conceive something new and then together we can make it happen!

Salathiel, Guardian Angel of Seekers:

If you are one who chooses to read and absorb the words of angels then you are a Seeker after Truth. Now is the time when your Way may be found, and your inner self revealed, for you have much strength that you have had to conceal in the past because of others. Like the old year, this time has passed, and you can decide to set your heart free. Forgiveness will be needed, as you have waited long for this moment, but I urge you to cast aside the veils and step into your personal power, for the good of All.

Cambiel, Ruler of January and Aquarius:

Bring me your aspirations so that I can guide your spiritual steps. In this festival when Farlas and Ariel advocate earth and re-birth for you, through my zodiac sign I encompass fire and water. This means that if you so choose, I assist you by holding all three energies in balance for this period of time. Like sun, my fire empowers you to act, while like moon my water aids calmness and your intuitive skills; if this is what you need right now in your life, call on me and I will answer your call until progress is made.

Working with angels: step one

LEARNING THE POWER OF THE WORD OR LOGOS

Though they can appear in any form, I believe that angels are *Spiritus Dei*, the breath of the Creator, essence of Love and Light. When we pronounce an angel name out loud this is a sacred sound, a pure vibration like a mini-prayer. The first connection you can make is to invoke the sacred name three times, from the heart with loving intent, as this 'calls in' the angelic ray. You can learn to feel this energy on your hands, within your heart or crown, or simply enfolding you. When you've learnt this you can move on to more sophisticated ways of connecting – see page 36.

THE SACRED LAW OF THREE OF HERMES TRISMEGISTOS

Why do you call an angel's name three times? Because to follow the sacred Law of Three maximises the energy of our invocations. There are many examples of the power of three: religious trinities of Father, Son and Holy Spirit; Isis, Osiris, Horus; the three Magi of the Bible. The composition of the world: animal, vegetable, mineral; of man: carbon, oxygen, hydrogen, who is also mind, body, spirit; the measurement of time: past, present, future. More importantly, perhaps, from Hermes Trismegistos/Thoth's Emerald Tablets we learn, amongst other things:

* Three is the mystery, come from the great One. Hear, and Light on thee will dawn.
* Three are the qualities of God in his Light-home: infinite Power, infinite Wisdom, infinite Love.
* Three are the Paths of the Soul: Man, Liberty, Light.

MAKING THE INVOCATION FROM YOUR HEART

Hold out your hands palms up and relax them. Call on your chosen angel by name three times, and then make your request, e.g. *Raphael, Raphael, Raphael, please be with me, in Love and Light, Love and Light, Love and Light* (this shows positive and honest intent). Always thank the angel once you have completed your request for help.

THE ANGELIC RESPONSES YOU MAY FEEL (INVOLVING ONE OR MORE SENSES)

TOUCH: you may feel one or more of the following:
* Tingling or tickling around fingers or palms, particularly in the left hand (the left is the 'taking' hand in Universal terms, while the right is the 'giving' hand, though occasionally this may be reversed).
* You could find yourself aware of energy flowing within the body.
* Warmth on palms, in heart, or gently flooding your whole being.
* Coolness on fingers, palms, wrists or along arms.
* Soft, gentle, yet strong pressure on the hands, arms or fingers.

SIGHT: depending on whether your eyes are open or closed:
* A brief, bright flash of light in your mind.
* A glimpse of the angel or a symbolic creature.
* A sparkling in the air, or swirling mist, on the edge/periphery of vision.
* A subtle change in the quality of how the air feels around you.

SMELL: a sudden fragrance that comes and goes. You wonder if you really smelled this scent or imagined it! Then it comes again.

SOUND: tones, faint booming or drumming sounds within your ear(s).

Impulse births desire

Yusamin, Guardian Angel of Fertility, offers advice:
I am fashioned from Light itself, and within my wings I hold the sum of all you could possibly have achieved in your past, or will in your present and future. For I encapsulate every potential opportunity and heart's desire that your fertile brain could seize and make its own. Though the past may be gone, I heal it for you, and it is I who can aid you to conceive something new in your life from now onwards, whether your quest is fertility of body, or mind.

Of course not all these opportunities bear fruit, because your life is about choices. The paths can vary, according to each and every decision you make, but with my help pure Light shines around you, offering clarity with the different routes. With this, an informed choice is possible, because your quest should be a true heart's desire that is also in line with your soul journey.

At this point in the year all is permissible; do not lose this special facility that I offer you. For the fertility I bring comes from the wellsprings of Light and, if you breathe it in with me and absorb it into your heart, it chases away those past disappointments, dark or wasted chances, making space for a brand new impulse to be generated. From this impulse you can perceive a true heart's desire and it is I who helps you with the fertility of thought processes, to create a real quest to pursue during the year until it is made manifest with Love.

Allowing the angels in

These angelic messages give advice about whatever quest or new start you'd like to address, and how to make space for the angels to bring you messages.

Sandalphon, Guardian Angel of Prayer and Meditation:

I ask you this question: how often do you do even a simple meditation? No time, you say? My reply to you is that it is difficult to guide your prayers, heart's desires or true aspirations if you do not give me the opportunity. For it is I who listens to what you express from your heart and conveys this to Heaven on your behalf, as brilliant flowers of purple and red. You can choose to allow me to help you in this way, for whilst you are in meditation I return guidance back to your heart.

Eth, Guardian Angel of Time:

Perhaps you feel that if you only had time, you could consider what you really want in life? It is true that whatever knowledge you seek is already there, now, in the heart of your heart, but perhaps you don't know how to access it? Meditation is a way to do this, and I can help to expand time for you in your life, for your highest good, so that you can unlock the secret of your 'now'.

Recharge your batteries

During this mid-winter festival you may need to re-charge physical or spiritual energy. Angels advise on self-healing with relevant colours of brown, purple, and deep wine red.

Mumiah, Guardian Angel of Wellbeing:

As winter draws on, and spring is still some way off, perhaps you are feeling right at this moment that your batteries need to be re-charged? Call my name and visualise my ray as deepest wine red, filled with sparkles of life-force energy. Sit quietly and breathe this in, as deeply as you can. Will and intend it first to empower your heart, pumping new vitality around your body, and then send it to your head to energise your thoughts towards right actions.

Ariel, Ruler of the Elements of Earth and Air:

If there is purple and deep red-brown in your life and you love placing your hands in my earth, then you are very grounded. Yet to find harmony and new aspirations you must also prepare for your mind to spring forth into my blue-mauve air. Root and twig be ready to reach out, grow towards the sky and fulfil your destiny, for to reach from earth to sky is to begin to free mind, body and spirit.

EARTH: The grounding from which spirit is re-born

Ariel, Guardian of Earth and Air, says:

I rule the elements of earth and air and the marriage of the two, by which I mean the very life of your world as well as its conjoining with other dimensions beyond your own. Earth sustains your physical self, while air, Breath of Life, brings spiritual manna or nourishment. Bridge the two on my shining violet Light wings as you commence your spiritual re-birth.

First we work on your grounding in this reality, so you have a safe foundation from which to be re-born. I bring deepest purples and magenta, sparkling with crystalline vitality into your life, to allow forgiveness for the past and form foundations for the future. During my earth festival I offer you steps for emotional grounding, transmuting negative thought processes, preparing you for a position of earthly strength.

Imagine yourself enjoying a new start within my earth, a tiny, perfect seed that Mother Earth and I love, nurture and protect. As you grow, earth heals you, for it is capable of absorbing all negativity that arises during this process. As the season turns, Raphael's sun warms you and you safely reach the surface. When you burst through you turn your face to the sun and sky, ready to flower and form a new seed for the future; thus the shining seed of your spirit emerges at last from the veils that hid its secrets and perfection from Light.

Overcoming obstacles

The angels suggest ways to help you focus more on positive energy and spiritual re-birth.

Haadiah, one of the 72 Quinary Star Guardian Angels:

The winter nights may still be long and dark, but the sublime melody of the Quinary angels comes to you always from the starry night sky. We connect to you through the flower of your heart, for one of us resides within its petals. If you are star-born and wish to be guided towards your star path, work with your own Quinary guardian angel and the power of Love until you emerge through the veils from darkness into Light.

Barakiel, Zodiac Ruler of February and Pisces:

If you feel the troubles of the world too deeply, then you can invoke me for aid and spiritual protection. However, do not dwell on negative aspects of world issues, for this just adds to and exacerbates them. Keep sending positive Love and Light energy out through your heart, and you will really help to counteract those dark situations, making a valuable contribution to heal Mother Earth who returns this to you with gratitude to aid your own quest.

Rikbiel, Guardian Angel of Power of Love:

My symbol is a Light Chariot filled with Love. Think of this as winged, moving ever onwards, its path undeviating in the cause of disseminating the Creator's Love and Light, with the power to solve all problems. It is goodness that powers the wheels, truth that sets the course, while beauty guides my Chariot on its unswerving course to illuminate your life from now onwards.

Pistis Sophia, Heavenly and Earthly Mother:

I am the Heavenly Mother whose love does not judge. Like an earthly mother I encourage and support your lifelong learning about your world. At the same time I nourish your spirit, sustaining you with self-belief through trials and tribulations until you reach your personal goals. Though you may not see me, I applaud your victories, so be aware of and draw on my loving presence at this, the start of your journey through the eternal Wheel of Life towards greater harmony and balance.

Guardian angels and energy vibration

CALLING ON ANGELS

All angels can be called upon at any time – their energy is omnipresent in our universe. Do not feel guilty about calling on them. They welcome our invocations, so long as we have loving will and intent, for their true role as designated by the Creator is to bring us support through unconditional love.

THE THREE TIERS (HIERARCHIES) OF ANGELS

There are three tiers of angels, each containing a triad (three groups). At the top, closest to the Creator, are Seraphim, Cherubim and Thrones. The second triad is Dominions, Powers and Virtues. The third triad (formerly nearest mankind) comprises Angel Princes (or Principalities), Archangels and Angels. These nine groups encompass all qualities or virtues of the Creator, to which we should aspire. Once it was thought that mankind could only communicate with the lowest triad. Now I believe that if we open our higher hearts, and keep working with angels to raise our own vibration, we are able to commune with all three, including the Seraphim who are guiding the Ascension. It is a question of combining heart with an intention guided by love, beauty and compassion.

ANGELS' WINGS

A white feather is a symbol of spirituality that we recognise as being a communication from angels, but if we see an angel in humanoid form the wings are actually shining streamers of Light, stretching out on either side, hence angels are sometimes called the Shining Ones.

WHAT ARE GUARDIAN ANGELS?

It is not just each individual who has a guardian angel (in fact several), but every single thing in the universe also has a designated guardian angel. All guardian angels are responsible for supporting with unconditional love, but they cannot interfere with free will, as given to humans, so we have to choose whether or not we invite these and other angels into our lives. And of course we should bear in mind that our free will affects other sentient life forms.

Apart from our guardian angel assigned from birth, other special angels are the angel ruling the weekday on which we were born, the ruler of our zodiac sign, and one of the three elemental angels, according to whether our zodiac sign is earth, air, water or fire. Finally we have a star guardian angel: one of the 72 Quinary Angels ruling the heavens. On the CD and in Part Two of this book you will be guided on how to identify your various guardian angels.

Grounding, balancing and harmonising with the Caduceus

The Caduceus image opposite (equated with the Tree of Life) is an ancient symbol of grounding, balance and healing. The staff itself (*sushumna* in Sanscrit) signifies Ariel's earth wisdom, plus grounding of the physical self, joining with his air wisdom – Breath of Life and third-eye spiritual connection. This is the meeting between physical and spiritual worlds, yet also represents the human spine, thus manifesting this energy for self-healing and healing All. Entwining the staff are two (gold and silver) snakes of wisdom (*ida* and *pingala* in Sanscrit) for balance of both solar (Raphael) and lunar (Gabriel) energy.

As mentioned earlier, the sun's rays influence masculine balance, and the moon's rays are feminine. Your personality (affecting all energy centres) blends masculine and feminine attributes (duality). The first priority of Caduceus healing is to be grounded and to balance these aspects for your ultimate highest good. The snakes' crossing points over the staff (spine) represent six of the seven main chakras (base to third eye) as the Caduceus aids balance to that point where duality ends. From crown chakra there is only Unity (Oneness).

Work firstly with the Caduceus/Tree of Life on the next pages (see also *Harmony Angel Cards* or *Gold & Silver Guardian Angels*) as often as you need to, to attain solar and lunar balance. Then consider the material on page 48 at the next level of vibration. This begins to move you on towards the vibration of the Sacred Eden Tree itself, gateway to the 44:44 Angel Star Gate, with Metatron (white-silver) and Shekinah (white-gold), in a series of increasingly spiritually powerful exercises culminating in Sacred Eden Tree 3 on page 88.

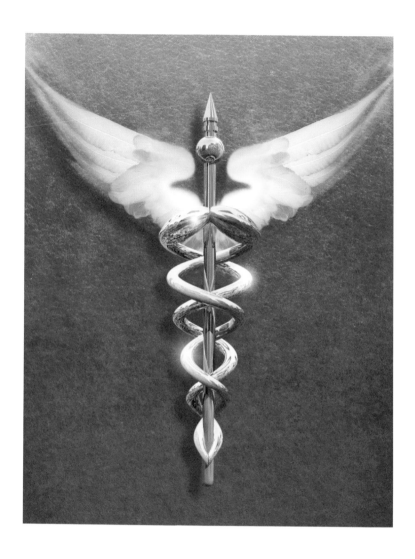

Working with the Tree of Life

- Invoke Raphael, Gabriel and Ariel.
- Hold your arms above, either side of you, making the Tree of Life shape, visualising your spine as the trunk of the Tree, your crown in air, Breath of Life, and your roots in the heart of Mother Earth.
- Say: My *will and intention is to become Tree of Life reaching from All Above down to the heart of Mother Earth, and from there to All Below.*
- Now draw down the solar and lunar energy spirals, using your own spine and Ariel's connection, to manifest gold and silver healing energies of sun and moon to heal and balance polarities within Mother Earth. In gratitude, Mother Earth will send energy to aid your own healing and balancing.
- Visualise the two bright, shining rays (snakes of wisdom) starting to spiral back up your spine, with gold spirals from left and silver spirals from right. You may actually feel this, but even if you don't, be assured it is still happening.
- The spiral snakes of wisdom cross each chakra centre in turn (they will cross six times). As they do so you can mentally say, starting from base chakra: *Please heal and balance me: left and right, masculine and feminine, ida and pingala, sun and moon, silver and gold, earth and air, in Love and Light, Love and Light, Love and Light.*
- As you complete your request, the two rays link back to your third-eye chakra, and when you have attained the right level of balance, you will start to feel them move to crown. At this point you can move to the first Sacred Eden Tree exercise, see page 48.
- If you feel you need to, or have a block preventing a feeling of balance, work separately with Raphael and Gabriel (or Metatron and Shekinah) in their exercises for gold and silver healing starting on page 208.
- Remember to thank Raphael, Gabriel and Ariel for their help.

WATER: Nourishing and growing your heart's desire

Spugliguel, Guardian Angel of Spring, says:

My festival is one of great beauty, promise and vigour. As a fern uncoils towards the warming sun, I tenderly unfurl my wings of leaf green, yellow, aqua and blue, giving direction to nature. All is possible, for this is the time when according to the strength of the roots, the greatest advance will be made. What is needed for this surge is water, the essential element for both mankind and nature, without which there is neither germination nor growth of even one of nature's seeds.

As my season progresses and Phuel's Water of Life flows into Mother Earth, my shining Light wings form a vivid green halo over the land and my colours deepen in strength, signifying triumphant new vitality. I send fast-flowing, regenerative, life-force energy that helps nature ensure all plants grow strongly, forming the flowers and seeds they need to guarantee survival. In mankind this spring survival instinct manifests as a time to follow your desire – a quest for change, for development, for love, for fulfilment.

Winter birthed your first impulse for change, creating and planting the seed of desire in the earth. Spring gives strength to the impulse; Water of Life nurtures your heart with energy and enthusiasm, and as my Love lifts your desire towards its flowering, together we propel your quest into vibrant reality.

How to progress your quest

Zuphlas, Guardian Angel of Trees, says:

See yourself as being like one of my trees. You may be young and slender, or older and a little gnarled, but it is never too late to nurture your new, life-changing desires. What is important is that your roots (foundations) are firm and strong, and your branches (aspirations) touch the sky. If it is strength that you need for your new ideas to take shape, take a newly unfurled leaf from one of my re-awakened trees and view its delicate, fine symmetry; its design is perfect for its purpose. Imagine yourself to be one with a leaf, that derives its nourishment and strength from the branches, but these in turn are sustained by the roots within Mother Earth herself. Connect and invoke me to help you with strength and sustenance, to better follow your quest.

Zadkiel, Guardian Angel of Jupiter and Thursday:

I am the power of Jupiter, abundance, wisdom and success. If you need one of my qualities then call my name, and if possible hold (and programme in meditation) one of my crystals of lapis lazuli or turquoise. These can aid you with the wisdom to know whether or not you are asking for something for your highest good, as well as to recognise your abundance when you receive it.

Isiael, Guardian Angel of Prophecy
or Phanuel, Guardian of Atonement:

Are you held back by the realisation that your future is blocked by your past? You must let go of past issues, and resulting energy imbalances, before we angels can begin to aid you with your future. If you determine what you need to do, you can invoke one of us to work with you on this, so that you can start to transform into the person you are meant to be.

Ithuriel, Guardian Angel of True Self:

As the chrysalis does not know it will become the beautiful butterfly, so do you not know the true beauty of your inner self. Set yourself free, with my aid, and become the unfettered spirit that you were destined to be, before life enclosed you in chains of your own making and acceptance. It is not too late to free yourself and be transformed, but you are the one who must make the choice.

Ruhiel, Guardian Angel of Winds:

I bring you the message of the winds, be they soft and soothing breezes heralding spring, or strong, full of power and potential, reminding us that earth is yet still clothed in winter. All will be apparent at some point at this time of the year. Call upon me to blow some fresh meaning into your life, according to what you need, and you may be sure that I will answer your call.

Working with angels: step two

SACRED BREATHING OF ANGELIC ENERGY

On the CD accompanying this book, immediately before the third meditation, I teach you how to do a form of sacred breathing. This is very simple, yet effective in holding energy within your heart in a special way, maximising its effect. But even more importantly, it is said that All That Is dwells in the pause between the sacred in-breath and sacred out-breath of the Creator. I believe that we can add this wonder to our angelic invocation (as I taught on page 16) and sacred breathing. In the pause, we actually connect directly to the angelic vibration and hold this within our hearts for those few seconds.

The reason is that when we mentally invoke the angel three times, and simultaneously breathe in the specific energy of that angel, we are breathing in also the subtle vibration of what that angel represents. For example, if we take a sacred in-breath and at the same time invoke Raphael, we are breathing in angelic healing rays of sun and holding these in our heart. Therefore when we take these breaths with the aid of the angels, there is limitless potential in what we can achieve with them, provided that we have loving and honest intention. If we work at this the angels help us to become ready to carry a higher and higher energy vibration within; this is a step towards changing from carbon to gem (Divine) self. This means a stronger immune system, a deeper connection with All, and therefore we gradually attain physical and spiritual harmony and balance.

HEART SONG OF ANGELS

There is nothing purer, sweeter or clearer than angelic energy. Although, like the music of the spheres, most of us don't hear it, we can sense it through our heart. If you could hear it, it would be like the most beautiful, sublime melody ever written. When you call in an angel, breathe this essence of Love and Light into your heart; then trust and surrender to the beauty of angels.

UNITY CONSCIOUSNESS AND ONENESS WITH ALL

These are linked states and have different levels of meaning. Oneness firstly means being joined through the higher heart to everything in earth and sky, and feeling love and compassion for any and all sentient life, from mankind to trees, plants, animals, birds and insects – even earth, rock, crystal and mountain. Unity Consciousness takes a wider view, and to me implies also working in the level of unfallen, pure Light through the higher heart; a Oneness that goes far beyond this world into the universe and multiverse; this means respecting All, helping to heal All, working for the benefit of All. I shall explain more of this as the Wheel of Life rolls onwards.

Furthering your true heart's desires

Pagiel, Guardian Angel of Heart's Desire, says:

This is the festival of the year when you can truly focus with me on achieving your heart's desire, that you birthed in mid-winter, for your highest good. Regard my image, and visualise yourself as the flower that my wings tenderly enclose. See how my delicate colours of rose and gold, and Phuel's emerald water, surround you. The gold aids your resolve, while the rose and emerald-green are also vital, for these are the colours of love, growth and expansion that also calm and heal your heart of hurts. For so many of you are held back by damage in the personal heart that blocks your own bright future.

This can be the start of a mystical journey – one that we angels say is part of your Heart Quest. When your heart is healed your focus and your love can spread outwards, like the Flower of Life fractal on my image, into all aspects of daily life and physical existence. Then, when you feel ready, we urge you to move on to consider your soul path, for the Soul Quest is a desire to use the higher heart to help heal Mother Earth and All Life. To begin this journey, use my colours and other delicate shades of this season, to clear some of these blocks within you and help you manifest the heart's desire you want to achieve this year. Then we will gladly guide you on to other colours, priorities and goals.

Increasing your awareness

Angels urge you to value and appreciate the beauty that exists all around you.

Zephon, Guardian Angel of Awareness:

When you look at nature you can see the Creator's work, pure and unsullied, vibrant with all Colours of Creation. But better still if you also interact with Creation itself. Touch the leaves, spiral pinecones or smooth tree bark. The very geometry of a seed or crystal is echoed in mankind. Run sand through your hands; this is quartz, a crystal of general healing.

There is simplicity and magic here if you would but become more aware of it. It is my role to heighten your awareness of all around you, to enhance your appreciation of what is really important, and to help you open your consciousness to new opportunity. In this season re-examine your own core values, separate your needs from your wants, and determine a new way forward into harmony with All.

Haniel, Ruler of Venus and Friday:

Have you ever wondered why you feel so peaceful in a special, green and gentle place of nature? One reason is because you are instinctively absorbing the many different shades of the colour and, as you now know, healing your personal heart chakra. The heart can then expand into love, joy and happiness, opening the higher heart chakra of pink: the bridge to the soul.

Help in decision making

Learn to focus on the solar and heart chakras in order to make informed and balanced decisions.

Raphael, Ruler of the Sun and Sunday:

Yellow and gold are my colours, and they can be used for willpower and to balance your masculine aspects. Breathe them in with my sun rays to the solar chakra, to help you take the decisions you need to work towards your heart's desire, though only when properly thought through. For what is important is that you combine powers of will and mind and heart, basing your decisions and actions on all three, for then they will be for your highest good.

Gabriel, Ruler of the Moon and Monday:

I work with Phuel, for the waters of his tides are governed by my moon powers. Together we bring silver, green and palest aqua to aid your emotions and creative ability and to balance the feminine within you, no matter what your gender. Breathe in these shades to help heal and empower the heart, so that your decisions and actions are, as Raphael says, truly balanced.

WATER OF LIFE: Helps your re-born spirit to prepare for flight

Phuel: Lord of the Waters, Powers of the Moon:

Mine are all the waters of earth, from the mighty, turbulent seas from which your ancestors first crawled on to the land, to emerald lakes, bubbling streams and tiny pools. I guard and guide every one of them for they are my playgrounds and yours (for you are mainly composed of water) and in the contrast between them the understanding of my powers will be found.

At this glorious time I speak of my smallest duty of care: the clear and sparkling drop of morning dew on the velvety May Day flower, for dew is borne out of Ariel's air, Breath of Life, to manifest as my Water of Life on Mother Earth. Bathe your face in morning dew and sense its strong yet gentle power in heart and soul. Connect with Ariel and me, for my message tells you of the link between water and air: both elements hold alchemy to nourish your newly determined spiritual re-birth.

Let my Water of Life metaphorically flow around you, a dazzling stream to bring you calmness and clarity so that you can see where to fly, for like my mystical dragonfly you will soar from water into air on rainbow wings, as your spiritual consciousness rises. Even more important, now, that Water of Life continues to nurture you, so that growth is strong and sturdy, your quest leading ever onwards and upwards, further into the sky and Light.

Learn from the creatures of the earth

Thuriel, Guardian Angel of Wild Animals, advises you on respecting his creatures and instructs on messages he sends via real animals or even relevant photographs or pictures you may see:

At this time of the year you may walk in parks or countryside. If you are alone and proceed quietly you may see the playful fox, the timid deer, or other creatures that graze, burrow or leap over Mother Earth. Perhaps they regard you warily, for in general they have much to fear from mankind. But send them love, for do they not have as much right as you to be there? Respect All in your heart, and All will likewise respect you as well as guide you.

* *A deer shows a current need for circumspection and gentleness over a certain issue, urging you to avoid force and dogmatism.*

* *A bull means you should stand firm and be patient in a certain situation, for if you can do this it will soon be resolved.*

* *A fox is a symbol that you should make a proper plan for whatever you wish to start, for then the outcome will be more satisfactory.*

For further guidance, see Moon Wisdom, starting on page 94.

Anpiel, Guardian Angel of Wild Birds, speaks of caring for his wild birds, as well as their spiritual meanings. If you see a group of the same species there is also numerical significance:

When you see one of my birds, or hear a fluting call, open your heart and invoke me to help you send them love, for love costs nothing yet means so much. Be vigilant for signs from me when you see certain of my birds, for these hold subtleties of spiritual meaning for you:

* *A robin is a sign from a dead loved one or spirit guide, who wishes to show you that he/she is always near you and loves you.*

* *A swan means transformation or important spiritual development is imminent. Watch or ask for further guidance that will come.*

* *A lark tumbling in the sky tells of freedom and urges you to speak your truth now before it is too late.*

* *A peacock or peacock feather links to green and suggests you research nature's secrets in some way, for you are, or will be, close to nature and the animal kingdom.*

Energy vibration, Unity Consciousness, Personal and Planetary Ascension

Once earth and mankind (Adam Kadmon) had a high vibration full of peace and love, but this vibration has fallen through man's misdeeds. The first fall was said to be that of Lucifer, who became chief of the Fallen Angels and took many angels (none in this book) with him after his rebellion. There was the fall over Eden, a loss in vibration through intermingling of races with the Nephilim (giant ones). The Adam Kadmon divine template that had been created was later lost. The final fall was during Atlantean times, when man misused crystal energy for his own ends, resulting in the complete destruction of Atlantis.

The Ascension will happen when there is enough Love and Light present to allow us and Mother Earth to regain our former vibration: when all sentient life is One with All. If we wish to aid Mother Earth to regain her pure vibration – the vibration of peace that she enjoyed before the falls – we can start by working towards Personal Heart Ascension. This can be attained with the help of the angels by opening the flower within our hearts and filling this flower with Love and Light. A true desire to send out this energy in fractals can take us from carbon towards our gem self, thus we can greatly increase the Love and Light quotient in Mother Earth herself. Therefore at the same time as we move towards Oneness with All, we aid Mother Earth to do the same.

The Tree of Life/Sacred Eden Tree and 44:44 Angel Star Gate

A key step towards Ascension is to work with the Tree of Life. At a certain vibration this is also known as the Sacred Eden Tree; its guardians are Metatron: Above (at crown, or *Kether*), and Shekinah: Below (at roots, Earthly Kingdom or *Malkuth*). The tree is a bridge between Above and Below, that connects to the 44:44 Angel Star Gate, about which more later.

Because Above and Below are in fact the same when we reach Oneness, in ancient prints the roots are sometimes shown at the top, and the crown of the Tree of Life at the bottom. In fact the roots and branches of the Sacred Eden Tree finally become joined together to form a complete circle, because the Eden Tree is an allegory of our own personal journey to Unity Consciousness or Oneness, and One is All. This circle of course mirrors the Wheel of Life and the Star Gate itself.

You may have worked with the Caduceus and Tree of Life up to this point and feel you have attained, or are steadily attaining, energy balance to third eye. Now you will be able to move on to start to work within the Eden Tree, and its guardians, Metatron and Shekinah, who guide you to Oneness.

Metatron and Shekinah, Twin Guardians of the Tree of Life, say:

In midwinter your days are short and Light in your world seems fleeting. We urge you to use this opportunity to focus on growing your Light within. This is the spark of divine Light that resides in your own higher heart and, through your will and intention, this spark can be fanned into pure white angelic Light of the 'flame that does not burn'.

Our Sacred Eden Tree is the archetype of all trees on earth, as well as the means of mankind returning, through the power of Love to the pure Angelic Light spectrum. The master number of all angels is 444 (unconditional love), but as guardians of the Sacred Eden Tree we embody 44:44, for the Eden Tree also accesses the Angel Star Gate. This is the portal between the fallen Light of most of mankind's present reality and the pure Angelic Light (that of Mother Earth before the falls). Together with the Eden Tree we form a bridge of Love and Light that can allow you access through the Star Gate.

The first priority is to have worked to balance your solar and lunar aspects with the Caduceus; secondly, with the Tree of Life vibration (white-gold and white-silver). Then, as you attain balance and begin to move to the white crown chakra in pursuit of Oneness, you take this wisdom back to your higher heart. Having made this link you can take the third magical step and go within, to become One with us and our Sacred Eden Tree vibration – truly a major leap on your Soul Quest and the Way of Love and Light.

Time to simplify

In this festival of May and June, you are now at a point when you may need to let go of certain things to follow your truth and quest.

Tual, Guardian Angel of the Zodiac Sign of Taurus:
My star form of the bull signifies strength and vigour, plus my horns radiate unconquerable power, yet also they guard and protect. If you need my qualities call on me, especially during my time of dominion, for I help you to develop and conserve these special attributes.

If you are one who suffers from tension or pain in upper back and shoulders, it may be because your dependability and reliability cause you to be overloaded. Though you have much inner strength, it does not extend to refusing to aid others, even to your own detriment. You can invoke my name to give you the means to say no, in order to safeguard your own precious health.

Michael, Guardian Angel of Wednesday and Mercury:

All that exists is energy; Light is All That Is. My Light Sword holds the power that shows you all levels of truth. Do you wish you were living your truth? Call my name to aid you at any time and remember that Love is the Key.

To angels there are no favoured ones. Rest assured that you are all favoured. Do not feel that by calling on us you are bothering us, or that we have preferences, for our role is to offer mankind unconditional love, to support equally all those who choose to seek our assistance. We cannot win your battles for you, but we can aid you with the strength to address karmic issues, surmount challenge and move ever onwards, spiritually, on the Way of Love and Light, towards personal, and through this, absolute, truth.

Phuel, Lord of the Waters of Earth:

Spring is the time when water is of utmost importance for all to grow, but water has many guises and aspects. A still blue-green pool of my water holds a perfect reflection of you, but ruffle the water and it fragments. Is your life still or fragmented? If the latter, call on me to bring the emotional calmness that you need to return your life to stillness. Only from a position of calm can you consider how to develop your newly birthed ideas, desires or quest.

AIR: Your quest leads to abundant, joyful and airy thoughts

Tubiel, Guardian Angel of Summer, says:

As the delicate shades of spring make way for summer's brilliance, I shake my Light wings and perfume caresses your senses, wafting on the breeze to enfold you in gladness. This is the time of Air, Breath of Life, when the seeds sown earlier in the year, will, if watered and nurtured carefully in spring, reach glorious flowering. My season is one of great profusion, filled with fragrance and colour as nature wears her most radiant garments; you, too, can wear bright colours to express your joyful mood as you celebrate your accomplishments.

In mid-winter Ariel urged you towards firm foundations to ground and birth your quest towards a heart's desire. Phuel's mid-spring water allowed your desire to grow towards Light. As rising sap caused nature's plants to burst into life, filled with morning dew and promise, this promise found resonance in your own body, especially your heart. Now, I hope the promise is fulfilled in a swirl of bright summer air. So send your thoughts soaring and delight in what you have achieved on your quest so far. As my festival continues I festoon the land with emerald, bronze, violet, crimson and vivid blue – the colours of determination, courage, action and truth, preparing to take you yet further as the year progresses, for who knows how far you will go?

Advice for the mid-summer festival

Verchiel, Ruler of July and the Sign of Leo:

I rule the star sign of Leo, the Lion, a sovereign creature of indomitable power and strength on earth, but who also connects through the power of sun to life-force energy. Therefore if you call on me you make this connection, from sun to earth and back through sun to stars. In ancient times it was said that I erased my footprints with my tail, therefore some of my power is concealed, except to those who seek through heart and soul the Way of Love and Light.

Sahaqiel, Guardian Angel of the Sky:

Mine is the angel-wing cloud, a cloud of knowing. You glance at the blue summer sky as if (but not really) by chance, and there it is, above you. When you look at this cloud with the eye of your heart, suddenly something clicks into place; it all seems so right and your heart can perceive, hold and understand a little of the true mystery of All. Ask me to help you identify how this understanding furthers your quest.

Colour healing messages

Hahlii, Guardian Angel of Colours:

As the bright sun of summer streams down and pure crystal divides his glory, a kaleidoscope of colours is created – nine colours of Creation. Together with gold and silver these form masculine/ feminine balance and, as they blend together to make the pure white light of Unity with All, perfect energy balance is achieved. Of these, the colour that you instinctively choose is the colour you need most, as well as your self-healing priority.

Camael, Guardian Angel of Tuesday and Mars:

This message is of the colour crimson – of courage, and stamina, of firmness and strength. This is the colour of blood and your physical well being. Invoke me for power of radiant crimson, like the summer roses, to energise your mind or body, and breathe bright rays into the part of you that needs this vitality.

Michael, Guardian Angel of Wednesday and Mercury:

My cloak is cobalt blue, or ultramarine. Call on me and breathe in this colour. In your mind, see this cloak of cobalt wrapped around yourself whenever you need protection from negative energy of people, places or situations, or place it around those you love.

Introduction to angelic numerology

Single and double numbers relate to Heart Quest (healing physical self) while triple master numbers are for Soul Quest (spiritual development).

NUMBER 1

One is the One, the Creator from which All That Is comes, the circle is the void that births All and Oneness is that to which All returns. The number of energy itself, so 11 is twice the energy. 111 is the angelic master number. If you see 111 or further multiples on clocks, car plates, or in any other way, then it means the angels are helping you to energise whatever it is you are trying to do for self, life, or spiritually.

NUMBER 2

This is the number of a potential new phase in life, while 22 signifies this change is important for your quest(s). 222 is the angelic master number indicating possible spiritual transformation, but this is still a matter of your own personal choice. Two is duality; the sun and the moon also represent the two aspects of mankind that must come into balance to find Oneness.

NUMBER 3

This number indicates a decision about a potential new phase in life, while 33 means the decision/phase is important. Angelic master number 333 means the decision relates to your spiritual development. See also the Law of Three of Hermes Trismegistos (page 16) regarding spiritual alchemy.

NUMBER 4

The number of the fourth (personal heart) chakra, representing love and compassion, while with 44 the angels urge opening of higher heart. 444 is the master number of the angels themselves, signifying unconditional love. If you see 444 it corroborates your study of angels and angel wisdom and desire to incorporate this into your life. 44:44 is the Angel Star Gate of Love and Light.

NUMBER 5

This is the number of raising of spiritual consciousness, linked to the five-point star of Microcosm (see also page 222). The number 55 means you are reaching the next, higher level, while 555 mean you have now attained a certain level of mastery in a healing discipline or of angelic wisdom, or in an esoteric subject; any of these will greatly further your own Soul Quest.

A time for widening horizons

Elemiah, Guardian Angel of Exploration, says:

Regard how a vine encircles a pillar, until in the end the one seems to support the other; so do I support you with my love. As your pillar I urge you and your quest to turn now towards exploration and adventure, finding new challenges that take you ever onwards in mind, body and spirit towards the blue sky above. It could be that it's time for your life to take on a new dimension, or perhaps your inner self needs to break free and be shown to the world; either way, your heart knows what you should do.

Imagine my verdant wings around you, and see how my precious summer flowers embrace your heart. You rest in the shade when the sun shines, preparing to unfold into true glory as you grow in wisdom. The message is one of continuously working towards harmony and balance at each level.

My fellow angels and I offer you healing messages for summer with which to further your own self-exploration, within and without. Our task is to help you to understand yourself and to lovingly support both your quests, so that like the vine you achieve further and further airy heights in this physical life and the spiritual life beyond.

Exploring nature's magic

Aratron, Guardian Angel of Nature's Magic:

If for some reason you feel disconnected from All I ask you to look closely at nature and behold her beauty, especially in this glorious month of the year. For the Creator's wisdom is found in the number of petals of every flower, in the tracery of the trees, the form of each crystal and the intricate activity of the humble bee. You, too, are part of this magic, and I aid you to weave yourself once more into this marvellous pattern that underpins All.

Raguel, Guardian Angel of Spiritual Perception:

A thread of blue runs through your life right now, and also through these words; let them resonate in your throat chakra to soothe and heal. What blue do you see in your mind's eye? If you see dark, indigo blue then you are wise and will become wiser. Pale blue shows you are now able to work intelligently towards spiritual development by starting to live your personal truth.

Cassiel, Guardian Angel of Saturday and Saturn:

Sometimes a black-and-white animal, such as a horse or dog, is a sign that I am near you. For black and white signify the two extremes, highest to lowest, darkest to lightest, without and within, from life to emotions. For I am the power that connects the two extremes, showing you the route between the two, that ultimately brings you to harmony and balance. I guide you in the vital knowledge of one, to enable the recognition and understanding of the other.

Zuphlas, Guardian Angel of Trees:

I am the dappling of light and shade that flows around you when you look at the sky from under one of my magnificent forest trees. Both are necessary for nature herself, as well as for you; together they are harmony.

Tagas, Guardian Angel of Music:

The universe resembles a giant tuning fork emitting a dancing wave of sound, whose purity knows no bounds. Sing out! Become part of this wave with me, starting today, as my vibration allows you to begin to harmonise with All.

AIR, BREATH OF LIFE: Lifts you to Above, returns you to Below

Ariel, Ruler of Air and Earth, says:

See how morning mist lies on a meadow, there and yet not there. This is how I interface with earth. You may enter the mist in a certain sense and be touched by it, and similarly I invite you to enter my world of violet and lavender-blue, and be enveloped by glorious Love and Light. You have reached a vital stage of spiritual growth. You stand on the awesome precipice from which you will now take flight skywards on shimmering wings, wreathed in Light. This is a quantum leap, for my summer element, air, is Breath of Life, and to reach from earth (Below) to air (Above) is to actively seek expansion of spiritual consciousness, freeing the spirit to move between worlds.

To do this, become a great white bird, spiralling on thermals to Above. Presently you encounter a shower of rain, and a rainbow appears. Enter the rainbow and absorb its brilliant hues, finally encompassing the power of the violet ray itself. The endgame is for your higher consciousness to acquire the third-eye wisdom to understand you must return Below to manifest these secrets for All. Light moves in waves or spirals, and so you spiral down to Mother Earth, your first medium of nurture for past, present and future, so that your Love can benefit all earth's sentient life forms. This is Oneness.

Aspirations take flight

Spread your wings and fly, for you are full of Light, yet also must remain grounded and balanced in this reality.

Alphun, Guardian Angel of Doves:

When you see one of my white doves shining against a blue sky do you not marvel at its beauty? Think of your spirit in this way, desiring to soar into the sky, to become part of that expanse that seems limitless. There is nothing to stop your spirit actually doing this – only the choice of your own free will.

Sahaqiel, Guardian Angel of the Sky:

An eagle flying is a magnificent creature, soaring so high and swiftly into the blue – a king of the air. Yet it must return to earth to nest, feed and roost. So must you have aspirations that take you skywards, but also be grounded to fulfil them.

Hermes Trismegistos, Guardian of Spiritual Alchemy:

As the eagle soars aloft you marvel at his strength and fierceness, while the flight of the dove suggests purity and gentleness. However, in mankind, only when these two opposites are reconciled can true Oneness be attained.

Spiralling into wisdom

Seraphiel, Zadkiel and Rikbiel tell you of the importance of spirals.

Seraphiel, Ruler of the Seraphim:
Spirals are very important in this reality – from the mighty spiral arms of the galaxies, to the delicate spirals of ferns and shells. You can heal and balance with spirals, and be lifted to the stars. If you so choose, I will teach you the Way.

Zadkiel, Ruler of Jupiter and Thursday:
See the spiral shell with its beautiful geometry. Trace the spiral either way; you will always return to the same point. This is like the spiral of wisdom, though wisdom spirals have many dimensions. From the dawn of time to the present day, my wisdom does not change, it is as it always was, just retrieved when needed. Your own wisdom spiral is similar, and your revelation is a point on this spiral, waiting for when the time is right for you to remember.

Rikbiel, Driver of the Creator's Chariot of Love:
The positive energy of Love is a like a pure Light spiralling around and even through your world. Hate is the same, yet a dark, negative version. Why not choose Love? Visualise your heart sending spirals of rose, gold and white; these hold the power of Love to solve all problems, given time, and through your choice you help me direct this energy to where it is most needed.

Melchisadec and seven

Melchisadec, Ruler of Sacred Seven, says:
The spiritual path that we angels call the Way of Love and Light stretches before you across time and space, ever leading your heart and soul towards the 44:44 Angel Star Gate through which you reach Oneness with All. The Way starts with Heart, Rainbows and Sacred Seven: Hope, Courage, Truth, Wisdom, Beauty, Harmony and Healing before moving on to Soul. If you are not yet on this Way is now not the time for you to make a start?

SACRED SEVEN
Seven is sacred in almost all belief systems. The ancient writings tell of seven heavens. The Sacred Seven angel rulers of the weekdays and seven major planets of our solar system are also the angel rulers of each of the Heavens, although the ruler of the seventh (Cassiel) is actually classified as the Gatekeeper for God/The Creator who dwells in Seventh Heaven. Melchisadec, father to the Sacred Seven, rules the seventh ray (violet).

ABOUT MELCHISADEC, RULER OF SEVEN
Sources speak of him as the Holy Ghost, or Prince of Peace, or even that he incarnated as one of the sons of Noah (Shem). Abraham paid tithes to Melchisadec (also spelled Melchizedek). A statue of him holding the chalice (that contains the key, as depicted in ancient engravings and in the *Harmony Angel Cards*) adorns Chartres Cathedral, beside Abraham and Moses.

Modern angelic wisdom

WHAT IS THE HOLY GRAIL?

I believe it is the chalice of the heart, as held by Melchisadec, and containing a special key. This is the key that in fact is the centre of Melchisadec's seven-turn labyrinth, where we can find and open our higher heart, our spiritual Divine Self. When we open the flower that is within the higher heart we can return to Oneness with All – truly a prize that is worth having!

THE VIOLET RAY

This, the seventh ray of Melchisadec, is composed of the pink ray of unconditional love combined with the blue ray of truth. There are many variations of violet, from the warm pink-violet, to the cool blue-violet, and the higher vibration of silvery violet. All serve different purposes in transmuting negative, dark energy back to pure white and sparkling angelic Light.

HALOES OF PURE LIGHT

What is termed a halo is actually the radiance of the crown chakra that shines pure white when a person has found Unity Consciousness or Oneness with All. Because the energy of each chakra is three dimensional, this forms a kind of sphere or helmet of white light around the head.

The Sacred Eden Tree 2

As previously mentioned (page 48), the Sacred Eden Tree is the etheric archetype of all trees on earth. Its heart is a hollow channel of highest spiritual potential, in which you can ignite the wisdom flame in your own soul.

Following the work you did in earlier solar festivals, and if your desire is to benefit All, you can now will and intend that your own spirit is within the Sacred Tree – at One with its Sacred Consciousness. Allow the divine Shekinah energy to flow into your feet from her earthly kingdom and then bring her white-gold energy up through your body to your heart. The love in your heart, and desire to serve, magnifies this energy (it becomes paler); send it to Metatron at crown level. Transmuted now to white-silver, bring the energy back into your heart to self-heal. Cause it then to return to Shekinah, for through the roots it is also healing Mother Earth and all sentient life.

Because of your desire to help heal Mother Earth, now Melchisadec aids your Light vibration to rise further, while Pistis Sophia lifts your Love vibration; and so the flower of your heart will open – a great spiritual step. Through the power of Love and Light, through your branches your Light touches Metatron at crown, while through your roots your Love embraces Shekinah and earthly kingdom. They return manifold energy to you in gratitude; enjoy a wonderful feeling of inner peace in the heart as you complete this second step of three.

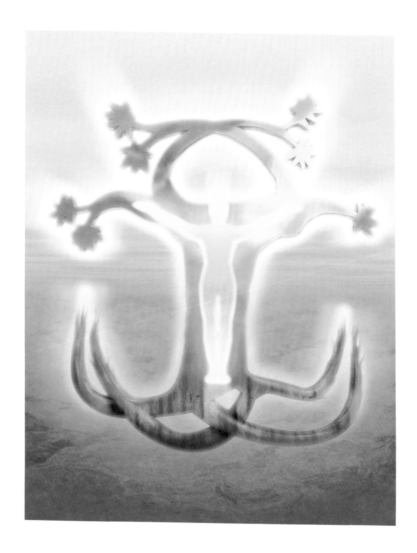

Helping to heal All

Haadiah, one of the 72 Quinary Star Angels:

We angels applaud when you gather in a group to aid your spiritual development. But if you are one who prefers to do this alone, spending a few minutes each day opening your heart, to send Love and Light to All, then we want you to know that this is every bit as valuable and important.

Asfael, Leader of 1,000 Ministering Angels:

I lead a troop of 1,000 angels. When you invoke my name our collective energy swirls like a cloak around you, with the softness of feathers yet with iron strength. We uphold you and keep you safe, until you come to know your way towards your own higher heart and inner peace, and then we urge you to call on us to learn how to use your special talents to aid All.

Violet and diamond rays

Melchisadec, Ruler of Sacred Seven:

Violet is the spiritual antiseptic that transmutes dark energy, returning it to pure white light. If you feel any darkness within, invoke my name (and you can also invoke Ariel) and mentally say, three times: 'I channel the power of violet fire, that brings the purity I desire' to transmute this darkness. If you are in a negative atmosphere, say it out loud to clear the space.

Seraphiel, Ruler of the Seraphim:

The diamond star path is the journey back to Light through the temple of soul. My crystalline energy spirals down to you; when you breathe it in, you breathe in a Divine breath that infuses heart and soul, offering the potential to reach your own star of destiny. If you accept my gift, when you breathe it out you will find you are on the Way of Love and Light – the rest is up to you.

FIRE: Celebrate what succeeded, cleanse and purify to
move on once again

Torquaret, Guardian Angel of Autumn, says:

*As glorious summer wanes, trailing her skirts of crimson,
orange and gold, I reach out to touch my autumn leaves,
echoing and deepening these colours. And as the leaves turn
to ochre, russet and brown, it is your time of reckoning.*

*At the start of my festival my warm amber wings are like
autumn sunshine; they caress your spirit as the year inexorably
draws to its conclusion, urging you to consider what you have
achieved so far. Have you found greater fulfilment? Did the
seed of your transformation that commenced with earth and
re-birth grow through the power of water, flourish in the sun,
then lift into the potential of the endless horizon? If so, your
heart rejoices and my honeyed sun feels sweet upon your face.
But if not, now is the time to re-evaluate matters for next year.*

*Then as the leaves fall marvel at their beauty and the living
art that they make when they come to rest, but do not be sad!
Hold always in your heart the promise of spring. For soon the
skies will darken and fires will be lit to cleanse and purify the
land; amber turns to bright flame as Uriel kindles Fire of Life
above as well as beneath Mother Earth. Let this become your
own flame of passion, allowing endings to ever empower
another new beginning.*

An autumn assessment

The angels remind you that it is time to evaluate your year so far, and to make new plans. They praise your achievements, but if all did not go totally right, there is always next year.

Hermes Trismegistos, Guardian of Spiritual Alchemy:

My message is of Love (rose pink), Power (yellow-gold) and Wisdom (blue-violet), the three parts of All that I wish to teach you. If during this year you have worked with these colours, and truly combined head and heart in all that you do, I applaud you, for you have found the key to Power with Love, and this will bring Wisdom.

Zuriel, Guardian Angel of the Zodiac Sign of Libra:

Many times will the scales of your existence be finely balanced, affecting your present and your future. There is still all to play for in your life, so be sure to take your time and involve your heart in all decisions that you are making, for I counsel that one is coming soon and it will be crucial to your quest.

Arad, Guardian Angel of Self-Belief:

When the clouds part in an oval, through which a cone of sun rays stream down to earth, it is like the eye in the sky. All that the rays touch turns to gold. I am the eye within your heart and soul that waits for the opportunity to gild you with golden rays that will flow out from you as self-belief. If you've been hurt, try to let this go, for my golden radiance waits to comfort and heal you.

Shamshiel, Guardian Angel of the Light of Day:

Oftentimes, in this season, the sun sets in a blaze of glory, streaming copper and rose-gold tinted clouds across the sky. On other days you see only shades of dove grey and slate. At times your life can be like this, but I bring you Love and Light even on grey days, and I comfort you with the thought that tomorrow you may see the splendour of colours once again grace the day.

The Quinary Guardian Angels:

We, the angels of the firmament, are called the Quinaries. Collectively our bottomless well of energy touches and can lift your soul back to our vibration to help guide it towards its destiny.

Some angel facts

THE SMILING ANGEL OF REIMS.
This famous angel, one of the stone carvings on the outside of Reims Cathedral, is believed to be Gabriel. If so, although the angel's hands are now empty, they originally held the lily with which Gabriel is associated. Gabriel is said to have appeared to Joan of Arc to inspire her to aid the French king. If you smell the lily fragrance as a response to calling in angels (see page 17), then this is almost certainly Gabriel's presence around you.

FLEUR DE LYS – THE LILY
The fleur de lys, a stylised representation of a lily, is the emblem of French royalty (and of secret wisdom), linked with both Hermes Trismegistos and Gabriel. If your heart resonates with the fleur de lys, it may be because Hermes Trismegistos is urging you towards spiritual development (alchemy), or Gabriel is bringing hope and aspirations.

ANGEL FRAGRANCES

Carnation, frankincense, hyacinth and rose are all general fragrances said to resemble perfumes in the angelic realms themselves, and will help to 'call' angels to you. You can either burn a candle perfumed with one of these, or use an essential oil to enhance your ability to communicate with angels.

ANGELICA

The herb angelica (*Angelica archangelica*) has an angelic significance. The seeds suggest the lightness of the angelic realms, and protect your thoughts from unwelcome intrusions, while allowing the angels to assist you. The fragrance is said to conjure up cosmic awareness, while the oil can encourage spiritual vision.

VARIATIONS IN ANGELS' NAMES

In ancient times, papyrus was used to record the names of angels. This crumbled after a certain time so the angel names had to be copied and re-copied, also translated, over the centuries. This gave rise to small variations appearing in the same names.

Harvesting your achievements

Sofiel: Guardian Angel of Nature's Bounty:

I am the pure gold of the field of corn that shines with Light, but flows like bright water when ruffled by the autumn breeze. When the time comes I aid the harvest to be gathered, and as it moves through the thresher, separating the wheat from the chaff, my strong wings cradle the abundant grain that is destined to feed mankind and I rejoice. It is also a time of thanksgiving for all that you've gained this year, as well as a reckoning for anything you lost.

In this season, when all is gathered and the fields are cleared and cleansed, see what bounty Mother Nature has bestowed. None of this is possible without care and commitment, for that which is worth having is not won without effort.

I come to help you take stock of your year and to prepare and make plans for the next. Nothing can or even should ever remain exactly the same in your life, for your aspirations should be to try to move ever onwards. If you are willing to continue with your quests next year, pledging time when needed, whether for heart or soul healing and development, you may call on my golden energy at any time to help you to receive and conserve the precious bounty you deserve to enrich your future.

A time of reckoning

Pistis Sophia, Heavenly and Earthly Mother:

At this time of the year I exhort you to review your progress. Have you done good things, have you freely given of yourself to help another? Or have you done something you now have cause to regret? We angels see all that you do, rejoicing when we see compassion and weeping when we see wrong or thoughtless actions. Though we forgive all, we ask you to remember that the Eight Roads to Heaven include Rightness of Thought, Action and Speech, as well as meditations through which we guide your onward steps.

Raphael, Guardian Angel of the Sun, and Sunday:

When in the presence of your loved ones, is your shadow too deep? By this I do not mean dark, I mean intense. If so, perhaps you are trying to exercise too much control over them. Allow some of my golden sun energy in to lighten the shadow, for the ultimate benefit of all.

Words of comfort

Rachmiel, Guardian Angel of Compassion:

As the year draws to an end have you lost someone? Do you feel alone in life, bereft? In fact, you need never be alone, as I love and protect you always, bringing unlimited compassion and surrounding you with rosy gold rays. Whatever has happened, or is happening, I am there with you, day by day, in the dark night of the soul, to support and guide you until your heart is healed.

Uriel, Ruler of Uranus, Guardian Angel of Transformation:

I bring the clear and vibrant ray of orange, for sensuality, creativity, change and transformation. If this is what you seek, allow me into your life, for when you breathe in my orange fire to your sacral chakra you immediately create the potential for all these dormant qualities within self. But even more than this, you breathe in the power to realise this potential.

Nathaniel, Guardian Angel of Passion:

To ignite passion within, think coral red; it is a joyful colour – a shade that may be needed in your life to make things happen for you. For this is the shade of passion, and whatever passion you desire – for life, for love, for work, for play – then you can invoke my name to help ignite within the passion you need.

FIRE OF LIFE: Illumines the soul and the Phoenix
rises again

Uriel, Guardian Angel of Fire Alchemy, says:
*During my festival I rule with radiant Fire of Life, and if
you are one who loves life I bring you joy. I am woven of
living flame, burning orange, yellow-gold and blue-white,
and as I clap my wings fire flickers and rolls across the land,
burning away dross, cleansing and purifying as the year dies.
From the golden ashes of the old, you too, like the Phoenix,
can be re-born once more. If your quest has already achieved
self-transformation, by year's end you will be at a higher
vibration than before, when the whole cycle begins again.*

*My Fire of Life is connected with Ariel's Breath of Life, for
fire comes from and returns to air. These two elements enable
retrieval of ancient wisdom or healing of soul fragments you
may have lost when a loved one departed. Uniquely for
mankind I bring the blue-white alchemy flame that illumines
the path of your soul – a cosmic flash by which I descend to
earth. If you so choose you can work with Ariel and me to
breathe in this special flame, and hold it within higher heart
for a seminal moment. It is a flame of angelic initiation that
Lights All; it can instantly purify, alter, clarify or transmute,
empowering your soul to retrieve what it has lost to hold for
ever afterwards.*

Using power of the heart for healing

Rachmiel, Guardian Angel of Compassion:

If you read or hear that something dire has happened in your world today let your heart feel compassion for all involved and mentally send it to them. In gratitude for this I help you open the flower of Love and Light that waits in your heart, through which you will come to find inner peace.

Gazardiel, Ruler of the Sun's Passage in the Heavens:

When the crimson pearl of the sun rises above the horizon the rays can be seen as six-fold, like the petals of a flower. This flower is called the Blood Rose and has the power to heal at all levels, even cellular. You may ask me to aid you in breathing sun radiance into your solar energy centre to start off a healing process within, culminating in forming the Blood Rose in your heart. When you have mastered the art of self-healing with this, then send it to All.

Working with the Sacred Eden Tree

Metatron, Guardian Angel of the Tree of Life/Sacred Eden Tree: *I am called by some 'the tallest angel'. My energy reaches to the seven heavens and beyond, for I guard the crown of the Tree of Life and am the bridge to the stars. Through me you can reach the 44:44 Angel Star Gate and Oneness with All. Yet when my energy touches the crown of your head it feels like the tiniest, softest feather. I urge you to send your Spirit skywards, deepening your connection to All.*

Shekinah, Guardian Angel of the Tree of Life/Sacred Eden Tree: *While with Metatron you climb through the Star Gate to Oneness Above, with me you go to the very heart of Mother Earth, called the atoma, and then link from there through Below to the heart of Venus, her sister planet. Whatever you do or learn with Metatron, you ground through me to Mother Earth, so that all sentient life benefits from your growing spiritual knowledge and wisdom, for in the circle or Wheel of Life: 'as Above so Below, as Below so Above'.*

Introduction to angelic numerology

Remember you can receive numerology messages through clocks and watches, number plates, totals on computer printouts, bills, birds flying, or animals in fields – all numbers are important guides especially triples.

SACRED GEOMETRY

Behind the structure of All, or Oneness, are numbers and sacred geometry; music is but a ratio of numbers; sacred spirals are growth through numbers, Nature and mankind are constructed to this same pattern. Form is sacred geometry made manifest. The universe is like a sacred geometry jigsaw, and when you plug yourself back into this jigsaw then you go back into Oneness, and thus have the potential of infinite spiritual awareness.

NUMBER 6

This is reaching a level of healing and completion, as symbolised in the six-pointed star of Macrocosm (All That Is – also known as the Star of David). The number 66 means a new level of healing has been reached. 666 is not, in my view, anything to do with 'the beast' (believed to be a Biblical mistranslation), but is an angelic master number referring to attainment of a key level of spiritual development connected with the decision you took with 3, 33, or 333.

NUMBER 7

An important esoteric number figuring in almost all belief systems. Also the number of Melchisadec (ruler of the rainbow, the Sacred Seven and the seventh violet ray. He is the seventh central point in the six-pointed star. The number 777 is the angelic master number of the mysteries, urging you to complete Heart Quest to focus on Soul Quest.

NUMBER 8

If you see the number 8 this represents eternity, connected with Pistis Sophia, Heavenly and Earthly Mother. Personification of faith, wisdom and compassion, she guides your Heart and Soul Quests and directs you also to her zodiac angels (see page 164-191). The number 88 means you can overcome adversity with her help. The angelic master number 888 means you have reached a key level of learning angelic wisdom (444) and can move on in your Soul Quest.

NUMBERS 9 AND 10

If you see 9, or 99, this indicates that what you started in 3, or 33 is now fully complete and it is time to look for fresh guidance from the angels. The number 999 is an angelic master number linked to the Ascension (see also Part 3 of this book) and Blue Star. If this resonates you are, or will be working on Ascension. After 9, the number 10 returns to Oneness and perfection, but if you've followed the angelic master numbers you will be at your next vibration level.

The Sacred Eden Tree 3

You are ready for the third stage of working with the Sacred Eden Tree, guided to the Angel Star Gate by Metatron and Shekinah.

After the inner peace you reached in the second step, you should be ready to move to the third step in this book. Now from within the tree you reach higher into Unity Consciousness, and combine crown with your open higher heart. Ask Metatron to deepen your Divine connection, allowing you to reach through the 44:44 Angel Star Gate to truly embrace All That Is. The vibration of Light beyond is Metatron and Shekinah's pure white fire called the Love flame of spiritual alchemy that does not burn, is unfallen, heals All.

When this flame fills your higher heart flower, will and intend it to go down to the heart (atoma) of Mother Earth herself, and also to her sister planet, Venus. In accordance with the Star Gate's resonance of 16, the angels help you attain a pure harmonic of Love within your roots (Shekinah: 44 of Love), and so these become eight in number. Also a pure harmonic of Light at crown (Metatron: 44 of Light) take your branches to eight. All 16 extend further and wider, so that you become the Circle of Life itself through heart and soul.

In the same way that the pure flame radiates from the Sacred Tree, when you and the tree are One it will shine out from you also, and in time it can become diamond. Its power derives from beyond the Star Gate and it is accessed only with the higher heart. If a true heart's desire has been to become One with the Sacred Eden Tree you may be sure this is part of your soul's purpose.

The place of peace

The angels advise how to find and keep within you the place of peace.

Anafiel, Guardian Angel of Heavenly Peace:

Heavenly peace is a place within the heart of your heart, and you can reach it if you try. Put up my name, and invoke me every day when you have a quiet moment, to show you how to find this place of refuge. Once you know the Way you can always return there in times of need.

Tabris, Guardian Angel of Free Will:

Let us say you walk in a corridor, and two doors appear side by side. One of them is marked 'happiness' and the other 'contentment'. You may walk through either one of these, but as Guardian of Free Will I give you counsel. Happiness is gratifying but may be fleeting, while if you can but find what brings you contentment, this wisdom endures for a lifetime.

Och, Guardian Angel of Crystal Alchemy:

Crystals hold much energy to enhance your healing or meditations. Use clear quartz in any capacity for it holds information, or a crystal of the colour matching the energy centre on which you wish to focus. Not only the colour, but also the crystalline structure and geometry of the crystal are all linked to that of mankind and will add extra power for alchemy of mind, body and spirit.

Diamond and sapphire energy

Seraphiel, Ruler of the Seraphim:

*Once again, it is the season when days are short and nights long.
When you look at the stars they seem so very distant, yet I tell you
that there is a way in which the diamond energy of Creation can be
held in your own heart, establishing a permanent connection to the
star angels of Light. If these words resonate, you will be drawn to
learn more from the Seraphim.*

Sanusemi, of the Blue Star Angels:

*I am a Seraph of the Blue Star Ennead: nine angels guiding
Ascension. If my name resonates within then you are a Blue Star
child. Breathe in my sapphire energy, beam it down to Mother Earth
to heal her, and then see this beam extending from her heart to the
Blue Star itself – your wisdom path of Truth.*

Mirabiel, Guardian Angel of the Two Moons of Earth:

*My two moons when full are called the eyes of heaven, and when
they are the eyes of the Thunderbird of the Blue Star you would see
perfect stillness in them. Combine this with the powerhouse of the
Thunderbird's heart and deep spiritual balance is attained; you can
reach the Blue Star and beyond.*

THE 28 MANSIONS OF THE MOON

This year gives you the chance to work continuously with Raphael's solar cycles, but now Gabriel, ruler of the moon, also guides you through her 13 Lunar Cycles. For you must weave Gabriel's silver moon thread into Raphael's golden sun to really achieve your true heart's desires or find your soul purpose. And the human heart, like the solar and lunar cycles, has many phases that should be taken gently, not rushed, if you wish to work towards inner peace and harmony.

The Caduceus and Sacred Eden Tree exercises were to help you personally achieve solar and lunar balance. This, now, is slightly different. The ruler of the entire Wheel of the Moon (called the 28 Mansions of the Moon, one angel for each day) is Ophaniel, pictured opposite. His 28 mansions can be used as a focus to deal with an issue that you realize needs to be started, climaxed, wound down or closed. It could be a project, a relationship, a problem – your heart knows what this is, so decide to do something about it!

The 14 days of the waxing moon (growing towards full moon) are for helping a project to grow; the 14 days of waning (when the moon diminishes) are for obtaining closure or ridding yourself of anything unwanted. If working on a waxing moon, start the day of the new moon; if working on a waning moon, start the day after full moon. Your chosen project must be something for your highest good, and to harm none. The day or night before the lunar cycle begins, make this invocation to ask for support from Gabriel and Ophaniel:

Gabriel, Gabriel, Gabriel, Ophaniel, Ophaniel, Ophaniel (for a third angel choose one of your other Guardians), *I have chosen this coming lunar cycle as my heart and intuition tell me I must now focus on this issue for my highest good. Please guide me daily through the Mansions of the Moon angels, in Love and Light, Love and Light, Love and Light.*

MOON WISDOM: Working with the Mansions of the Moon Angels

● full moon ○ new moon

2009	● JAN 11	○ JAN 26	● FEB 9	○ FEB 25	● MAR 11	○ MAR 26	● APR 9	○ APR 25	● MAY 9	○ MAY 24	● JUN 7	○ JUN 22
2010	○ JAN 15	● JAN 30	○ FEB 14	● FEB 28	○ MAR 15	● MAR 30	○ APR 14	● APR 28	○ MAY 14	● MAY 27	○ JUN 12	● JUN 26
2011	○ JAN 4	● JAN 19	○ FEB 3	● FEB 18	○ MAR 4	● MAR 19	○ APR 3	● APR 18	○ MAY 3	● MAY 17	○ JUN 1	● JUN 15
2012	● JAN 9	○ JAN 23	● FEB 7	○ FEB 21	● MAR 8	○ MAR 22	● APR 6	○ APR 21	● MAY 6	○ MAY 20	● JUN 4	○ JUN 19
2013	○ JAN 11	● JAN 27	○ FEB 10	● FEB 25	○ MAR 11	● MAR 27	○ APR 10	● APR 25	○ MAY 10	● MAY 25	○ JUN 8	● JUN 23

Choose the moon on which you wish to work from the chart below. On the following pages you will find the angels of the 28 Mansions divided into four quarters. Make the same affirmation over the seven days, but invoke the relevant angel of the Mansion before you do so.

JUL 7	JUL 22	AUG 6	AUG 20	SEP 4	SEP 18	OCT 4	OCT 18	NOV 2	NOV 16	DEC 2	DEC 16	DEC 31

JUL 11	JUL 26	AUG 10	AUG 24	SEP 8	SEP 23	OCT 7	OCT 23	NOV 6	NOV 21	DEC 5	DEC 21

JUL 1	JUL 15	JUL 30	AUG 13	AUG 29	SEP 12	SEP 27	OCT 12	OCT 26	NOV 10	NOV 25	DEC 10	DEC 24

JUL 3	JUL 19	AUG 2	AUG 17	AUG 31	SEP 16	SEP 30	OCT 15	OCT 29	NOV 13	NOV 28	DEC 13	DEC 28

JUL 8	JUL 22	AUG 6	AUG 21	SEP 5	SEP 19	OCT 5	OCT 18	NOV 3	NOV 17	DEC 3	DEC 17

95

WAXING MOON: First quarter

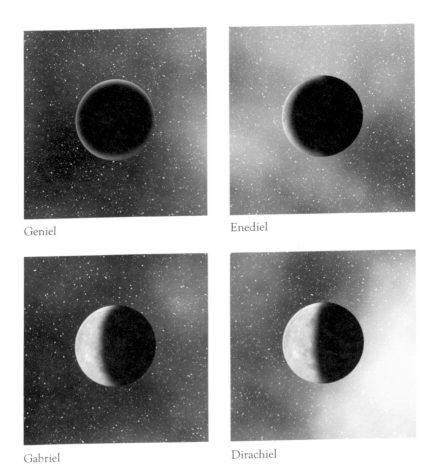

Geniel

Enediel

Gabriel

Dirachiel

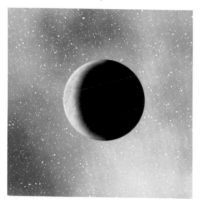

Anixiel

Asariel

Scheliel

The time has come when I want and need to make this happen in my life. Please guide me day by day to work at this, so that by the end of this week my goal is getting closer, for my highest good.

WAXING MOON: Second quarter

Amnediel

Barbiel

Abdizuel

Jazeriel

Ardifiel

Neciel

Ergediel

*With your support my focus is
building, and day by day I am
working towards my chosen
goal. Please help my efforts to
achieve a climax by full moon,
for my highest good.*

WANING MOON: Third quarter

Adiel

Azerel

Amutiel

Kyriel

Adriel

Egibiel

Bethnael

My goal is that I want and need to conclude this issue in my life. Please help me day by day to wind it down, so that my goal is getting closer and closer, for my highest good.

WANING MOON: Fourth quarter

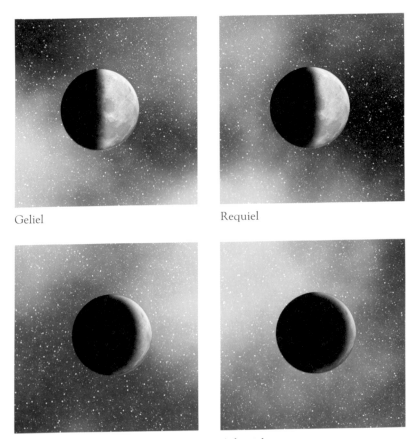

Geliel

Requiel

Tagriel

Atheniel

Abrinael

Aziel

Amitiel

With your support, day by day I am building my resolve to completely conclude this issue in my life. Please help me to achieve closure by the dark moon, for my highest good.

Part Two: Working with your guardian angels

Many people know there is a personal guardian angel assigned to us from birth that remains throughout life, but it is for us to find the name of this angel. As I mention in my first book, *A Harmony of Angels*, if you ask from your heart to be given the name, you may see or hear a name three times in fairly rapid succession. This follows the sacred Law of Three, and represents Divine Truth. It may not be a traditional angel name, but invoking this name would give you a special feeling, like warmth in your heart. The first meditation on the CD is designed to help you see and connect with this guardian angel. It may take a little time and patience, so persevere! But what many people don't realise is that we each have another four special angels who could also be termed guardians, with whom we can work in a variety of ways. Five is the number of spiritual growth.

YOUR GUARDIAN RULER OF THE DAYS OF THE WEEK
The ruling angels of the days of the week are called the Sacred Seven, each of whom has a key life-transforming role within our life as assigned by the Creator; they themselves are ruled by Melchisadec, Prince of Peace, a type of angelic director or father figure, and who fast-tracks our spiritual development. These are the angels with whom I started to transform my own life in 1999. Although you can invoke all Sacred Seven, your own second guardian angel is the one ruling the day of the week on which you were born. Charts within this section will enable you to find the day of your birth so that you can identify this important angel's guardianship attributes and start to work with this being.

YOUR ZODIAC RULER

Your third guardian angel is the
one ruling your zodiac sign. Again,
working with these angels will deepen
your personal angelic connection. Zodiac
angels strengthen us, help us to overcome
weaknesses and are also traditionally linked to
parts of the body. These angels are ruled by Pistis
Sophia, an ancient symbol of heavenly motherhood,
wisdom and faith in self who is as old as time, and who
has had many names over the years according to different
belief systems and religions.

YOUR ELEMENTAL GUARDIAN ANGEL

A fourth guardian angel will be the angel connected with the element
in your own zodiac sign – earth, air, water or fire. These elements are
ruled by Ariel (earth and air), Uriel (fire) and Phuel (water).
According to your zodiac sign you/your life will be aided by one of
these three angels.

YOUR STAR GUARDIAN ANGEL

Your fifth guardian angel is your star angel. The heavens are divided
into 72 parts, and each segment is ruled by one of the Quinary Star
Angels. One of these will be guiding your own destiny and here you
will discover how to find your personal star angel.

You are invited to work with any and all of these guardian angels as
often as you can to take you further along the Way of Love and
Light, until at last you reach Seraphiel and the Seraphim Star Angels
of Creation.

MELCHISADEC: Spiritual director of mankind

Melchisadec, ruler of the Sacred Seven Angels, says:
*I am Melchisadec, Prince of Peace. From the highest and
most perfect vibration of Light, the pure universal
Harmonic, I descend, offering you my chalice of life, filled
with manna for spiritual nourishment. Within my chalice I
also hold the key to Sacred Seven, for it is filled with this
pure harmonic, an iridescent sevenfold Light or Rainbow
Eye that reflects all the healing aspects and potential of
seven shades of my rainbow colours: seven times seven levels
of spiritual peace and wholeness. To wish to absorb this
Light is to seek my rainbow eye on a pathway called the Way
of Love and Light. I urge you to take this path, leading also
to the heart of my seven-turn labyrinth, towards finding and
accepting your true self. For then you, too, will hold my key
to wholeness that is also Oneness with All.*

*How to start? I am father to the Sacred Seven planetary
angels who are rulers of your weekdays. In total we are
eight: another turn of the Wheel of Life and Fate. I counsel
you to work with me as well as my seven angels – especially
the one who is your special guardian. Together we assist
your focus on spiritual harmony and, as you venture deeper
into the circles of my Rainbow Eye, the colours move you
further on the Way of Love and Light.*

Monday: Gabriel

IF YOUR DAY OF BIRTH IS MONDAY: Gabriel rules and is one of your six guardian angels. Gabriel's healing rays are white, silver and palest aqua, her metal is silver, crystals/stones are moonstone, selenite and pearls. Attributes for Gabriel on which to focus are: hopes, dreams, aspirations, intuition and feminine balance.

Gabriel is ruler of the moon and Monday, 1st Heaven and north wind. Her name means 'God is my strength' and she is also known as the 'heavenly awakener'. Although angels don't really have genders, Gabriel is thought of in female terms because the power of the moon is feminine while the sun's power is considered masculine. She is the angel who reveals the meaning of our dreams and supports our aspirations in life; above all she brings her gift of awakening hope in us. Gabriel dictated the Koran to Mohammed and is said to have inspired Joan of Arc to come to the aid of her king. To the Moslems, Gabriel (known as Jibral) is the spirit of truth, to the Jews she is credited with being the adviser of Joseph and the Children of Israel, to the Christians she revealed to Mary that she would conceive and bear the baby Jesus.

Whether we are born male or female we are each composed of golden masculine energy (the sun: left brain hemisphere and right hand) and silver feminine energy (the moon: right brain/left hand). Raphael's energy is essential to make things happen in your life, but you must ensure that decisions taken with head are balanced with heart.

This is where Gabriel comes in, as Gabriel's feminine energy develops your intuition and appreciation for art, music and poetry, subtle and emotive life influences that need to be felt and experienced rather than measured or analysed.

We can all call on Gabriel any time any day, whenever we need her special help in life. However, if she is the angel of the day of your birth, then she will be one of your guardian angels and therefore be continually guiding your life, especially on Mondays. Here is an invocation, as well as a useful tip:

Gabriel, Gabriel, Gabriel please bring me hope (or another of this angel's attributes, i.e. new aspirations, intuition, feminine balance), *in Love and Light, Love and Light, Love and Light.*

For temporary invisibility, ask Gabriel to envelop someone or something in silver energy for a short period, and/or wear silver on your left hand or wrist as a reminder of Gabriel's divine attributes and presence.

Monday birthdays

1940 Jan: 1, 8, 15, 22, 29; Feb: 5, 12, 19, 26; Mar: 4, 11, 18, 25; Apr: 1, 8, 15, 22, 29; May: 6, 13, 20, 27; Jun: 3, 10, 17, 24; Jul: 1, 8, 15, 22, 29; Aug: 5, 12, 19, 26; Sep: 2, 9, 16, 23, 30; Oct: 7, 14, 21, 28; Nov: 4, 11, 18, 25; Dec: 2, 9, 16, 23, 30

1941 Jan: 6, 13, 20, 27; Feb: 3, 10, 17, 24; Mar: 3, 10, 17, 24, 31; Apr: 7, 14, 21, 28; May: 5, 12, 19, 26; Jun: 2, 9, 16, 23, 30; Jul: 7, 14, 21, 28; Aug: 4, 11, 18, 25; Sep: 1, 8, 15, 22, 29; Oct: 6, 13, 20, 27; Nov: 3, 10, 17, 24; Dec: 1, 8, 15, 22, 29

1942 Jan: 5, 12, 19, 26; Feb: 2, 9, 16, 23; Mar: 2, 9, 16, 23, 30; Apr: 6, 13, 20, 27; May: 4, 11, 18, 25; Jun: 1, 8, 15, 22, 29; Jul: 6, 13, 20, 27; Aug: 3, 10, 17, 24, 31; Sep: 7, 14, 21, 28; Oct: 5, 12, 19, 26; Nov: 2, 9, 16, 23, 30; Dec: 7, 14, 21, 28

1943 Jan: 4, 11, 18, 25; Feb: 1, 8, 15, 22; Mar: 1, 8, 15, 22, 29; Apr: 5, 12, 19, 26; May: 3, 10, 17, 24, 31; Jun: 7, 14, 21, 28; Jul: 5, 12, 19, 26; Aug: 2, 9, 16, 23, 30; Sep: 6, 13, 20, 27; Oct: 4, 11, 18, 25; Nov: 1, 8, 15, 22, 29; Dec: 6, 13, 20, 27

1944 Jan: 3, 10, 17, 24, 31; Feb: 7, 14, 21, 28; Mar: 6, 13, 20, 27; Apr: 3, 10, 17, 24; May: 1, 8, 15, 22, 29; Jun: 5, 12, 19, 26; Jul: 3, 10, 17, 24, 31; Aug: 7, 14, 21, 28; Sep: 4, 11, 18, 25; Oct: 2, 9, 16, 23, 30; Nov: 6, 13, 20, 27; Dec: 4, 11, 18, 25

1945 Jan: 1, 8, 15, 22, 29; Feb: 5, 12, 19, 26; Mar: 5, 12, 19, 26; Apr: 2, 9, 16, 23, 30; May: 7, 14, 21, 28; Jun: 4, 11, 18, 25; Jul: 2, 9, 16, 23, 30; Aug: 6, 13, 20, 27; Sep: 3, 10, 17, 24; Oct: 1, 8, 15, 22, 29; Nov: 5, 12, 19, 26; Dec: 3, 10, 17, 24, 31

1946 Jan: 7, 14, 21, 28; Feb: 4, 11, 18, 25; Mar: 4, 11, 18, 25; Apr: 1, 8, 15, 22, 29; May: 6, 13, 20, 27; Jun: 3, 10, 17, 24; Jul: 1, 8, 15, 22, 29; Aug: 5, 12, 19, 26; Sep: 2, 9, 16, 23, 30; Oct: 7, 14, 21, 28; Nov: 4, 11, 18, 25; Dec: 2, 9, 16, 23, 30

1947 Jan: 6, 13, 20, 27; Feb: 3, 10, 17, 24; Mar: 3, 10, 17, 24, 31; Apr: 7, 14, 21, 28; May: 5, 12, 19, 26; Jun: 2, 9, 16, 23, 30; Jul: 7, 14, 21, 28; Aug: 4, 11, 18, 25; Sep: 1, 8, 15, 22, 29; Oct: 6, 13, 20, 27; Nov: 3, 10, 17, 24; Dec: 1, 8, 15, 22, 29

1948 Jan: 5, 12, 19, 26; Feb: 2, 9, 16, 23; Mar: 1, 8, 15, 22, 29; Apr: 5, 12, 19, 26; May: 3, 10, 17, 24, 31; Jun: 7, 14, 21, 28; Jul: 5, 12, 19, 26; Aug: 2, 9, 16, 23, 30; Sep: 6, 13, 20, 27; Oct: 4, 11, 18, 25; Nov: 1, 8, 15, 22, 29; Dec: 6, 13, 20, 27

1949 Jan: 3, 10, 17, 24, 31; Feb: 7, 14, 21, 28; Mar: 7, 14, 21, 28; Apr: 4, 11, 18, 25; May: 2, 9, 16, 23, 30; Jun: 6, 13, 20, 27; Jul: 4, 11, 18, 25; Aug: 1, 8, 15, 22, 29; Sep: 5, 12, 19, 26; Oct: 3, 10, 17, 24, 31; Nov: 7, 14, 21, 28; Dec: 5, 12, 19, 26

1950 Jan: 2, 9, 16, 23, 30; Feb: 6, 13, 20, 27; Mar: 6, 13, 20, 27; Apr: 3, 10, 17, 24; May: 1, 8, 15, 22, 29; Jun: 5, 12, 19, 26; Jul: 3, 10, 17, 24, 31; Aug: 7, 14, 21, 28; Sep: 4, 11, 18, 25; Oct: 2, 9, 16, 23, 30; Nov: 6, 13, 20, 27; Dec: 4, 11, 18, 25

1951 Jan: 1, 8, 15, 22, 29; Feb: 5, 12, 19, 26; Mar: 5, 12, 19, 26; Apr: 2, 9, 16, 23, 30; May: 7, 14, 21, 28; Jun: 4, 11, 18, 25; Jul: 2, 9, 16, 23, 30; Aug: 6, 13, 20, 27; Sep: 3, 10, 17, 24; Oct: 1, 8, 15, 22, 29; Nov: 5, 12, 19, 26; Dec: 3, 10, 17, 24, 31

1952 Jan: 7, 14, 21, 28; Feb: 4, 11, 18, 25; Mar: 3, 10, 17, 24, 31; Apr: 7, 14, 21, 28; May: 5, 12, 19, 26; Jun: 2, 9, 16, 23, 30; Jul: 7, 14, 21, 28; Aug: 4, 11, 18, 25; Sep: 1, 8, 15, 22, 29; Oct: 6, 13, 20, 27; Nov: 3, 10, 17, 24; Dec: 1, 8, 15, 22, 29

1953 Jan: 5, 12, 19, 26; Feb: 2, 9, 16, 23; Mar: 2, 9, 16, 23, 30; Apr: 6, 13, 20, 27; May: 4, 11, 18, 25; Jun: 1, 8, 15, 22, 29; Jul: 6, 13, 20, 27; Aug: 3, 10, 17, 24, 31; Sep: 7, 14, 21, 28; Oct: 5, 12, 19, 26; Nov: 2, 9, 16, 23, 30; Dec: 7, 14, 21, 28

1954 Jan: 4, 11, 18, 25; Feb: 1, 8, 15, 22; Mar: 1, 8, 15, 22, 29; Apr: 5, 12, 19, 26; May: 3, 10, 17, 24, 31; Jun: 7, 14, 21, 28; Jul: 5, 12, 19, 26; Aug: 2, 9, 16, 23, 30; Sep: 6, 13, 20, 27; Oct: 4, 11, 18, 25; Nov: 1, 8, 15, 22, 29; Dec: 6, 13, 20, 27

1955 Jan: 3, 10, 17, 24, 31; Feb: 7, 14, 21, 28; Mar: 7, 14, 21, 28; Apr: 4, 11, 18, 25; May: 2, 9, 16, 23, 30; Jun: 6, 13, 20, 27; Jul: 4, 11, 18, 25; Aug: 1, 8, 15, 22, 29; Sep: 5, 12, 19, 26; Oct: 3, 10, 17, 24, 31; Nov: 7, 14, 21, 28; Dec: 5, 12, 19, 26

1956 Jan: 2, 9, 16, 23, 30; Feb: 6, 13, 20, 27; Mar: 5, 12, 19, 26; Apr: 2, 9, 16, 23, 30; May: 7, 14, 21, 28; Jun: 4, 11, 18, 25; Jul: 2, 9, 16, 23, 30; Aug: 6, 13, 20, 27; Sep: 3, 10, 17, 24; Oct: 1, 8, 15, 22, 29; Nov: 5, 12, 19, 26; Dec: 3, 10, 17, 24, 31

1957 Jan: 7, 14, 21, 28; Feb: 4, 11, 18, 25; Mar: 4, 11, 18, 25; Apr: 1, 8, 15, 22, 29; May: 6, 13, 20, 27; Jun: 3, 10, 17, 24; Jul: 1, 8, 15, 22, 29; Aug: 5, 12, 19, 26; Sep: 2, 9, 16, 23, 30; Oct: 7, 14, 21, 28; Nov: 4, 11, 18, 25; Dec: 2, 9, 16, 23, 30

1958 Jan: 6, 13, 20, 27; Feb: 3, 10, 17, 24; Mar: 3, 10, 17, 24, 31; Apr: 7, 14, 21, 28; May: 5, 12, 19, 26; Jun: 2, 9, 16, 23, 30; Jul: 7, 14, 21, 28; Aug: 4, 11, 18, 25; Sep: 1, 8, 15, 22, 29; Oct: 6, 13, 20, 27; Nov: 3, 10, 17, 24; Dec: 1, 8, 15, 22, 29

1959 Jan: 5, 12, 19, 26; Feb: 2, 9, 16, 23; Mar: 2, 9, 16, 23, 30; Apr: 6, 13, 20, 27; May: 4, 11, 18, 25; Jun: 1, 8, 15, 22, 29; Jul: 6, 13, 20, 27; Aug: 3, 10, 17, 24, 31; Sep: 7, 14, 21, 28; Oct: 5, 12, 19, 26; Nov: 2, 9, 16, 23, 30; Dec: 7, 14, 21, 28

1960 Jan: 4, 11, 18, 25; Feb: 1, 8, 15, 22, 29; Mar: 7, 14, 21, 28; Apr: 4, 11, 18, 25; May: 2, 9, 16, 23, 30; Jun: 6, 13, 20, 27; Jul: 4, 11, 18, 25; Aug: 1, 8, 15, 22, 29; Sep: 5, 12, 19, 26; Oct: 3, 10, 17, 24, 31; Nov: 7, 14, 21, 28; Dec: 5, 12, 19, 26

1961 Jan: 2, 9, 16, 23, 30; Feb: 6, 13, 20, 27; Mar: 6, 13, 20, 27; Apr: 3, 10, 17, 24; May: 1, 8, 15, 22, 29; Jun: 5, 12, 19, 26; Jul: 3, 10, 17, 24, 31; Aug: 7, 14, 21, 28; Sep: 4, 11, 18, 25; Oct: 2, 9, 16, 23, 30; Nov: 6, 13, 20, 27; Dec: 4, 11, 18, 25

1962 Jan: 1, 8, 15, 22, 29; Feb: 5, 12, 19, 26; Mar: 5, 12, 19, 26; Apr: 2, 9, 16, 23, 30; May: 7, 14, 21, 28; Jun: 4, 11, 18, 25; Jul: 2, 9, 16, 23, 30; Aug: 6, 13, 20, 27; Sep: 3, 10, 17, 24; Oct: 1, 8, 15, 22, 29; Nov: 5, 12, 19, 26; Dec: 3, 10, 17, 24, 31

1963 Jan: 7, 14, 21, 28; Feb: 4, 11, 18, 25; Mar: 4, 11, 18, 25; Apr: 1, 8, 15, 22, 29; May: 6, 13, 20, 27; Jun: 3, 10, 17, 24; Jul: 1, 8, 15, 22, 29; Aug: 5, 12, 19, 26; Sep: 2, 9, 16, 23, 30; Oct: 7, 14, 21, 28; Nov: 4, 11, 18, 25; Dec: 2, 9, 16, 23, 30

1964 Jan: 6, 13, 20, 27; Feb: 3, 10, 17, 24; Mar: 2, 9, 16, 23, 30; Apr: 6, 13, 20, 27; May: 4, 11, 18, 25; Jun: 1, 8, 15, 22, 29; Jul: 6, 13, 20, 27; Aug: 3, 10, 17, 24, 31; Sep: 7, 14, 21, 28; Oct: 5, 12, 19, 26; Nov: 2, 9, 16, 23, 30; Dec: 7, 14, 21, 28

1965 *Jan:* 4, 11, 18, 25; *Feb:* 1, 8, 15, 22; *Mar:* 1, 8, 15, 22, 29; *Apr:* 5, 12, 19, 26; *May:* 3, 10, 17, 24, 31; *Jun:* 7, 14, 21, 28; *Jul:* 5, 12, 19, 26; *Aug:* 2, 9, 16, 23, 30; *Sep:* 6, 13, 20, 27; *Oct:* 4, 11, 18, 25; *Nov:* 1, 8, 15, 22, 29; *Dec:* 6, 13, 20, 27

1966 *Jan:* 3, 10, 17, 24, 31; *Feb:* 7, 14, 21, 28; *Mar:* 7, 14, 21, 28; *Apr:* 4, 11, 18, 25; *May:* 2, 9, 16, 23, 30; *Jun:* 6, 13, 20, 27; *Jul:* 4, 11, 18, 25; *Aug:* 1, 8, 15, 22, 29; *Sep:* 5, 12, 19, 26; *Oct:* 3, 10, 17, 24, 31; *Nov:* 7, 14, 21, 28; *Dec:* 5, 12, 19, 26

1967 *Jan:* 2, 9, 16, 23, 30; *Feb:* 6, 13, 20, 27; *Mar:* 6, 13, 20, 27; *Apr:* 3, 10, 17, 24; *May:* 1, 8, 15, 22, 29; *Jun:* 5, 12, 19, 26; *Jul:* 3, 10, 17, 24, 31; *Aug:* 7, 14, 21, 28; *Sep:* 4, 11, 18, 25; *Oct:* 2, 9, 16, 23, 30; *Nov:* 6, 13, 20, 27; *Dec:* 4, 11, 18, 25

1968 *Jan:* 1, 8, 15, 22, 29; *Feb:* 5, 12, 19, 26; *Mar:* 4, 11, 18, 25; *Apr:* 1, 8, 15, 22, 29; *May:* 6, 13, 20, 27; *Jun:* 3, 10, 17, 24; *Jul:* 1, 8, 15, 22, 29; *Aug:* 5, 12, 19, 26; *Sep:* 2, 9, 16, 23, 30; *Oct:* 7, 14, 21, 28; *Nov:* 4, 11, 18, 25; *Dec:* 2, 9, 16, 23, 30

1969 *Jan:* 6, 13, 20, 27; *Feb:* 3, 10, 17, 24; *Mar:* 3, 10, 17, 24, 31; *Apr:* 7, 14, 21, 28; *May:* 5, 12, 19, 26; *Jun:* 2, 9, 16, 23, 30; *Jul:* 7, 14, 21, 28; *Aug:* 4, 11, 18, 25; *Sep:* 1, 8, 15, 22, 29; *Oct:* 6, 13, 20, 27; *Nov:* 3, 10, 17, 24; *Dec:* 1, 8, 15, 22, 29

1970 *Jan:* 5, 12, 19, 26; *Feb:* 2, 9, 16, 23; *Mar:* 2, 9, 16, 23, 30; *Apr:* 6, 13, 20, 27; *May:* 4, 11, 18, 25; *Jun:* 1, 8, 15, 22, 29; *Jul:* 6, 13, 20, 27; *Aug:* 3, 10, 17, 24, 31; *Sep:* 7, 14, 21, 28; *Oct:* 5, 12, 19, 26; *Nov:* 2, 9, 16, 23, 30; *Dec:* 7, 14, 21, 28

1971 *Jan:* 4, 11, 18, 25; *Feb:* 1, 8, 15, 22; *Mar:* 1, 8, 15, 22, 29; *Apr:* 5, 12, 19, 26; *May:* 3, 10, 17, 24, 31; *Jun:* 7, 14, 21, 28; *Jul:* 5, 12, 19, 26; *Aug:* 2, 9, 16, 23, 30; *Sep:* 6, 13, 20, 27; *Oct:* 4, 11, 18, 25; *Nov:* 1, 8, 15, 22, 29; *Dec:* 6, 13, 20, 27

1972 *Jan:* 3, 10, 17, 24, 31; *Feb:* 7, 14, 21, 28; *Mar:* 6, 13, 20, 27; *Apr:* 3, 10, 17, 24; *May:* 1, 8, 15, 22, 29; *Jun:* 5, 12, 19, 26; *Jul:* 3, 10, 17, 24, 31; *Aug:* 7, 14, 21, 28; *Sep:* 4, 11, 18, 25; *Oct:* 2, 9, 16, 23, 30; *Nov:* 6, 13, 20, 27; *Dec:* 4, 11, 18, 25

1973 *Jan:* 1, 8, 15, 22, 29; *Feb:* 5, 12, 19, 26; *Mar:* 5, 12, 19, 26; *Apr:* 2, 9, 16, 23, 30; *May:* 7, 14, 21, 28; *Jun:* 4, 11, 18, 25; *Jul:* 2, 9, 16, 23, 30; *Aug:* 6, 13, 20, 27; *Sep:* 3, 10, 17, 24; *Oct:* 1, 8, 15, 22, 29; *Nov:* 5, 12, 19, 26; *Dec:* 3, 10, 17, 24, 31

1974 *Jan:* 7, 14, 21, 28; *Feb:* 4, 11, 18, 25; *Mar:* 4, 11, 18, 25; *Apr:* 1, 8, 15, 22, 29; *May:* 6, 13, 20, 27; *Jun:* 3, 10, 17, 24; *Jul:* 1, 8, 15, 22, 29; *Aug:* 5, 12, 19, 26; *Sep:* 2, 9, 16, 23, 30; *Oct:* 7, 14, 21, 28; *Nov:* 4, 11, 18, 25; *Dec:* 2, 9, 16, 23, 30

1975 *Jan:* 6, 13, 20, 27; *Feb:* 3, 10, 17, 24; *Mar:* 3, 10, 17, 24, 31; *Apr:* 7, 14, 21, 28; *May:* 5, 12, 19, 26; *Jun:* 2, 9, 16, 23, 30; *Jul:* 7, 14, 21, 28; *Aug:* 4, 11, 18, 25; *Sep:* 1, 8, 15, 22, 29; *Oct:* 6, 13, 20, 27; *Nov:* 3, 10, 17, 24; *Dec:* 1, 8, 15, 22, 29

1976 *Jan:* 5, 12, 19, 26; *Feb:* 2, 9, 16, 23; *Mar:* 1, 8, 15, 22, 29; *Apr:* 5, 12, 19, 26; *May:* 3, 10, 17, 24, 31; *Jun:* 7, 14, 21, 28; *Jul:* 5, 12, 19, 26; *Aug:* 2, 9, 16, 23, 30; *Sep:* 6, 13, 20, 27; *Oct:* 4, 11, 18, 25; *Nov:* 1, 8, 15, 22, 29; *Dec:* 6, 13, 20, 27

1977 *Jan:* 3, 10, 17, 24, 31; *Feb:* 7, 14, 21, 28; *Mar:* 7, 14, 21, 28; *Apr:* 4, 11, 18, 25; *May:* 2, 9, 16, 23, 30; *Jun:* 6, 13, 20, 27; *Jul:* 4, 11, 18, 25; *Aug:* 1, 8, 15, 22, 29; *Sep:* 5, 12, 19, 26; *Oct:* 3, 10, 17, 24, 31; *Nov:* 7, 14, 21, 28; *Dec:* 5, 12, 19, 26

1978 Jan: 2, 9, 16, 23, 30; Feb: 6, 13, 20, 27; Mar: 6, 13, 20, 27; Apr: 3, 10, 17, 24; May: 1, 8, 15, 22, 29; Jun: 5, 12, 19, 26; Jul: 3, 10, 17, 24, 31; Aug: 7, 14, 21, 28; Sep: 4, 11, 18, 25; Oct: 2, 9, 16, 23, 30; Nov: 6, 13, 20, 27; Dec: 4, 11, 18, 25

1979 Jan: 1, 8, 15, 22, 29, Feb: 5, 12, 19, 26, Mar: 5, 12, 19, 26, Apr: 2, 9, 16, 23, 30, May: 7, 14, 21, 28, Jun: 4, 11, 18, 25Jul: 2, 9, 16, 23, 30, Aug: 6, 13, 20, 27, Sep: 3, 10, 17, 24, Oct: 1, 8, 15, 22, 29, Nov: 5, 12, 19, 26, Dec: 3, 10, 17, 24, 31

1980 Jan: 7, 14, 21, 28; Feb: 4, 11, 18, 25; Mar: 3, 10, 17, 24, 31; Apr: 7, 14, 21, 28; May: 5, 12, 19, 26; Jun: 2, 9, 16, 23, 30; Jul: 7, 14, 21, 28; Aug: 4, 11, 18, 25; Sep: 1, 8, 15, 22, 29; Oct: 6, 13, 20, 27; Nov: 3, 10, 17, 24; Dec: 1, 8, 15, 22, 29

1981 Jan: 5, 12, 19, 26; Feb: 2, 9, 16, 23; Mar: 2, 9, 16, 23, 30; Apr: 6, 13, 20, 27; May: 4, 11, 18, 25; Jun: 1, 8, 15, 22, 29; Jul: 6, 13, 20, 27; Aug: 3, 10, 17, 24, 31; Sep: 7, 14, 21, 28; Oct: 5, 12, 19, 26; Nov: 2, 9, 16, 23, 30; Dec: 7, 14, 21, 28

1982 Jan: 4, 11, 18, 25; Feb: 1, 8, 15, 22; Mar: 1, 8, 15, 22, 29; Apr: 5, 12, 19, 26; May: 3, 10, 17, 24, 31; Jun: 7, 14, 21, 28; Jul: 5, 12, 19, 26; Aug: 2, 9, 16, 23, 30; Sep: 6, 13, 20, 27; Oct: 4, 11, 18, 25; Nov: 1, 8, 15, 22, 29, Dec: 6, 13, 20, 27

1983 Jan: 3, 10, 17, 24, 31, Feb: 7, 14, 21, 28, Mar: 7, 14, 21, 28, Apr: 4, 11, 18, 25, May: 2, 9, 16, 23, 30, Jun: 6, 13, 20, 27, Jul: 4, 11, 18, 25, Aug: 1, 8, 15, 22, 29, Sep: 5, 12, 19, 26, Oct: 3, 10, 17, 24, 31, Nov: 7, 14, 21, 28, Dec: 5, 12, 19, 26

1984 Jan: 2, 9, 16, 23, 30; Feb: 6, 13, 20, 27; Mar: 5, 12, 19, 26; Apr: 2, 9, 16, 23, 30; May: 7, 14, 21, 28; Jun: 4, 11, 18, 25; Jul: 2, 9, 16, 23, 30; Aug: 6, 13, 20, 27; Sep: 3, 10, 17, 24; Oct: 1, 8, 15, 22, 29; Nov: 5, 12, 19, 26; Dec: 3, 10, 17, 24, 31

1985 Jan: 7, 14, 21, 28; Feb: 4, 11, 18, 25; Mar: 4, 11, 18, 25; Apr: 1, 8, 15, 22, 29; May: 6, 13, 20, 27; Jun: 3, 10, 17, 24; Jul: 1, 8, 15, 22, 29; Aug: 5, 12, 19, 26; Sep: 2, 9, 16, 23, 30; Oct: 7, 14, 21, 28; Nov: 4, 11, 18, 25; Dec: 2, 9, 16, 23, 30

1986 Jan: 6, 13, 20, 27; Feb: 3, 10, 17, 24; Mar: 3, 10, 17, 24, 31; Apr: 7, 14, 21, 28; May: 5, 12, 19, 26; Jun: 2, 9, 16, 23, 30; Jul: 7, 14, 21, 28; Aug: 4, 11, 18, 25; Sep: 1, 8, 15, 22, 29; Oct: 6, 13, 20, 27; Nov: 3, 10, 17, 24; Dec: 1, 8, 15, 22, 29

1987 Jan: 5, 12, 19, 26; Feb: 2, 9, 16, 23; Mar: 2, 9, 16, 23, 30; Apr: 6, 13, 20, 27; May: 4, 11, 18, 25; Jun: 1, 8, 15, 22, 29; Jul: 6, 13, 20, 27; Aug: 3, 10, 17, 24, 31; Sep: 7, 14, 21, 28; Oct: 5, 12, 19, 26; Nov: 2, 9, 16, 23; Dec: 1, 4, 21, 28, 30

1988 Jan: 4, 11, 18, 25; Feb: 1, 8, 15, 22, 29; Mar: 7, 14, 21, 28; Apr: 4, 11, 18, 25; May: 2, 9, 16, 23, 30; Jun: 6, 13, 20, 27; Jul: 4, 11, 18, 25; Aug: 1, 8, 15, 22, 29; Sep: 5, 12, 19, 26; Oct: 3, 10, 17, 24, 31; Nov: 7, 14, 21, 28; Dec: 5, 12, 19, 26

1989 Jan: 2, 9, 16, 23, 30; Feb: 6, 13, 20, 27; Mar: 6, 13, 20, 27; Apr: 3, 10, 17, 24; May: 1, 8, 15, 22, 29; Jun: 5, 12, 19, 26; Jul: 3, 10, 17, 24, 31; Aug: 7, 14, 21, 28; Sep: 4, 11, 18, 25; Oct: 2, 9, 16, 23, 30; Nov: 6, 13, 20, 27; Dec: 4, 11, 18, 25

1990 Jan: 1, 8, 15, 22, 29; Feb: 5, 12, 19, 26; Mar: 5, 12, 19, 26; Apr: 2, 9, 16, 23, 30; May: 7, 14, 21, 28; Jun: 4, 11, 18, 25; Jul: 2, 9, 16, 23, 30; Aug: 6, 13, 20, 27; Sep: 3, 10, 17, 24; Oct: 1, 8, 15, 22, 29; Nov: 5, 12, 19, 26; Dec: 3, 10, 17, 24, 31

1991 *Jan:* 7, 14, 21, 28; *Feb:* 4, 11, 18, 25; *Mar:* 4, 11, 18, 25; *Apr:* 1, 8, 15, 22, 29; *May:* 6, 13, 20, 27; *Jun:* 3, 10, 17, 24; *Jul:* 1, 8, 15, 22, 29; *Aug:* 5, 12, 19, 26; *Sep:* 2, 9, 16, 23, 30; *Oct:* 7, 14, 21, 28; *Nov:* 4, 11, 18, 25; *Dec:* 2, 9, 16, 23, 30

1992 *Jan:* 6, 13, 20, 27, *Feb:* 3, 10, 17, 24, *Mar:* 2, 9, 16, 23, 30, *Apr:* 6, 13, 20, 27, *May:* 4, 11, 18, 25, *Jun:* 1, 8, 15, 22, 29, *Jul:* 6, 13, 20, 27, *Aug:* 3, 10, 17, 24, 31, *Sep:* 7, 14, 21, 28, *Oct:* 5, 12, 19, 26, *Nov:* 2, 9, 16, 23, 30, *Dec:* 7, 14, 21, 28

1993 *Jan:* 4, 11, 18, 25; *Feb:* 1, 8, 15, 22; *Mar:* 1, 8, 15, 22, 29; *Apr:* 5, 12, 19, 26; *May:* 3, 10, 17, 24, 31; *Jun:* 7, 14, 21, 28; *Jul:* 5, 12, 19, 26; *Aug:* 2, 9, 16, 23, 30; *Sep:* 6, 13, 20, 27; *Oct:* 4, 11, 18, 25; *Nov:* 1, 8, 15, 22, 29; *Dec:* 6, 13, 20, 27

1994 *Jan:* 3, 10, 17, 24, 31; *Feb:* 7, 14, 21, 28; *Mar:* 7, 14, 21, 28; *Apr:* 4, 11, 18, 25; *May:* 2, 9, 16, 23, 30; *Jun:* 6, 13, 20, 27; *Jul:* 4, 11, 18, 25; *Aug:* 1, 8, 15, 22, 29; *Sep:* 5, 12, 19, 26; *Oct:* 3, 10, 17, 24, 31; *Nov:* 7, 14, 21, 28; *Dec:* 5, 12, 19, 26

1995 *Jan:* 2, 9, 16, 23, 30, *Feb:* 6, 13, 20, 27, *Mar:* 6, 13, 20, 27, *Apr:* 3, 10, 17, 24, *May:* 1, 8, 15, 22, 29, *Jun:* 5, 12, 19, 26, *Jul:* 3, 10, 17, 24, 31, *Aug:* 7, 14, 21, 28, *Sep:* 4, 11, 18, 25, *Oct:* 2, 9, 16, 23, 30, *Nov:* 6, 13, 20, 27, *Dec:* 4, 11, 18, 25

1996 *Jan:* 1, 8, 15, 22, 29; *Feb:* 5, 12, 19, 26; *Mar:* 4, 11, 18, 25; *Apr:* 1, 8, 15, 22, 29; *May:* 6, 13, 20, 27; *Jun:* 3, 10, 17, 24; *Jul:* 1, 8, 15, 22, 29; *Aug:* 5, 12, 19, 26; *Sep:* 2, 9, 16, 23, 30; *Oct:* 7, 14, 21, 28; *Nov:* 4, 11, 18, 25; *Dec:* 2, 9, 16, 23, 30

1997 *Jan:* 6, 13, 20, 27; *Feb:* 3, 10, 17, 24; *Mar:* 3, 10, 17, 24, 31; *Apr:* 7, 14, 21, 28; *May:* 5, 12, 19, 26; *Jun:* 2, 9, 16, 23, 30; *Jul:* 7, 14, 21, 28; *Aug:* 4, 11, 18, 25; *Sep:* 1, 8, 15, 22, 29; *Oct:* 6, 13, 20, 27; *Nov:* 3, 10, 17, 24; *Dec:* 1, 8, 15, 22, 29

1998 *Jan:* 5, 12, 19, 26; *Feb:* 2, 9, 16, 23; *Mar:* 2, 9, 16, 23, 30; *Apr:* 6, 13, 20, 27; *May:* 4, 11, 18, 25; *Jun:* 1, 8, 15, 22, 29; *Jul:* 6, 13, 20, 27; *Aug:* 3, 10, 17, 24, 31; *Sep:* 7, 14, 21, 28; *Oct:* 5, 12, 19, 26; *Nov:* 2, 9, 16, 23, 30; *Dec:* 7, 14, 21, 28

1999 *Jan:* 4, 11, 18, 25; *Feb:* 1, 8, 15, 22; *Mar:* 1, 8, 15, 22, 29; *Apr:* 5, 12, 19, 26; *May:* 3, 10, 17, 24, 31; *Jun:* 7, 14, 21, 28; *Jul:* 5, 12, 19, 26; *Aug:* 2, 9, 16, 23, 30; *Sep:* 6, 13, 20, 27; *Oct:* 4, 11, 18, 25; *Nov:* 1, 8, 15, 22, 29; *Dec:* 6, 13, 20, 27

2000 *Jan:* 3, 10, 17, 24, 31; *Feb:* 7, 14, 21, 28; *Mar:* 6, 13, 20, 27; *Apr:* 3, 10, 17, 24; *May:* 1, 8, 15, 22, 29; *Jun:* 5, 12, 19, 26; *Jul:* 3, 10, 17, 24, 31; *Aug:* 7, 14, 21, 28; *Sep:* 4, 11, 18, 25; *Oct:* 2, 9, 16, 23, 30; *Nov:* 6, 13, 20, 27; *Dec:* 4, 11, 18, 25

2001 *Jan:* 1, 8, 15, 22, 29; *Feb:* 5, 12, 19, 26; *Mar:* 5, 12, 19, 26; *Apr:* 2, 9, 16, 23, 30; *May:* 7, 14, 21, 28; *Jun:* 4, 11, 18, 25; *Jul:* 2, 9, 16, 23, 30; *Aug:* 6, 13, 20, 27; *Sep:* 3, 10, 17, 24; *Oct:* 1, 8, 15, 22, 29; *Nov:* 5, 12, 19, 26; *Dec:* 3, 10, 17, 24, 31

2002 *Jan:* 7, 14, 21, 28; *Feb:* 4, 11, 18, 25; *Mar:* 4, 11, 18, 25; *Apr:* 1, 8, 15, 22, 29; *May:* 6, 13, 20, 27; *Jun:* 3, 10, 17, 24; *Jul:* 1, 8, 15, 22, 29; *Aug:* 5, 12, 19, 26; *Sep:* 2, 9, 16, 23, 30; *Oct:* 7, 14, 21, 28; *Nov:* 4, 11, 18, 25; *Dec:* 2, 9, 16, 23, 30

2003 *Jan:* 6, 13, 20, 27; *Feb:* 3, 10, 17, 24; *Mar:* 3, 10, 17, 24, 31; *Apr:* 7, 14, 21, 28; *May:* 5, 12, 19, 26; *Jun:* 2, 9, 16, 23, 30; *Jul:* 7, 14, 21, 28; *Aug:* 4, 11, 18, 25; *Sep:* 1, 8, 15, 22, 29; *Oct:* 6, 13, 20, 27; *Nov:* 3, 10, 17, 24; *Dec:* 1, 8, 15, 22, 29

2004 *Jan:* 5, 12, 19, 26; *Feb:* 2, 9, 16, 23; *Mar:* 1, 8, 15, 22, 29; *Apr:* 5, 12, 19, 26; *May:* 3, 10, 17, 24, 31; *Jun:* 7, 14, 21, 28; *Jul:* 5, 12, 19, 26; *Aug:* 2, 9, 16, 23, 30; *Sep:* 6, 13, 20, 27; *Oct:* 4, 11, 18, 25; *Nov:* 1, 8, 15, 22, 29; *Dec:* 6, 13, 20, 27

2005 *Jan:* 3, 10, 17, 24, 31; *Feb:* 7, 14, 21, 28; *Mar:* 7, 14, 21, 28; *Apr:* 4, 11, 18, 25; *May:* 2, 9, 16, 23, 30; *Jun:* 6, 13, 20, 27; *Jul:* 4, 11, 18, 25; *Aug:* 1, 8, 15, 22, 29; *Sep:* 5, 12, 19, 26; *Oct:* 3, 10, 17, 24, 31; *Nov:* 7, 14, 21, 28; *Dec:* 5, 12, 19, 26

2006 *Jan:* 2, 9, 16, 23, 30; *Feb:* 6, 13, 20, 27; *Mar:* 6, 13, 20, 27; *Apr:* 3, 10, 17, 24; *May:* 1, 8, 15, 22, 29; *Jun:* 5, 12, 19, 26; *Jul:* 3, 10, 17, 24, 31; *Aug:* 7, 14, 21, 28; *Sep:* 4, 11, 18, 25; *Oct:* 2, 9, 16, 23, 30; *Nov:* 6, 13, 20, 27; *Dec:* 4, 11, 18, 25

2007 *Jan:* 1, 8, 15, 22, 29; *Feb:* 5, 12, 19, 26; *Mar:* 5, 12, 19, 26; *Apr:* 2, 9, 16, 23, 30; *May:* 7, 14, 21, 28; *Jun:* 4, 11, 18, 25; *Jul:* 2, 9, 16, 23, 30; *Aug:* 6, 13, 20, 27; *Sep:* 3, 10, 17, 24; *Oct:* 1, 8, 15, 22, 29; *Nov:* 5, 12, 19, 26; *Dec:* 3, 10, 17, 24, 31

2008 *Jan:* 7, 14, 21, 28; *Feb:* 4, 11, 18, 25; *Mar:* 3, 10, 17, 24, 31; *Apr:* 7, 14, 21, 28; *May:* 5, 12, 19, 26; *Jun:* 2, 9, 16, 23, 30; *Jul:* 7, 14, 21, 28; *Aug:* 4, 11, 18, 25; *Sep:* 1, 8, 15, 22, 29; *Oct:* 6, 13, 20, 27; *Nov:* 3, 10, 17, 24; *Dec:* 1, 8, 15, 22, 29

2009 *Jan:* 5, 12, 19, 26; *Feb:* 2, 9, 16, 23; *Mar:* 2, 9, 16, 23, 30; *Apr:* 6, 13, 20, 27; *May:* 4, 11, 18, 25; *Jun:* 1, 8, 15, 22, 29; *Jul:* 6, 13, 20, 27; *Aug:* 3, 10, 17, 24, 31; *Sep:* 7, 14, 21, 28; *Oct:* 5, 12, 19, 26; *Nov:* 2, 9, 16, 23, 30; *Dec:* 7, 14, 21, 28

2010 *Jan:* 4, 11, 18, 25; *Feb:* 1, 8, 15, 22; *Mar:* 1, 8, 15, 22, 29; *Apr:* 5, 12, 19, 26; *May:* 3, 10, 17, 24, 31; *Jun:* 7, 14, 21, 28; *Jul:* 5, 12, 19, 26; *Aug:* 2, 9, 16, 23, 30; *Sep:* 6, 13, 20, 27; *Oct:* 4, 11, 18, 25; *Nov:* 1, 8, 15, 22, 29; *Dec:* 6, 13, 20, 27

2011 *Jan:* 3, 10, 17, 24, 31; *Feb:* 7, 14, 21, 28; *Mar:* 7, 14, 21, 28; *Apr:* 4, 11, 18, 25; *May:* 2, 9, 16, 23, 30; *Jun:* 6, 13, 20, 27; *Jul:* 4, 11, 18, 25; *Aug:* 1, 8, 15, 22, 29; *Sep:* 5, 12, 19, 26; *Oct:* 3, 10, 17, 24, 31; *Nov:* 7, 14, 21, 28; *Dec:* 5, 12, 19, 26

2012 *Jan:* 2, 9, 16, 23, 30; *Feb:* 6, 13, 20, 27; *Mar:* 5, 12, 19, 26; *Apr:* 2, 9, 16, 23, 30; *May:* 7, 14, 21, 28; *Jun:* 4, 11, 18, 25; *Jul:* 2, 9, 16, 23, 30; *Aug:* 6, 13, 20, 27; *Sep:* 3, 10, 17, 24; *Oct:* 1, 8, 15, 22, 29; *Nov:* 5, 12, 19, 26; *Dec:* 3, 10, 17, 24, 31

2013 *Jan:* 7, 14, 21, 28; *Feb:* 4, 11, 18, 25; *Mar:* 4, 11, 18, 25; *Apr:* 1, 8, 15, 22, 29; *May:* 6, 13, 20, 27; *Jun:* 3, 10, 17, 24; *Jul:* 1, 8, 15, 22, 29; *Aug:* 5, 12, 19, 26; *Sep:* 2, 9, 16, 23, 30; *Oct:* 7, 14, 21, 28; *Nov:* 4, 11, 18, 25; *Dec:* 2, 9, 16, 23, 30

Tuesday: Camael

IF YOUR DAY OF BIRTH IS TUESDAY: Camael rules. Camael's healing rays are shades of red, including rose gold, his metal is iron, his crystals are ruby, garnet, red carnelian and red agate. Attributes on which to focus are: courage, justice and empowerment through forgiveness.

Camael is ruler of Mars and Tuesday. His name means 'He who sees God'. He represents courage with nobility, sometimes being depicted in the guise of a leopard crouched on a rock. In the *History of Magic* (written 150 years ago), Camael is described as 'a name that personifies divine justice'. He is associated with Mars, the red planet, hence his day is Tuesday, day of Mars. In the angelic hierarchy of nine groups, he is ruler of the Order of Powers and 5th Heaven.

Camael is the angel to invoke to offer strength and encouragement in aid of a just cause. Many of us feel fearful at times, about life, about the future, about the world in general. This is perfectly understandable, but while love expands, fear constricts, contracting the spirit and creating boundaries. Fear, therefore, prevents us from developing our potential and spiritual growth. Camael offers ways for you to become stronger, more empowered and with secure foundations, for Camael and red are linked with root chakra. Symbols associated with root chakra are a red rose (forgiveness) or cube (earth: secure foundations).

We can all call on Camael whenever we need his special help in our life. However, if you were born on Tuesday then he is one of your guardian angels who will always be in evidence, guiding you. Invoke Camael to enhance or transform your life, but you will derive even more energy with him on a Tuesday. Here is an invocation as well as a tip for the colour red:

Camael, Camael, Camael, please be with me to bring courage (or justice or empowerment or forgiveness), *in Love and Light, Love and Light, Love and Light.*

For empowerment, wear something red to aid focus on Camael, and try colour breathing with red to bolster your courage and stamina or heal root chakra (see page 203 for more on this).

Tuesday birthdays

1940 Jan: 02, 09, 16, 23, 30; Feb: 06, 13, 20, 27; Mar: 05, 12, 19, 26; Apr: 02, 09, 16, 23, 30; May: 07, 14, 21, 28; Jun: 04, 11, 18, 25; Jul: 02, 09, 16, 23, 30; Aug: 06, 13, 20, 27; Sep: 03, 10, 17, 24; Oct: 01, 08, 15, 22, 29; Nov: 05, 12, 19, 26; Dec: 03, 10, 17, 24, 31

1941 Jan: 07, 14, 21, 28, Feb: 04, 11, 18, 25, Mar: 04, 11, 18, 25, Apr: 01, 08, 15, 22, 29, May: 06, 13, 20, 27, Jun: 03, 10, 17, 24; Jul: 01, 08, 15, 22, 29; Aug: 05, 12, 19, 26; Sep: 02, 09, 16, 23, 30; Oct: 07, 14, 21, 28; Nov: 04, 11, 18, 25; Dec: 02, 09, 16, 23, 30

1942 Jan: 06, 13, 20, 27; Feb: 03, 10, 17, 24; Mar: 03, 10, 17, 24, 31; Apr: 07, 14, 21, 28; May: 05, 12, 19, 26; Jun: 02, 09, 16, 23, 30; Jul: 07, 14, 21, 28; Aug: 04, 11, 18, 25; Sep: 01, 08, 15, 22, 29; Oct: 06, 13, 20, 27; Nov: 03, 10, 17, 24; Dec: 01, 08, 15, 22, 29

1943 Jan: 05, 12, 19, 26; Feb: 02, 09, 16, 23; Mar: 02, 09, 16, 23, 30; Apr: 06, 13, 20, 27; May: 04, 11, 18, 25; Jun: 01, 08, 15, 22, 29; Jul: 06, 13, 20, 27; Aug: 03, 10, 17, 24, 31; Sep: 07, 14, 21, 28; Oct: 05, 12, 19, 26; Nov: 02, 09, 16, 23, 30; Dec: 07, 14, 21, 28

1944 Jan: 04, 11, 18, 25; Feb: 01, 08, 15, 22, 29; Mar: 07, 14, 21, 28; Apr: 04, 11, 18, 25; May: 02, 09, 16, 23, 30; Jun: 06, 13, 20, 27; Jul: 04, 11, 18, 25; Aug: 01, 08, 15, 22, 29; Sep: 05, 12, 19, 26; Oct: 03, 10, 17, 24, 31; Nov: 07, 14, 21, 28; Dec: 05, 12, 19, 26

1945 Jan: 02, 09, 16, 23, 30; Feb: 06, 13, 20, 27; Mar: 06, 13, 20, 27; Apr: 03, 10, 17, 24; May: 01, 08, 15, 22, 29; Jun: 05, 12, 19, 26; Jul: 03, 10, 17, 24, 31; Aug: 07, 14, 21; 28; Sep: 04, 11, 18, 25; Oct: 02, 09, 16, 23, 30; Nov: 06, 13, 20, 27; Dec: 04, 11, 18, 25

1946 Jan: 01, 08, 15, 22, 29; Feb: 05, 12, 19, 26; Mar: 05, 12, 19, 26; Apr: 02, 09, 16, 23, 30; May: 07, 14, 21, 28; Jun: 04, 11, 18, 25; Jul: 02, 09, 16, 23, 30; Aug: 06, 13, 20, 27; Sep: 03, 10, 17, 24; Oct: 01, 08, 15, 22, 29; Nov: 05, 12, 19, 26; Dec: 03, 10, 17, 24, 31

1947 Jan: 07, 14, 21, 28; Feb: 04, 11, 18, 25; Mar: 04, 11, 18, 25; Apr: 01, 08, 15, 22, 29; May: 06, 13, 20, 27; Jun: 03, 10, 17, 24; Jul: 01, 08, 15, 22, 29; Aug: 05, 12, 19, 26; Sep: 02, 09, 16, 23, 30; Oct: 07, 14, 21, 28; Nov: 04, 11, 18, 25; Dec: 02, 09, 16, 23, 30

1948 Jan: 06, 13, 20, 27; Feb: 03, 10, 17, 24; Mar: 02, 09, 16, 23, 30; Apr: 06, 13, 20, 27; May: 04, 11, 18, 25; Jun: 01, 08, 15, 22, 29; Jul: 06, 13, 20, 27; Aug: 03, 10, 17, 24, 31; Sep: 07, 14, 21, 28; Oct: 05, 12, 19, 26; Nov: 02, 09, 16, 23, 30; Dec: 07, 14, 21, 28

1949 Jan: 04, 11, 18, 25; Feb: 01, 08, 15, 22; Mar: 01, 08, 15, 22, 29; Apr: 05, 12, 19, 26; May: 03, 10, 17, 24, 31; Jun: 07, 14, 21, 28; Jul: 05, 12, 19, 26; Aug: 02, 09, 16, 23, 30; Sep: 06, 13, 20, 27; Oct: 04, 11, 18, 25; Nov: 01, 08, 15, 22, 29; Dec: 06, 13, 20, 27

1950 Jan: 03, 10, 17, 24, 31; Feb: 07, 14, 21, 28; Mar: 07, 14, 21, 28; Apr: 04, 11, 18, 25; May: 02, 09, 16, 23, 30; Jun: 06, 13, 20, 27; Jul: 04, 11, 18, 25; Aug: 01, 08, 15, 22, 29; Sep: 05, 12, 19, 26; Oct: 03, 10, 17, 24, 31; Nov: 07, 14, 21, 28; Dec: 05, 12, 19, 26

1951 Jan: 02, 09, 16, 23, 30; Feb: 06, 13, 20, 27; Mar: 06, 13, 20, 27; Apr: 03, 10, 17, 24; May: 01, 08, 15, 22, 29; Jun: 05, 12, 19, 26; Jul: 03, 10, 17, 24, 31; Aug: 07, 14, 21, 28; Sep: 04, 11, 18, 25; Oct: 02, 09, 16, 23, 30; Nov: 06, 13, 20, 27; Dec: 04, 11, 18, 25

1952 *Jan:* 01, 08, 15, 22, 29; *Feb:* 05, 12, 19, 26; *Mar:* 04, 11, 18, 25; *Apr:* 01, 08, 15, 22, 29; *May:* 06, 13, 20, 27; *Jun:* 03, 10, 17, 24; *Jul:* 01, 08, 15, 22, 29; *Aug:* 05, 12, 19, 26; *Sep:* 02, 09, 16, 23, 30; *Oct:* 07, 14, 21, 28; *Nov:* 04, 11, 18, 25; *Dec:* 02, 09, 16, 23, 30

1953 *Jan:* 06, 13, 20, 27; *Feb:* 03, 10, 17, 24; *Mar:* 03, 10, 17, 24, 31; *Apr:* 07, 14, 21, 28; *May:* 05, 12, 19, 26; *Jun:* 02, 09, 16, 23, 30; *Jul:* 07, 14, 21, 28; *Aug:* 04, 11, 18, 25; *Sep:* 01, 08, 15, 22, 29; *Oct:* 06, 13, 20, 27; *Nov:* 03, 10, 17, 24; *Dec:* 01, 08, 15, 22, 29

1954 *Jan:* 05, 12, 19, 26; *Feb:* 02, 09, 16, 23; *Mar:* 02, 09, 16, 23, 30; *Apr:* 06, 13, 20, 27; *May:* 04, 11, 18, 25; *Jun:* 01, 08, 15, 22, 29; *Jul:* 06, 13, 20, 27; *Aug:* 03, 10, 17, 24, 31; *Sep:* 07, 14, 21, 28; *Oct:* 05, 12, 19, 26; *Nov:* 02, 09, 16, 23, 30; *Dec:* 07, 14, 21, 28

1955 *Jan:* 04, 11, 18, 25; *Feb:* 01, 08, 15, 22; *Mar:* 01, 08, 15, 22, 29; *Apr:* 05, 12, 19, 26; *May:* 03, 10, 17, 24, 31; *Jun:* 07, 14, 21, 28; *Jul:* 05, 12, 19, 26; *Aug:* 02, 09, 16, 23, 30; *Sep:* 06, 13, 20, 27; *Oct:* 04, 11, 18, 25; *Nov:* 01, 08, 15, 22, 29; *Dec:* 06, 13, 20, 27

1956 *Jan:* 03, 10, 17, 24, 31; *Feb:* 07, 14, 21, 28; *Mar:* 06, 13, 20, 27; *Apr:* 03, 10, 17, 24; *May:* 01, 08, 15, 22, 29; *Jun:* 05, 12, 19, 26; *Jul:* 03, 10, 17, 24, 31; *Aug:* 07, 14, 21, 28; *Sep:* 04, 11, 18, 25; *Oct:* 02, 09, 16, 23, 30; *Nov:* 06, 13, 20, 27; *Dec:* 04, 11, 18, 25

1957 *Jan:* 01, 08, 15, 22, 29; *Feb:* 05, 12, 19, 26; *Mar:* 05, 12, 19, 26; *Apr:* 02, 09, 16, 23, 30; *May:* 07, 14, 21, 28; *Jun:* 04, 11, 18, 25; *Jul:* 02, 09, 16, 23, 30; *Aug:* 06, 13, 20, 27; *Sep:* 03, 10, 17, 24; *Oct:* 01, 08, 15, 22, 29; *Nov:* 05, 12, 19, 26; *Dec:* 03, 10, 17, 24, 31

1958 *Jan:* 07, 14, 21, 28; *Feb:* 04, 11, 18, 25; *Mar:* 04, 11, 18, 25; *Apr:* 01, 08, 15, 22, 29; *May:* 06, 13, 20, 27; *Jun:* 03, 10, 17, 24; *Jul:* 01, 08, 15, 22, 29; *Aug:* 05, 12, 19, 26; *Sep:* 02, 09, 16, 23, 30; *Oct:* 07, 14, 21, 28; *Nov:* 04, 11, 18, 25; *Dec:* 02, 09, 16, 23, 30

1959 *Jan:* 06, 13, 20, 27; *Feb:* 03, 10, 17, 24; *Mar:* 03, 10, 17, 24, 31; *Apr:* 07, 14, 21, 28; *May:* 05, 12, 19, 26; *Jun:* 02, 09, 16, 23, 30; *Jul:* 07, 14, 21, 28; *Aug:* 04, 11, 18, 25; *Sep:* 01, 08, 15, 22, 29; *Oct:* 06, 13, 20, 27; *Nov:* 03, 10, 17, 24; *Dec:* 01, 08, 15, 22, 29

1960 *Jan:* 05, 12, 19, 26; *Feb:* 02, 09, 16, 23; *Mar:* 01, 08, 15, 22, 29; *Apr:* 05, 12, 19, 26; *May:* 03, 10, 17, 24, 31; *Jun:* 07, 14, 21, 28; *Jul:* 05, 12, 19, 26; *Aug:* 02, 09, 16, 23, 30; *Sep:* 06, 13, 20, 27; *Oct:* 04, 11, 18, 25; *Nov:* 01, 08, 15, 22, 29; *Dec:* 06, 13, 20, 27

1961 *Jan:* 03, 10, 17, 24, 31; *Feb:* 07, 14, 21, 28; *Mar:* 07, 14, 21, 28; *Apr:* 04, 11, 18, 25; *May:* 02, 09, 16, 23, 30; *Jun:* 06, 13, 20, 27; *Jul:* 04, 11, 18, 25; *Aug:* 01, 08, 15, 22, 29; *Sep:* 05, 12, 19, 26; *Oct:* 03, 10, 17, 24, 31; *Nov:* 07, 14, 21, 28; *Dec:* 05, 12, 19, 26

1962 *Jan:* 02, 09, 16, 23, 30; *Feb:* 06, 13, 20, 27; *Mar:* 06, 13, 20, 27; *Apr:* 03, 10, 17, 24; *May:* 01, 08, 15, 22, 29; *Jun:* 05, 12, 19, 26; *Jul:* 03, 10, 17, 24, 31; *Aug:* 07, 14, 21, 28; *Sep:* 04, 11, 18, 25; *Oct:* 02, 09, 16, 23, 30; *Nov:* 06, 13, 20, 27; *Dec:* 04, 11, 18, 25

1963 *Jan:* 01, 08, 15, 22, 29; *Feb:* 05, 12, 19, 26; *Mar:* 05, 12, 19, 26; *Apr:* 02, 09, 16, 23, 30; *May:* 07, 14, 21, 28; *Jun:* 04, 11, 18, 25; *Jul:* 02, 09, 16, 23, 30; *Aug:* 06, 13, 20, 27; *Sep:* 03, 10, 17, 24; *Oct:* 01, 08, 15, 22, 29; *Nov:* 05, 12, 19, 26; *Dec:* 03, 10, 17, 24, 31

1964 *Jan:* 07, 14, 21, 28; *Feb:* 04, 11, 18, 25; *Mar:* 03, 10, 17, 24, 31; *Apr:* 07, 14, 21, 28; *May:* 05, 12, 19, 26; *Jun:* 02, 09, 16, 23, 30; *Jul:* 07, 14, 21, 28; *Aug:* 04, 11, 18, 25; *Sep:* 01, 08, 15, 22, 29; *Oct:* 06, 13, 20, 27; *Nov:* 03, 10, 17, 24; *Dec:* 01, 08, 15, 22, 29

1965 *Jan:* 05, 12, 19, 26, *Feb:* 02, 09, 16, 23, *Mar:* 02, 09, 16, 23, 30, *Apr:* 06, 13, 20, 27, *May:* 04, 11, 18, 25, *Jun:* 01, 08, 15, 22, 29, *Jul:* 06, 13, 20, 27, *Aug:* 03, 10, 17, 24, 31, *Sep:* 07, 14, 21, 28, *Oct:* 05, 12, 19, 26, *Nov:* 02, 09, 16, 23, 30, *Dec:* 07, 14, 21, 28

1966 *Jan:* 04, 11, 18, 25, *Feb:* 01, 08, 15, 22, *Mar:* 01, 08, 15, 22, 29, *Apr:* 05, 12, 19, 26, *May:* 03, 10, 17, 24, 31, *Jun:* 07, 14, 21, 28, *Jul:* 05, 12, 19, 26, *Aug:* 02, 09, 16, 23, 30, *Sep:* 06, 13, 20, 27, *Oct:* 04, 11, 18, 25, *Nov:* 01, 08, 15, 22, 29, *Dec:* 06, 13, 20, 27

1967 *Jan:* 03, 10, 17, 24, 31, *Feb:* 07, 14, 21, 28, *Mar:* 07, 14, 21, 28, *Apr:* 04, 11, 18, 25, *May:* 02, 09, 16, 23, 30, *Jun:* 06, 13, 20, 27, *Jul:* 04, 11, 18, 25, *Aug:* 01, 08, 15, 22, 29, *Sep:* 05, 12, 19, 26, *Oct:* 03, 10, 17, 24, 31, *Nov:* 07, 14, 21, 28, *Dec:* 05, 12, 19, 26

1968 *Jan:* 02, 09, 16, 23, 30, *Feb:* 06, 13, 20, 27, *Mar:* 05, 12, 19, 26, *Apr:* 02, 09, 16, 23, 30, *May:* 07, 14, 21, 28, *Jun:* 04, 11, 18, 25, *Jul:* 02, 09, 16, 23, 30, *Aug:* 06, 13, 20, 27, *Sep:* 03, 10, 17, 24, *Oct:* 01, 08, 15, 22, 29, *Nov:* 05, 12, 19, 26, *Dec:* 03, 10, 17, 24, 31

1969 *Jan:* 07, 14, 21, 28, *Feb:* 04, 11, 18, 25, *Mar:* 04, 11, 18, 25, *Apr:* 01, 08, 15, 22, 29, *May:* 06, 13, 20, 27, *Jun:* 03, 10, 17, 24, *Jul:* 01, 08, 15, 22, 29, *Aug:* 05, 12, 19, 26, *Sep:* 02, 09, 16, 23, 30, *Oct:* 07, 14, 21, 28, *Nov:* 04, 11, 18, 25, *Dec:* 02, 09, 16, 23, 30

1970 *Jan:* 06, 13, 20, 27, *Feb:* 03, 10, 17, 24, *Mar:* 03, 10, 17, 24, 31, *Apr:* 07, 14, 21, 28, *May:* 05, 12, 19, 26, *Jun:* 02, 09, 16, 23, 30, *Jul:* 07, 14, 21, 28, *Aug:* 04, 11, 18, 25, *Sep:* 01, 08, 15, 22, 29, *Oct:* 06, 13, 20, 27, *Nov:* 03, 10, 17, 24, *Dec:* 01, 08, 15, 22, 29

1971 *Jan:* 05, 12, 19, 26, *Feb:* 02, 09, 16, 23, *Mar:* 02, 09, 16, 23, 30, *Apr:* 06, 13, 20, 27, *May:* 04, 11, 18, 25, *Jun:* 01, 08, 15, 22, 29, *Jul:* 06, 13, 20, 27, *Aug:* 03, 10, 17, 24, 31, *Sep:* 07, 14, 21, 28, *Oct:* 05, 12, 19, 26, *Nov:* 02, 09, 16, 23, 30, *Dec:* 07, 14, 21, 28

1972 *Jan:* 04, 11, 18, 25, *Feb:* 01, 08, 15, 22, 29, *Mar:* 07, 14, 21, 28, *Apr:* 04, 11, 18, 25, *May:* 02, 09, 16, 23, 30, *Jun:* 06, 13, 20, 27, *Jul:* 04, 11, 18, 25, *Aug:* 01, 08, 15, 22, 29, *Sep:* 05, 12, 19, 26, *Oct:* 03, 10, 17, 24, 31, *Nov:* 07, 14, 21, 28, *Dec:* 05, 12, 19, 26

1973 *Jan:* 02, 09, 16, 23, 30, *Feb:* 06, 13, 20, 27, *Mar:* 06, 13, 20, 27, *Apr:* 03, 10, 17, 24, *May:* 01, 08, 15, 22, 29, *Jun:* 05, 12, 19, 26, *Jul:* 03, 10, 17, 24, 31, *Aug:* 07, 14, 21, 28, *Sep:* 04, 11, 18, 25, *Oct:* 02, 09, 16, 23, 30, *Nov:* 06, 13, 20, 27, *Dec:* 04, 11, 18, 25

1974 *Jan:* 01, 08, 15, 22, 29, *Feb:* 05, 12, 19, 26, *Mar:* 05, 12, 19, 26, *Apr:* 02, 09, 16, 23, 30, *May:* 07, 14, 21, 28, *Jun:* 04, 11, 18, 25, *Jul:* 02, 09, 16, 23, 30, *Aug:* 06, 13, 20, 27, *Sep:* 03, 10, 17, 24, *Oct:* 01, 08, 15, 22, 29, *Nov:* 05, 12, 19, 26, *Dec:* 03, 10, 17, 24, 31

1975 *Jan:* 07, 14, 21, 28, *Feb:* 04, 11, 18, 25, *Mar:* 04, 11, 18, 25, *Apr:* 01, 08, 15, 22, 29, *May:* 06, 13, 20, 27, *Jun:* 03, 10, 17, 24, *Jul:* 01, 08, 15, 22, 29, *Aug:* 05, 12, 19, 26, *Sep:* 02, 09, 16, 23, 30, *Oct:* 07, 14, 21, 28, *Nov:* 04, 11, 18, 25, *Dec:* 02, 09, 16, 23, 30

1976 *Jan:* 06, 13, 20, 27, *Feb:* 03, 10, 17, 24, *Mar:* 02, 09, 16, 23, 30, *Apr:* 06, 13, 20, 27, *May:* 04, 11, 18, 25, *Jun:* 01, 08, 15, 22, 29, *Jul:* 06, 13, 20, 27, *Aug:* 03, 10, 17, 24, 31, *Sep:* 07, 14, 21, 28, *Oct:* 05, 12, 19, 26, *Nov:* 02, 09, 16, 23, 30, *Dec:* 07, 14, 21, 28

1977 *Jan:* 04, 11, 18, 25, *Feb:* 01, 08, 15, 22, *Mar:* 01, 08, 15, 22, 29, *Apr:* 05, 12, 19, 26, *May:* 03, 10, 17, 24, 31, *Jun:* 07, 14, 21, 28, *Jul:* 05, 12, 19, 26, *Aug:* 02, 09, 16, 23, 30, *Sep:* 06, 13, 20, 27, *Oct:* 04, 11, 18, 25, *Nov:* 01, 08, 15, 22, 29, *Dec:* 06, 13, 20, 27

1978 Jan: 03, 10, 17, 24, 31, Feb: 07, 14, 21, 28, Mar: 07, 14, 21, 28, Apr: 04, 11, 18, 25, May: 02, 09, 16, 23, 30, Jun: 06, 13, 20, 27, Jul: 04, 11, 18, 25, Aug: 01, 08, 15, 22, 29, Sep: 05, 12, 19, 26, Oct: 03, 10, 17, 24, 31, Nov: 07, 14, 21, 28, Dec: 05, 12, 19, 26
1979 Jan: 02, 09, 16, 23, 30, Feb: 06, 13, 20, 27, Mar: 06, 13, 20, 27, Apr: 03, 10, 17, 24, May: 01, 08, 15, 22, 29, Jun: 05, 12, 19, 26, Jul: 03, 10, 17, 24, 31, Aug: 07, 14, 21, 28, Sep: 04, 11, 18, 25, Oct: 02, 09, 16, 23, 30, Nov: 06, 13, 20, 27, Dec: 04, 11, 18, 25
1980 Jan: 01, 08, 15, 22, 29, Feb: 05, 12, 19, 26, Mar: 04, 11, 18, 25, Apr: 01, 08, 15, 22, 29, May: 06, 13, 20, 27, Jun: 03, 10, 17, 24, Jul: 01, 08, 15, 22, 29, Aug: 05, 12, 19, 26, Sep: 02, 09, 16, 23, 30, Oct: 07, 14, 21, 28, Nov: 04, 11, 18, 25, Dec: 02, 09, 16, 23, 30
1981 Jan: 06, 13, 20, 27, Feb: 03, 10, 17, 24, Mar: 03, 10, 17, 24, 31, Apr: 07, 14, 21, 28, May: 05, 12, 19, 26, Jun: 02, 09, 16, 23, 30, Jul: 07, 14, 21, 28, Aug: 04, 11, 18, 25, Sep: 01, 08, 15, 22, 29, Oct: 06, 13, 20, 27, Nov: 03, 10, 17, 24, Dec: 01, 08, 15, 22, 29
1982 Jan: 05, 12, 19, 26, Feb: 02, 09, 16, 23, Mar: 02, 09, 16, 23, 30, Apr: 06, 13, 20, 27, May: 04, 11, 18, 25, Jun: 01, 08, 15, 22, 29, Jul: 06, 13, 20, 27, Aug: 03, 10, 17, 24, 31, Sep: 07, 14, 21, 28, Oct: 05, 12, 19, 26, Nov: 02, 09, 16, 23, 30, Dec: 07, 14, 21, 28
1983 Jan: 04, 11, 18, 25, Feb: 01, 08, 15, 22, Mar: 01, 08, 15, 22, 29, Apr: 05, 12, 19, 26, May: 03, 10, 17, 24, 31, Jun: 07, 14, 21, 28, Jul: 05, 12, 19, 26, Aug: 02, 09, 16, 23, 30, Sep: 06, 13, 20, 27, Oct: 04, 11, 18, 25, Nov: 01, 08, 15, 22, 29, Dec: 06, 13, 20, 27
1984 Jan: 03, 10, 17, 24, 31, Feb: 07, 14, 21, 28, Mar: 06, 13, 20, 27, Apr: 03, 10, 17, 24, May: 01, 08, 15, 22, 29, Jun: 05, 12, 19, 26, Jul: 03, 10, 17, 24, 31, Aug: 07, 14, 21, 28, Sep: 04, 11, 18, 25, Oct: 02, 09, 16, 23, 30, Nov: 06, 13, 20, 27, Dec: 04, 11, 18, 25
1985 Jan: 01, 08, 15, 22, 29, Feb: 05, 12, 19, 26, Mar: 05, 12, 19, 26, Apr: 02, 09, 16, 23, 30, May: 07, 14, 21, 28, Jun: 04, 11, 18, 25, Jul: 02, 09, 16, 23, 30, Aug: 06, 13, 20, 27, Sep: 03, 10, 17, 24, Oct: 01, 08, 15, 22, 29, Nov: 05, 12, 19, 26, Dec: 03, 10, 17, 24, 31
1986 Jan: 07, 14, 21, 28, Feb: 04, 11, 18, 25, Mar: 04, 11, 18, 25, Apr: 01, 08, 15, 22, 29, May: 06, 13, 20, 27, Jun: 03, 10, 17, 24, Jul: 01, 08, 15, 22, 29, Aug: 05, 12, 19, 26, Sep: 02, 09, 16, 23, 30, Oct: 07, 14, 21, 28, Nov: 04, 11, 18, 25, Dec: 02, 09, 16, 23, 30
1987 Jan: 06, 13, 20, 27, Feb: 03, 10, 17, 24, Mar: 03, 10, 17, 24, 31, Apr: 07, 14, 21, 28, May: 05, 12, 19, 26, Jun: 02, 09, 16, 23, 30, Jul: 07, 14, 21, 28, Aug: 04, 11, 18, 25, Sep: 01, 08, 15, 22, 29, Oct: 06, 13, 20, 27, Nov: 03, 10, 17, 24, Dec: 01, 08, 15, 22, 29
1988 Jan: 05, 12, 19, 26, Feb: 02, 09, 16, 23, Mar: 01, 08, 15, 22, 29, Apr: 05, 12, 19, 26, May: 03, 10, 17, 24, 31, Jun: 07, 14, 21, 28, Jul: 05, 12, 19, 26, Aug: 02, 09, 16, 23, 30, Sep: 06, 13, 20, 27, Oct: 04, 11, 18, 25, Nov: 01, 08, 15, 22, 29, Dec: 06, 13, 20, 27
1989 Jan: 03, 10, 17, 24, 31, Feb: 07, 14, 21, 28, Mar: 07, 14, 21, 28, Apr: 04, 11, 18, 25, May: 02, 09, 16, 23, 30, Jun: 06, 13, 20, 27, Jul: 04, 11, 18, 25, Aug: 01, 08, 15, 22, 29, Sep: 05, 12, 19, 26, Oct: 03, 10, 17, 24, 31, Nov: 07, 14, 21, 28, Dec: 05, 12, 19, 26
1990 Jan: 02, 09, 16, 23, 30, Feb: 06, 13, 20, 27, Mar: 06, 13, 20, 27, Apr: 03, 10, 17, 24, May: 01, 08, 15, 22, 29, Jun: 05, 12, 19, 26, Jul: 03, 10, 17, 24, 31, Aug: 07, 14, 21, 28, Sep: 04, 11, 18, 25, Oct: 02, 09, 16, 23, 30, Nov: 06, 13, 20, 27, Dec: 04, 11, 18, 25

1991 Jan: 01, 08, 15, 22, 29, Feb: 05, 12, 19, 26, Mar: 05, 12, 19, 26, Apr: 02, 09, 16, 23, 30, May: 07, 14, 21, 28, Jun: 04, 11, 18, 25, Jul: 02, 09, 16, 23, 30, Aug: 06, 13, 20, 27, Sep: 03, 10, 17, 24, Oct: 01, 08, 15, 22, 29, Nov: 05, 12, 19, 26, Dec: 03, 10, 17, 24, 31

1992 Jan: 07, 14, 21, 28, Feb: 04, 11, 18, 25, Mar: 03, 10, 17, 24, 31, Apr: 07, 14, 21, 28, May: 05, 12, 19, 26, Jun: 02, 09, 16, 23, 30, Jul: 07, 14, 21, 28, Aug: 04, 11, 18, 25, Sep: 01, 08, 15, 22, 29, Oct: 06, 13, 20, 27, Nov: 03, 10, 17, 24, Dec: 01, 08, 15, 22, 29

1993 Jan: 05, 12, 19, 26, Feb: 02, 09, 16, 23, Mar: 02, 09, 16, 23, 30, Apr: 06, 13, 20, 27, May: 04, 11, 18, 25, Jun: 01, 08, 15, 22, 29, Jul: 06, 13, 20, 27, Aug: 03, 10, 17, 24, 31, Sep: 07, 14, 21, 28, Oct: 05, 12, 19, 26, Nov: 02, 09, 16, 23, 30, Dec: 07, 14, 21, 28

1994 Jan: 04, 11, 18, 25, Feb: 01, 08, 15, 22, Mar: 01, 08, 15, 22, 29, Apr: 05, 12, 19, 26, May: 03, 10, 17, 24, 31, Jun: 07, 14, 21, 28, Jul: 05, 12, 19, 26, Aug: 02, 09, 16, 23, 30, Sep: 06, 13, 20, 27, Oct: 04, 11, 18, 25, Nov: 01, 08, 15, 22, 29, Dec: 06, 13, 20, 27

1995 Jan: 03, 10, 17, 24, 31, Feb: 07, 14, 21, 28, Mar: 07, 14, 21, 28, Apr: 04, 11, 18, 25, May: 02, 09, 16, 23, 30, Jun: 06, 13, 20, 27, Jul: 04, 11, 18, 25, Aug: 01, 08, 15, 22, 29, Sep: 05, 12, 19, 26, Oct: 03, 10, 17, 24, 31, Nov: 07, 14, 21, 28, Dec: 05, 12, 19, 26

1996 Jan: 02, 09, 16, 23, 30, Feb: 06, 13, 20, 27, Mar: 05, 12, 19, 26, Apr: 02, 09, 16, 23, 30, May: 07, 14, 21, 28, Jun: 04, 11, 18, 25, Jul: 02, 09, 16, 23, 30, Aug: 06, 13, 20, 27, Sep: 03, 10, 17, 24, Oct: 01, 08, 15, 22, 29, Nov: 05, 12, 19, 26, Dec: 03, 10, 17, 24, 31

1997 Jan: 07, 14, 21, 28, Feb: 04, 11, 18, 25, Mar: 04, 11, 18, 25, Apr: 01, 08, 15, 22, 29, May: 06, 13, 20, 27, Jun: 03, 10, 17, 24, Jul: 01, 08, 15, 22, 29, Aug: 05, 12, 19, 26, Sep: 02, 09, 16, 23, 30, Oct: 07, 14, 21, 28, Nov: 04, 11, 18, 25, Dec: 02, 09, 16, 23, 30

1998 Jan: 06, 13, 20, 27, Feb: 03, 10, 17, 24, Mar: 03, 10, 17, 24, 31, Apr: 07, 14, 21, 28, May: 05, 12, 19, 26, Jun: 02, 09, 16, 23, 30, Jul: 07, 14, 21, 28, Aug: 04, 11, 18, 25, Sep: 01, 08, 15, 22, 29, Oct: 06, 13, 20, 27, Nov: 03, 10, 17, 24, Dec: 01, 08, 15, 22, 29

1999 Jan: 05, 12, 19, 26, Feb: 02, 09, 16, 23, Mar: 02, 09, 16, 23, 30, Apr: 06, 13, 20, 27, May: 04, 11, 18, 25, Jun: 01, 08, 15, 22, 29, Jul: 06, 13, 20, 27, Aug: 03, 10, 17, 24, 31, Sep: 07, 14, 21, 28, Oct: 05, 12, 19, 26, Nov: 02, 09, 16, 23, 30, Dec: 07, 14, 21, 28

2000 Jan: 04, 11, 18, 25, Feb: 01, 08, 15, 22, 29, Mar: 07, 14, 21, 28, Apr: 04, 11, 18, 25, May: 02, 09, 16, 23, 30, Jun: 06, 13, 20, 27, Jul: 04, 11, 18, 25, Aug: 01, 08, 15, 22, 29, Sep: 05, 12, 19, 26, Oct: 03, 10, 17, 24, 31, Nov: 07, 14, 21, 28, Dec: 05, 12, 19, 26

2001 Jan: 02, 09, 16, 23, 30, Feb: 06, 13, 20, 27, Mar: 06, 13, 20, 27, Apr: 03, 10, 17, 24, May: 01, 08, 15, 22, 29, Jun: 05, 12, 19, 26, Jul: 03, 10, 17, 24, 31, Aug: 07, 14, 21, 28, Sep: 04, 11, 18, 25, Oct: 02, 09, 16, 23, 30, Nov: 06, 13, 20, 27, Dec: 04, 11, 18, 25

2002 Jan: 01, 08, 15, 22, 29, Feb: 05, 12, 19, 26, Mar: 05, 12, 19, 26, Apr: 02, 09, 16, 23, 30, May: 07, 14, 21, 28, Jun: 04, 11, 18, 25, Jul: 02, 09, 16, 23, 30, Aug: 06, 13, 20, 27, Sep: 03, 10, 17, 24, Oct: 01, 08, 15, 22, 29, Nov: 05, 12, 19, 26, Dec: 03, 10, 17, 24, 31

2003 Jan: 07, 14, 21, 28, Feb: 04, 11, 18, 25, Mar: 04, 11, 18, 25, Apr: 01, 08, 15, 22, 29, May: 06, 13, 20, 27, Jun: 03, 10, 17, 24, Jul: 01, 08, 15, 22, 29, Aug: 05, 12, 19, 26, Sep: 02, 09, 16, 23, 30, Oct: 07, 14, 21, 28, Nov: 04, 11, 18, 25, Dec: 02, 09, 16, 23, 30

2004 Jan: 06, 13, 20, 27, Feb: 03, 10, 17, 24, Mar: 02, 09, 16, 23, 30, Apr: 06, 13, 20, 27, May: 04, 11, 18, 25, Jun: 01, 08, 15, 22, 29, Jul: 06, 13, 20, 27, Aug: 03, 10, 17, 24, 31, Sep: 07, 14, 21, 28, Oct: 05, 12, 19, 26, Nov: 02, 09, 16, 23, 30, Dec: 07, 14, 21, 28

2005 Jan: 04, 11, 18, 25, Feb: 01, 08, 15, 22, Mar: 01, 08, 15, 22, 29, Apr: 05, 12, 19, 26, May: 03, 10, 17, 24, 31, Jun: 07, 14, 21, 28, Jul: 05, 12, 19, 26, Aug: 02, 09, 16, 23, 30, Sep: 06, 13, 20, 27, Oct: 04, 11, 18, 25, Nov: 01, 08, 15, 22, 29, Dec: 06, 13, 20, 27

2006 Jan: 03, 10, 17, 24, 31, Feb: 07, 14, 21, 28, Mar: 07, 14, 21, 28, Apr: 04, 11, 18, 25, May: 02, 09, 16, 23, 30, Jun: 06, 13, 20, 27, Jul: 04, 11, 18, 25, Aug: 01, 08, 15, 22, 29, Sep: 05, 12, 19, 26, Oct: 03, 10, 17, 24, 31, Nov: 07, 14, 21, 28, Dec: 05, 12, 19, 26

2007 Jan: 02, 09, 16, 23, 30, Feb: 06, 13, 20, 27, Mar: 06, 13, 20, 27, Apr: 03, 10, 17, 24, May: 01, 08, 15, 22, 29, Jun: 05, 12, 19, 26, Jul: 03, 10, 17, 24, 31, Aug: 07, 14, 21, 28, Sep: 04, 11, 18, 25, Oct: 02, 09, 16, 23, 30, Nov: 06, 13, 20, 27, Dec: 04, 11, 18, 25

2008 Jan: 01, 08, 15, 22, 29, Feb: 05, 12, 19, 26, Mar: 04, 11, 18, 25, Apr: 01, 08, 15, 22, 29, May: 06, 13, 20, 27, Jun: 03, 10, 17, 24, Jul: 01, 08, 15, 22, 29, Aug: 05, 12, 19, 26, Sep: 02, 09, 16, 23, 30, Oct: 07, 14, 21, 28, Nov: 04, 11, 18, 25, Dec: 02, 09, 16, 23, 30

2009 Jan: 06, 13, 20, 27, Feb: 03, 10, 17, 24, Mar: 03, 10, 17, 24, 31, Apr: 07, 14, 21, 28, May: 05, 12, 19, 26, Jun: 02, 09, 16, 23, 30, Jul: 07, 14, 21, 28, Aug:04, 11, 18, 25, Sep: 01, 08, 15, 22, 29, Oct: 06, 13, 20, 27, Nov: 03, 10, 17, 24, Dec: 01, 08, 15, 22, 29

2010 Jan: 05, 12, 19, 26, Feb: 02, 09, 16, 23, Mar: 02, 09, 16, 23, 30, Apr: 06, 13, 20, 27, May: 04, 11, 18, 25, Jun: 01, 08, 15, 22, 29, Jul: 06, 13, 20, 27, Aug: 03, 10, 17, 24, 31, Sep: 07, 14, 21, 28, Oct: 05, 12, 19, 26, Nov: 02, 09, 16, 23, 30, Dec: 07, 14, 21, 28

2011 Jan: 04, 11, 18, 25, Feb: 01, 08, 15, 22, Mar: 01, 08, 15, 22, 29, Apr: 05, 12, 19, 26, May: 03, 10, 17, 24, 31, Jun: 07, 14, 21, 28, Jul: 05, 12, 19, 26, Aug: 02, 09, 16, 23, 30, Sep: 06, 13, 20, 27, Oct: 04, 11, 18, 25, Nov: 01, 08, 15, 22, 29, Dec: 06, 13, 20, 27

2012 Jan: 03, 10, 17, 24, 31, Feb: 07, 14, 21, 28, Mar: 06, 13, 20, 27, Apr: 03, 10, 17, 24, May: 01, 08, 15, 22, 29, Jun: 05, 12, 19, 26, Jul: 03, 10, 17, 24, 31, Aug: 07, 14, 21, 28, Sep: 04, 11, 18, 25, Oct: 02, 09, 16, 23, 30, Nov: 06, 13, 20, 27, Dec: 04, 11, 18, 25

2013 Jan: 01, 08, 15, 22, 29, Feb: 05, 12, 19, 26, Mar: 05, 12, 19, 26, Apr: 02, 09, 16, 23, 30, May: 07, 14, 21, 28, Jun: 04, 11, 18, 25, Jul: 02, 09, 16, 23, 30, Aug: 06, 13, 20, 27, Sep: 03, 10, 17, 24, Oct: 01, 08, 15, 22, 29, Nov: 05, 12, 19, 26, Dec: 03, 10, 17, 24, 31

Wednesday: Michael

IF YOUR DAY OF BIRTH IS WEDNESDAY: Michael rules. Michael's healing rays are different shades of blue, including sky blue and cobalt, as well as orange-gold for the Light Sword. His metal is mercury, his crystals are sapphire and topaz. His attributes on which to focus are: strength, protection, personal and absolute (the Creator's) truth.

Wednesday is the day ruled by Michael and the planet Mercury. His name means 'Who is as God' and he has always been considered one of the greatest of all angels. Apart from being equated with St George, patron saint of England, he appears in Christian, Persian, Moslem and Jewish texts. Ruler of 4th Heaven, and east wind, he is the carrier of the Sword of Light, and chief warrior against darkness.

Michael represents strength in body and spirit, and brings rescue to us in the form of his Light Sword. This enables us to cut away fear and other negative emotions within in order to allow positive blue energy to come in, engendering a feeling of wellbeing coupled with protection that we can use for self and loved ones.

Michael is also described as 'the Logos' (the Word); in this context 'the Word' represents truth in all its guises: truth about ourselves, truth in our dealings with others, presenting our own truth to the world by being loyal to our principles.

Perhaps most importantly of all, having addressed your personal truth,

and released unwanted aspects of yourself with the help of his sword, you can start to become spiritually stronger and more aware, moving towards God's truth.

Every one of us can call on Michael any time, but if he is the angel of the day of your birth, then he is one of your guardian angels and always with you. Wednesday would be a good day for a special invocation. Below is an invocation for Michael, plus a protective measure you can use.

Michael, Michael, Michael, I ask for your guidance to find my truth (or strength, or to bring protection), *in Love and Light, Love and Light, Love and Light.*

Negative energy in or around your home? Ask Michael to envelop you (or a loved one) completely in his cobalt blue cloak so the negativity cannot reach you, and/or visualise his sword drawn on your door.

Wednesday birthdays

1940 *Jan:* 03, 10, 17, 24, 31, *Feb:* 07, 14, 21, 28, *Mar:* 06, 13, 20, 27, *Apr:* 03, 10, 17, 24, *May:* 01, 08, 15, 22, 29, *Jun:* 05, 12, 19, 26, *Jul:* 03, 10, 17, 24, 31, *Aug:* 07, 14, 21, 28, *Sep:* 04, 11, 18, 25, *Oct:* 02, 09, 16, 23, 30, *Nov:* 06, 13, 20, 27, *Dec:* 04, 11, 18, 25

1941 *Jan:* 01, 08, 15, 22, 29, *Feb:* 05, 12, 19, 26, *Mar:* 05, 12, 19, 26, *Apr:* 02, 09, 16, 23, 30, *May:* 07, 14, 21, 28, *Jun:* 04, 11, 18, 25, *Jul:* 02, 09, 16, 23, 30, *Aug:* 06, 13, 20, 27, *Sep:* 03, 10, 17, 24, *Oct:* 01, 08, 15, 22, 29, *Nov:* 05, 12, 19, 26, *Dec:* 03, 10, 17, 24, 31

1942 *Jan:* 07, 14, 21, 28, *Feb:* 04, 11, 18, 25, *Mar:* 04, 11, 18, 25, *Apr:* 01, 08, 15, 22, 29, *May:* 06, 13, 20, 27, *Jun:* 03, 10, 17, 24, *Jul:* 01, 08, 15, 22, 29, *Aug:* 05, 12, 19, 26, *Sep:* 02, 09, 16, 23, 30, *Oct:* 07, 14, 21, 28, *Nov:* 04, 11, 18, 25, *Dec:* 02, 09, 16, 23, 30

1943 *Jan:* 06, 13, 20, 27, *Feb:* 03, 10, 17, 24, *Mar:* 03, 10, 17, 24, 31, *Apr:* 07, 14, 21, 28, *May:* 05, 12, 19, 26, *Jun:* 02, 09, 16, 23, 30, *Jul:* 07, 14, 21, 28, *Aug:* 04, 11, 18, 25, *Sep:* 01, 08, 15, 22, 29, *Oct:* 06, 13, 20, 27, *Nov:* 03, 10, 17, 24, *Dec:* 01, 08, 15, 22, 29

1944 *Jan:* 05, 12, 19, 26, *Feb:* 02, 09, 16, 23, *Mar:* 01, 08, 15, 22, 29, *Apr:* 05, 12, 19, 26, *May:* 03, 10, 17, 24, 31, *Jun:* 07, 14, 21, 28, *Jul:* 05, 12, 19, 26, *Aug:* 02, 09, 16, 23, 30, *Sep:* 06, 13, 20, 27, *Oct:* 04, 11, 18, 25, *Nov:* 01, 08, 15, 22, 29, *Dec:* 06, 13, 20, 27

1945 *Jan:* 03, 10, 17, 24, 31, *Feb:* 07, 14, 21, 28, *Mar:* 07, 14, 21, 28, *Apr:* 04, 11, 18, 25, *May:* 02, 09, 16, 23, 30, *Jun:* 06, 13, 20, 27, *Jul:* 04, 11, 18, 25, *Aug:* 01, 08, 15, 22, 29, *Sep:* 05, 12, 19, 26, *Oct:* 03, 10, 17, 24, 31, *Nov:* 07, 14, 21, 28, *Dec:* 05, 12, 19, 26

1946 *Jan:* 02, 09, 16, 23, 30, *Feb:* 06, 13, 20, 27, *Mar:* 06, 13, 20, 27, *Apr:* 03, 10, 17, 24, *May:* 01, 08, 15, 22, 29, *Jun:* 05, 12, 19, 26, *Jul:* 03, 10, 17, 24, 31, *Aug:* 07, 14, 21, 28, *Sep:* 04, 11, 18, 25, *Oct:* 02, 09, 16, 23, 30, *Nov:* 06, 13, 20, 27, *Dec:* 04, 11, 18, 25

1947 *Jan:* 01, 08, 15, 22, 29, *Feb:* 05, 12, 19, 26, *Mar:* 05, 12, 19, 26, *Apr:* 02, 09, 16, 23, 30, *May:* 07, 14, 21, 28, *Jun:* 04, 11, 18, 25, *Jul:* 02, 09, 16, 23, 30, *Aug:* 06, 13, 20, 27, *Sep:* 03, 10, 17, 24, *Oct:* 01, 08, 15, 22, 29, *Nov:* 05, 12, 19, 26, *Dec:* 03, 10, 17, 24, 31

1948 *Jan:* 07, 14, 21, 28, *Feb:* 04, 11, 18, 25, *Mar:* 03, 10, 17, 24, 31, *Apr:* 07, 14, 21, 28, *May:* 05, 12, 19, 26, *Jun:* 02, 09, 16, 23, 30, *Jul:* 07, 14, 21, 28, *Aug:* 04, 11, 18, 25, *Sep:* 01, 08, 15, 22, 29, *Oct:* 06, 13, 20, 27, *Nov:* 03, 10, 17, 24, *Dec:* 01, 08, 15, 22, 29

1949 *Jan:* 05, 12, 19, 26, *Feb:* 02, 09, 16, 23, *Mar:* 02, 09, 16, 23, 30, *Apr:* 06, 13, 20, 27, *May:* 04, 11, 18, 25, *Jun:* 01, 08, 15, 22, 29, *Jul:* 06, 13, 20, 27, *Aug:* 03, 10, 17, 24, 31, *Sep:* 07, 14, 21, 28, *Oct:* 05, 12, 19, 26, *Nov:* 02, 09, 16, 23, 30, *Dec:* 07, 14, 21, 28

1950 *Jan:* 04, 11, 18, 25, *Feb:* 01, 08, 15, 22, *Mar:* 01, 08, 15, 22, 29, *Apr:* 05, 12, 19, 26, *May:* 03, 10, 17, 24, 31, *Jun:* 07, 14, 21, 28, *Jul:* 05, 12, 19, 26, *Aug:* 02, 09, 16, 23, 30, *Sep:* 06, 13, 20, 27, *Oct:* 04, 11, 18, 25, *Nov:* 01, 08, 15, 22, 29, *Dec:* 06, 13, 20, 27

1951 *Jan:* 03, 10, 17, 24, 31, *Feb:* 07, 14, 21, 28, *Mar:* 07, 14, 21, 28, *Apr:* 04, 11, 18, 25, *May:* 02, 09, 16, 23, 30, *Jun:* 06, 13, 20, 27, *Jul:* 04, 11, 18, 25, *Aug:* 01, 08, 15, 22, 29, *Sep:* 05, 12, 19, 26, *Oct:* 03, 10, 17, 24, 31, *Nov:* 07, 14, 21, 28, *Dec:* 05, 12, 19, 26

1952 Jan: 02, 09, 16, 23, 30, Feb: 06, 13, 20, 27, Mar: 05, 12, 19, 26, Apr: 02, 09, 16, 23, 30, May: 07, 14, 21, 28, Jun: 04, 11, 18, 25, Jul: 02, 09, 16, 23, 30, Aug: 06, 13, 20, 27, Sep: 03, 10, 17, 24, Oct: 01, 08, 15, 22, 29, Nov: 05, 12, 19, 26, Dec: 03, 10, 17, 24, 31

1953 Jan: 07, 14, 21, 28, Feb: 04, 11, 18, 25, Mar: 04, 11, 18, 25, Apr: 01, 08, 15, 22, 29, May: 06, 13, 20, 27, Jun: 03, 10, 17, 24, Jul: 01, 08, 15, 22, 29, Aug: 05, 12, 19, 26, Sep: 02, 09, 16, 23, 30, Oct: 07, 14, 21, 28, Nov: 04, 11, 18, 25, Dec: 02, 09, 16, 23, 30

1954 Jan: 06, 13, 20, 27, Feb: 03, 10, 17, 24, Mar: 03, 10, 17, 24, 31, Apr: 07, 14, 21, 28, May: 05, 12, 19, 26, Jun: 02, 09, 16, 23, 30, Jul: 07, 14, 21, 28, Aug: 04, 11, 18, 25, Sep: 01, 08, 15, 22, 29, Oct: 06, 13, 20, 27, Nov: 03, 10, 17, 24, Dec: 01, 08, 15, 22, 29

1955 Jan: 05, 12, 19, 26, Feb: 02, 09, 16, 23, Mar: 02, 09, 16, 23, 30, Apr: 06, 13, 20, 27, May: 04, 11, 18, 25, Jun: 01, 08, 15, 22, 29, Jul: 06, 13, 20, 27, Aug: 03, 10, 17, 24, 31, Sep: 07, 14, 21, 28, Oct: 05, 12, 19, 26, Nov: 02, 09, 16, 23, 30, Dec: 07, 14, 21, 28

1956 Jan: 04, 11, 18, 25, Feb: 01, 08, 15, 22, 29, Mar: 07, 14, 21, 28, Apr: 04, 11, 18, 25, May: 02, 09, 16, 23, 30, Jun: 06, 13, 20, 27, Jul: 04, 11, 18, 25, Aug: 01, 08, 15, 22, 29, Sep: 05, 12, 19, 26, Oct: 03, 10, 17, 24, 31, Nov: 07, 14, 21, 28, Dec: 05, 12, 19, 26

1957 Jan: 02, 09, 16, 23, 30, Feb: 06, 13, 20, 27, Mar: 06, 13, 20, 27, Apr: 03, 10, 17, 24, May: 01, 08, 15, 22, 29, Jun: 05, 12, 19, 26, Jul: 03, 10, 17, 24, 31, Aug: 07, 14, 21, 28, Sep: 04, 11, 18, 25, Oct: 02, 09, 16, 23, 30, Nov: 06, 13, 20, 27, Dec: 04, 11, 18, 25

1958 Jan: 01, 08, 15, 22, 29, Feb: 05, 12, 19, 26, Mar: 05, 12, 19, 26, Apr: 02, 09, 16, 23, 30, May: 07, 14, 21, 28, Jun: 04, 11, 18, 25, Jul: 02, 09, 16, 23, 30, Aug: 06, 13, 20, 27, Sep: 03, 10, 17, 24, Oct: 01, 08, 15, 22, 29, Nov: 05, 12, 19, 26, Dec: 03, 10, 17, 24, 31

1959 Jan: 07, 14, 21, 28, Feb: 04, 11, 18, 25, Mar: 04, 11, 18, 25, Apr: 01, 08, 15, 22, 29, May: 06, 13, 20, 27, Jun: 03, 10, 17, 24, Jul: 01, 08, 15, 22, 29, Aug: 05, 12, 19, 26, Sep: 02, 09, 16, 23, 30, Oct: 07, 14, 21, 28, Nov: 04, 11, 18, 25, Dec: 02, 09, 16, 23, 30

1960 Jan: 06, 13, 20, 27, Feb: 03, 10, 17, 24, Mar: 02, 09, 16, 23, 30, Apr: 06, 13, 20, 27, May: 04, 11, 18, 25, Jun: 01, 08, 15, 22, 29, Jul: 06, 13, 20, 27, Aug: 03, 10, 17, 24, 31, Sep: 07, 14, 21, 28, Oct: 05, 12, 19, 26, Nov: 02, 09, 16, 23, 30, Dec: 07, 14, 21, 28

1961 Jan: 04, 11, 18, 25, Feb: 01, 08, 15, 22, Mar: 01, 08, 15, 22, 29, Apr: 05, 12, 19, 26, May: 03, 10, 17, 24, 31, Jun: 07, 14, 21, 28, Jul: 05, 12, 19, 26, Aug: 02, 09, 16, 23, 30, Sep: 06, 13, 20, 27, Oct: 04, 11, 18, 25, Nov: 01, 08, 15, 22, 29, Dec: 06, 13, 20, 27

1962 Jan: 03, 10, 17, 24, 31, Feb: 07, 14, 21, 28, Mar: 07, 14, 21, 28, Apr: 04, 11, 18, 25, May: 02, 09, 16, 23, 30, Jun: 06, 13, 20, 27, Jul: 04, 11, 18, 25, Aug: 01, 08, 15, 22, 29, Sep: 05, 12, 19, 26, Oct: 03, 10, 17, 24, 31, Nov: 07, 14, 21, 28, Dec: 05, 12, 19, 26

1963 Jan: 02, 09, 16, 23, 30, Feb: 06, 13, 20, 27, Mar: 06, 13, 20, 27, Apr: 03, 10, 17, 24, May: 01, 08, 15, 22, 29, Jun: 05, 12, 19, 26, Jul: 03, 10, 17, 24, 31, Aug: 07, 14, 21, 28, Sep: 04, 11, 18, 25, Oct: 02, 09, 16, 23, 30, Nov: 06, 13, 20, 27, Dec: 04, 11, 18, 25

1964 Jan: 01, 08, 15, 22, 29, Feb: 05, 12, 19, 26, Mar: 04, 11, 18, 25, Apr: 01, 08, 15, 22, 29, May: 06, 13, 20, 27, Jun: 03, 10, 17, 24, Jul: 01, 08, 15, 22, 29, Aug: 05, 12, 19, 26, Sep: 02, 09, 16, 23, 30, Oct: 07, 14, 21, 28, Nov: 04, 11, 18, 25, Dec: 02, 09, 16, 23, 30

1965 Jan: 06, 13, 20, 27, Feb: 03, 10, 17, 24, Mar: 03, 10, 17, 24, 31, Apr: 07, 14, 21, 28, May: 05, 12, 19, 26, Jun: 02, 09, 16, 23, 30, Jul: 07, 14, 21, 28, Aug: 04, 11, 18, 25, Sep: 01, 08, 15, 22, 29, Oct: 06, 13, 20, 27, Nov: 03, 10, 17, 24, Dec: 01, 08, 15, 22, 29

1966 Jan: 05, 12, 19, 26, Feb: 02, 09, 16, 23, Mar: 02, 09, 16, 23, 30, Apr: 06, 13, 20, 27, May: 04, 11, 18, 25, Jun: 01, 08, 15, 22, 29, Jul: 06, 13, 20, 27, Aug: 03, 10, 17, 24, 31, Sep: 07, 14, 21, 28, Oct: 05, 12, 19, 26, Nov: 02, 09, 16, 23, 30, Dec: 07, 14, 21, 28

1967 Jan: 04, 11, 18, 25, Feb: 01, 08, 15, 22, Mar: 01, 08, 15, 22, 29, Apr: 05, 12, 19, 26, May: 03, 10, 17, 24, 31, Jun: 07, 14, 21, 28, Jul: 05, 12, 19, 26, Aug: 02, 09, 16, 23, 30, Sep: 06, 13, 20, 27, Oct: 04, 11, 18, 25, Nov: 01, 08, 15, 22, 29, Dec: 06, 13, 20, 27

1968 Jan: 03, 10, 17, 24, 31, Feb: 07, 14, 21, 28, Mar: 06, 13, 20, 27, Apr: 03, 10, 17, 24, May: 01, 08, 15, 22, 29, Jun: 05, 12, 19, 26, Jul: 03, 10, 17, 24, 31, Aug: 07, 14, 21, 28, Sep: 04, 11, 18, 25, Oct: 02, 09, 16, 23, 30, Nov: 06, 13, 20, 27, Dec: 04, 11, 18, 25

1969 Jan: 01, 08, 15, 22, 29, Feb: 05, 12, 19, 26, Mar: 05, 12, 19, 26, Apr: 02, 09, 16, 23, 30, May: 07, 14, 21, 28, Jun: 04, 11, 18, 25, Jul: 02, 09, 16, 23, 30, Aug: 06, 13, 20, 27, Sep: 03, 10, 17, 24, Oct: 01, 08, 15, 22, 29, Nov: 05, 12, 19, 26, Dec: 03, 10, 17, 24, 31

1970 Jan: 07, 14, 21, 28, Feb: 04, 11, 18, 25, Mar: 04, 11, 18, 25, Apr: 01, 08, 15, 22, 29, May: 06, 13, 20, 27, Jun: 03, 10, 17, 24, Jul: 01, 08, 15, 22, 29, Aug: 05, 12, 19, 26, Sep: 02, 09, 16, 23, 30, Oct: 07, 14, 21, 28, Nov: 04, 11, 18, 25, Dec: 02, 09, 16, 23, 30

1971 Jan: 06, 13, 20, 27, Feb: 03, 10, 17, 24, Mar: 03, 10, 17, 24, 31, Apr: 07, 14, 21, 28, May: 05, 12, 19, 26, Jun: 02, 09, 16, 23, 30, Jul: 07, 14, 21, 28, Aug: 04, 11, 18, 25, Sep: 01, 08, 15, 22, 29, Oct: 06, 13, 20, 27, Nov: 03, 10, 17, 24, Dec: 01, 08, 15, 22, 29

1972 Jan: 05, 12, 19, 26, Feb: 02, 09, 16, 23, Mar: 01, 08, 15, 22, 29, Apr: 05, 12, 19, 26, May: 03, 10, 17, 24, 31, Jun: 07, 14, 21, 28, Jul: 05, 12, 19, 26, Aug: 02, 09, 16, 23, 30, Sep: 06, 13, 20, 27, Oct: 04, 11, 18, 25, Nov: 01, 08, 15, 22, 29, Dec: 06, 13, 20, 27

1973 Jan: 03, 10, 17, 24, 31, Feb: 07, 14, 21, 28, Mar: 07, 14, 21, 28, Apr: 04, 11, 18, 25, May: 02, 09, 16, 23, 30, Jun: 06, 13, 20, 27, Jul: 04, 11, 18, 25, Aug: 01, 08, 15, 22, 29, Sep: 05, 12, 19, 26, Oct: 03, 10, 17, 24, 31, Nov: 07, 14, 21, 28, Dec: 05, 12, 19, 26

1974 Jan: 02, 09, 16, 23, 30, Feb: 06, 13, 20, 27, Mar: 06, 13, 20, 27, Apr: 03, 10, 17, 24, May: 01, 08, 15, 22, 29, Jun: 05, 12, 19, 26, Jul: 03, 10, 17, 24, 31, Aug: 07, 14, 21, 28, Sep: 04, 11, 18, 25, Oct: 02, 09, 16, 23, 30, Nov: 06, 13, 20, 27, Dec: 04, 11, 18, 25

1975 Jan: 01, 08, 15, 22, 29, Feb: 05, 12, 19, 26, Mar: 05, 12, 19, 26, Apr: 02, 09, 16, 23, 30, May: 07, 14, 21, 28, Jun: 04, 11, 18, 25, Jul: 02, 09, 16, 23, 30, Aug: 06, 13, 20, 27, Sep: 03, 10, 17, 24, Oct: 01, 08, 15, 22, 29, Nov: 05, 12, 19, 26, Dec: 03, 10, 17, 24, 31

1976 Jan: 07, 14, 21, 28, Feb: 04, 11, 18, 25, Mar: 03, 10, 17, 24, 31, Apr: 07, 14, 21, 28, May: 05, 12, 19, 26, Jun: 02, 09, 16, 23, 30, Jul: 07, 14, 21, 28, Aug: 04, 11, 18, 25, Sep: 01, 08, 15, 22, 29, Oct: 06, 13, 20, 27, Nov: 03, 10, 17, 24, Dec: 01, 08, 15, 22, 29

1977 Jan: 05, 12, 19, 26, Feb: 02, 09, 16, 23, Mar: 02, 09, 16, 23, 30, Apr: 06, 13, 20, 27, May: 04, 11, 18, 25, Jun: 01, 08, 15, 22, 29, Jul: 06, 13, 20, 27, Aug: 03, 10, 17, 24, 31, Sep: 07, 14, 21, 28, Oct: 05, 12, 19, 26, Nov: 02, 09, 16, 23, 30, Dec: 07, 14, 21, 28

1978 *Jan:* 04, 11, 18, 25, *Feb:* 01, 08, 15, 22, *Mar:* 01, 08, 15, 22, 29, *Apr:* 05, 12, 19, 26, *May:* 03, 10, 17, 24, 31, *Jun:* 07, 14, 21, 28, *Jul:* 05, 12, 19, 26, *Aug:* 02, 09, 16, 23, 30, *Sep:* 06, 13, 20, 27, *Oct:* 04, 11, 18, 25, *Nov:* 01, 08, 15, 22, 29, *Dec:* 06, 13, 20, 27

1979 *Jan:* 03, 10, 17, 24, 31, *Feb:* 07, 14, 21, 28, *Mar:* 07, 14, 21, 28, *Apr:* 04, 11, 18, 25, *May:* 02, 09, 16, 23, 30, *Jun:* 06, 13, 20, 27, *Jul:* 04, 11, 18, 25, *Aug:* 01, 08, 15, 22, 29, *Sep:* 05, 12, 19, 26, *Oct:* 03, 10, 17, 24, 31, *Nov:* 07, 14, 21, 28, *Dec:* 05, 12, 19, 26

1980 *Jan:* 02, 09, 16, 23, 30, *Feb:* 06, 13, 20, 27, *Mar:* 05, 12, 19, 26, *Apr:* 02, 09, 16, 23, 30, *May:* 07, 14, 21, 28, *Jun:* 04, 11, 18, 25, *Jul:* 02, 09, 16, 23, 30, *Aug:* 06, 13, 20, 27, *Sep:* 03, 10, 17, 24, *Oct:* 01, 08, 15, 22, 29, *Nov:* 05, 12, 19, 26, *Dec:* 03, 10, 17, 24, 31

1981 *Jan:* 07, 14, 21, 28, *Feb:* 04, 11, 18, 25, *Mar:* 04, 11, 18, 25, *Apr:* 01, 08, 15, 22, 29, *May:* 06, 13, 20, 27, *Jun:* 03, 10, 17, 24, *Jul:* 01, 08, 15, 22, 29, *Aug:* 05, 12, 19, 26, *Sep:* 02, 09, 16, 23, 30, *Oct:* 07, 14, 21, 28, *Nov:* 04, 11, 18, 25, *Dec:* 02, 09, 16, 23, 30

1982 *Jan:* 06, 13, 20, 27, *Feb:* 03, 10, 17, 24, *Mar:* 03, 10, 17, 24, 31, *Apr:* 07, 14, 21, 28, *May:* 05, 12, 19, 26, *Jun:* 02, 09, 16, 23, 30, *Jul:* 07, 14, 21, 28, *Aug:* 04, 11, 18, 25, *Sep:* 01, 08, 15, 22, 29, *Oct:* 06, 13, 20, 27, *Nov:* 03, 10, 17, 24, *Dec:* 01, 08, 15, 22, 29

1983 *Jan:* 05, 12, 19, 26, *Feb:* 02, 09, 16, 23, *Mar:* 02, 09, 16, 23, 30, *Apr:* 06, 13, 20, 27, *May:* 04, 11, 18, 25, *Jun:* 01, 08, 15, 22, 29, *Jul:* 06, 13, 20, 27, *Aug:* 03, 10, 17, 24, 31, *Sep:* 07, 14, 21, 28, *Oct:* 05, 12, 19, 26, *Nov:* 02, 09, 16, 23, 30, *Dec:* 07, 14, 21, 28

1984 *Jan:* 04, 11, 18, 25, *Feb:* 01, 08, 15, 22, 29, *Mar:* 07, 14, 21, 28, *Apr:* 04, 11, 18, 25, *May:* 02, 09, 16, 23, 30, *Jun:* 06, 13, 20, 27, *Jul:* 04, 11, 18, 25, *Aug:* 01, 08, 15, 22, 29, *Sep:* 05, 12, 19, 26, *Oct:* 03, 10, 17, 24, 31, *Nov:* 07, 14, 21, 28, *Dec:* 05, 12, 19, 26

1985 *Jan:* 02, 09, 16, 23, 30, *Feb:* 06, 13, 20, 27, *Mar:* 06, 13, 20, 27, *Apr:* 03, 10, 17, 24, *May:* 01, 08, 15, 22, 29, *Jun:* 05, 12, 19, 26, *Jul:* 03, 10, 17, 24, 31, *Aug:* 07, 14, 21, 28, *Sep:* 04, 11, 18, 25, *Oct:* 02, 09, 16, 23, 30, *Nov:* 06, 13, 20, 27, *Dec:* 04, 11, 18, 25

1986 *Jan:* 01, 08, 15, 22, 29, *Feb:* 05, 12, 19, 26, *Mar:* 05, 12, 19, 26, *Apr:* 02, 09, 16, 23, 30, *May:* 07, 14, 21, 28, *Jun:* 04, 11, 18, 25, *Jul:* 02, 09, 16, 23, 30, *Aug:* 06, 13, 20, 27, *Sep:* 03, 10, 17, 24, *Oct:* 01, 08, 15, 22, 29, *Nov:* 05, 12, 19, 26, *Dec:* 03, 10, 17, 24, 31

1987 *Jan:* 07, 14, 21, 28, *Feb:* 04, 11, 18, 25, *Mar:* 04, 11, 18, 25, *Apr:* 01, 08, 15, 22, 29, *May:* 06, 13, 20, 27, *Jun:* 03, 10, 17, 24, *Jul:* 01, 08, 15, 22, 29, *Aug:* 05, 12, 19, 26, *Sep:* 02, 09, 16, 23, 30, *Oct:* 07, 14, 21, 28, *Nov:* 04, 11, 18, 25, *Dec:* 02, 09, 16, 23, 30

1988 *Jan:* 06, 13, 20, 27, *Feb:* 03, 10, 17, 24, *Mar:* 02, 09, 16, 23, 30, *Apr:* 06, 13, 20, 27, *May:* 04, 11, 18, 25, *Jun:* 01, 08, 15, 22, 29, *Jul:* 06, 13, 20, 27, *Aug:* 03, 10, 17, 24, 31, *Sep:* 07, 14, 21, 28, *Oct:* 05, 12, 19, 26, *Nov:* 02, 09, 16, 23, 30, *Dec:* 07, 14, 21, 28

1989 *Jan:* 04, 11, 18, 25, *Feb:* 01, 08, 15, 22, *Mar:* 01, 08, 15, 22, 29, *Apr:* 05, 12, 19, 26, *May:* 03, 10, 17, 24, 31, *Jun:* 07, 14, 21, 28, *Jul:* 05, 12, 19, 26, *Aug:* 02, 09, 16, 23, 30, *Sep:* 06, 13, 20, 27, *Oct:* 04, 11, 18, 25, *Nov:* 01, 08, 15, 22, 29, *Dec:* 06, 13, 20, 27

1990 *Jan:* 03, 10, 17, 24, 31, *Feb:* 07, 14, 21, 28, *Mar:* 07, 14, 21, 28, *Apr:* 04, 11, 18, 25, *May:* 02, 09, 16, 23, 30, *Jun:* 06, 13, 20, 27, *Jul:* 04, 11, 18, 25, *Aug:* 01, 08, 15, 22, 29, *Sep:* 05, 12, 19, 26, *Oct:* 03, 10, 17, 24, 31, *Nov:* 07, 14, 21, 28, *Dec:* 05, 12, 19, 26

1991 *Jan:* 02, 09, 16, 23, 30, *Feb:* 06, 13, 20, 27, *Mar:* 06, 13, 20, 27, *Apr:* 03, 10, 17, 24, *May:* 01, 08, 15, 22, 29, *Jun:* 05, 12, 19, 26, *Jul:* 03, 10, 17, 24, 31, *Aug:* 07, 14, 21, 28, *Sep:* 04, 11, 18, 25, *Oct:* 02, 09, 16, 23, 30, *Nov:* 06, 13, 20, 27, *Dec:* 04, 11, 18, 25

1992 *Jan:* 01, 08, 15, 22, 29, *Feb:* 05, 12, 19, 26, *Mar:* 04, 11, 18, 25, *Apr:* 01, 08, 15, 22, 29, *May:* 06, 13, 20, 27, *Jun:* 03, 10, 17, 24, *Jul:* 01, 08, 15, 22, 29, *Aug:* 05, 12, 19, 26, *Sep:* 02, 09, 16, 23, 30, *Oct:* 07, 14, 21, 28, *Nov:* 04, 11, 18, 25, *Dec:* 02, 09, 16, 23, 30

1993 *Jan:* 06, 13, 20, 27, *Feb:* 03, 10, 17, 24, *Mar:* 03, 10, 17, 24, 31, *Apr:* 07, 14, 21, 28, *May:* 05, 12, 19, 26, *Jun:* 02, 09, 16, 23, 30, *Jul:* 07, 14, 21, 28, *Aug:* 04, 11, 18, 25, *Sep:* 01, 08, 15, 22, 29, *Oct:* 06, 13, 20, 27, *Nov:* 03, 10, 17, 24, *Dec:* 01, 08, 15, 22, 29

1994 *Jan:* 05, 12, 19, 26, *Feb:* 02, 09, 16, 23, *Mar:* 02, 09, 16, 23, 30, *Apr:* 06, 13, 20, 27, *May:* 04, 11, 18, 25, *Jun:* 01, 08, 15, 22, 29, *Jul:* 06, 13, 20, 27, *Aug:* 03, 10, 17, 24, 31, *Sep:* 07, 14, 21, 28, *Oct:* 05, 12, 19, 26, *Nov:* 02, 09, 16, 23, 30, *Dec:* 07, 14, 21, 28

1995 *Jan:* 04, 11, 18, 25, *Feb:* 01, 08, 15, 22, *Mar:* 01, 08, 15, 22, 29, *Apr:* 05, 12, 19, 26, *May:* 03, 10, 17, 24, 31, *Jun:* 07, 14, 21, 28, *Jul:* 05, 12, 19, 26, *Aug:* 02, 09, 16, 23, 30, *Sep:* 06, 13, 20, 27, *Oct:* 04, 11, 18, 25, *Nov:* 01, 08, 15, 22, 29, *Dec:* 06, 13, 20, 27

1996 *Jan:* 03, 10, 17, 24, 31, *Feb:* 07, 14, 21, 28, *Mar:* 06, 13, 20, 27, *Apr:* 03, 10, 17, 24, *May:* 01, 08, 15, 22, 29, *Jun:* 05, 12, 19, 26, *Jul:* 03, 10, 17, 24, 31, *Aug:* 07, 14, 21, 28, *Sep:* 04, 11, 18, 25, *Oct:* 02, 09, 16, 23, 30, *Nov:* 06, 13, 20, 27, *Dec:* 04, 11, 18, 25

1997 *Jan:* 01, 08, 15, 22, 29, *Feb:* 05, 12, 19, 26, *Mar:* 05, 12, 19, 26, *Apr:* 02, 09, 16, 23, 30, *May:* 07, 14, 21, 28, *Jun:* 04, 11, 18, 25, *Jul:* 02, 09, 16, 23, 30, *Aug:* 06, 13, 20, 27, *Sep:* 03, 10, 17, 24, *Oct:* 01, 08, 15, 22, 29, *Nov:* 05, 12, 19, 26, *Dec:* 03, 10, 17, 24, 31

1998 *Jan:* 07, 14, 21, 28, *Feb:* 04, 11, 18, 25, *Mar:* 04, 11, 18, 25, *Apr:* 01, 08, 15, 22, 29, *May:* 06, 13, 20, 27, *Jun:* 03, 10, 17, 24, *Jul:* 01, 08, 15, 22, 29, *Aug:* 05, 12, 19, 26, *Sep:* 02, 09, 16, 23, 30, *Oct:* 07, 14, 21, 28, *Nov:* 04, 11, 18, 25, *Dec:* 02, 09, 16, 23, 30

1999 *Jan:* 06, 13, 20, 27, *Feb:* 03, 10, 17, 24, *Mar:* 03, 10, 17, 24, 31, *Apr:* 07, 14, 21, 28, *May:* 05, 12, 19, 26, *Jun:* 02, 09, 16, 23, 30, *Jul:* 07, 14, 21, 28, *Aug:* 04, 11, 18, 25, *Sep:* 01, 08, 15, 22, 29, *Oct:* 06, 13, 20, 27, *Nov:* 03, 10, 17, 24, *Dec:* 01, 08, 15, 22, 29

2000 *Jan:* 05, 12, 19, 26, *Feb:* 02, 09, 16, 23, *Mar:* 01, 08, 15, 22, 29, *Apr:* 05, 12, 19, 26, *May:* 03, 10, 17, 24, 31, *Jun:* 07, 14, 21, 28, *Jul:* 05, 12, 19, 26, *Aug:* 02, 09, 16, 23, 30, *Sep:* 06, 13, 20, 27, *Oct:* 04, 11, 18, 25, *Nov:* 01, 08, 15, 22, 29, *Dec:* 06, 13, 20, 27

2001 *Jan:* 03, 10, 17, 24, 31, *Feb:* 07, 14, 21, 28, *Mar:* 07, 14, 21, 28, *Apr:* 04, 11, 18, 25, *May:* 02, 09, 16, 23, 30, *Jun:* 06, 13, 20, 27, *Jul:* 04, 11, 18, 25, *Aug:* 01, 08, 15, 22, 29, *Sep:* 05, 12, 19, 26, *Oct:* 03, 10, 17, 24, 31, *Nov:* 07, 14, 21, 28, *Dec:* 05, 12, 19, 26

2002 *Jan:* 02, 09, 16, 23, 30, *Feb:* 06, 13, 20, 27, *Mar:* 06, 13, 20, 27, *Apr:* 03, 10, 17, 24, *May:* 01, 08, 15, 22, 29, *Jun:* 05, 12, 19, 26, *Jul:* 03, 10, 17, 24, 31, *Aug:* 07, 14, 21, 28, *Sep:* 04, 11, 18, 25, *Oct:* 02, 09, 16, 23, 30, *Nov:* 06, 13, 20, 27, *Dec:* 04, 11, 18, 25

2003 *Jan:* 01, 08, 15, 22, 29, *Feb:* 05, 12, 19, 26, *Mar:* 05, 12, 19, 26, *Apr:* 02, 09, 16, 23, 30, *May:* 07, 14, 21, 28, *Jun:* 04, 11, 18, 25, *Jul:* 02, 09, 16, 23, 30, *Aug:* 06, 13, 20, 27, *Sep:* 03, 10, 17, 24, *Oct:* 01, 08, 15, 22, 29, *Nov:* 05, 12, 19, 26, *Dec:* 03, 10, 17, 24, 31

2004 *Jan:* 07, 14, 21, 28, *Feb:* 04, 11, 18, 25, *Mar:* 03, 10, 17, 24, 31, *Apr:* 07, 14, 21, 28, *May:* 05, 12,
19, 26, *Jun:* 02, 09, 16, 23, 30, *Jul:* 07, 14, 21, 28, *Aug:* 04, 11, 18, 25, *Sep:* 01, 08, 15, 22, 29, *Oct:* 06,
13, 20, 27, *Nov:* 03, 10, 17, 24, *Dec:* 01, 08, 15, 22, 29

2005 *Jan:* 05, 12, 19, 26, *Feb:* 02, 09, 16, 23, *Mar:* 02, 09, 16, 23, 30, *Apr:* 06, 13, 20, 27, *May:* 04, 11,
18, 25, *Jun:* 01, 08, 15, 22, 29, *Jul:* 06, 13, 20, 27, *Aug:* 03, 10, 17, 24, 31, *Sep:* 07, 14, 21, 28, *Oct:* 05,
12, 19, 26, *Nov:* 02, 09, 16, 23, 30, *Dec:* 07, 14, 21, 28

2006 *Jan:* 04, 11, 18, 25, *Feb:* 01, 08, 15, 22, *Mar:* 01, 08, 15, 22, 29, *Apr:* 05, 12, 19, 26, *May:* 03, 10,
17, 24, 31, *Jun:* 07, 14, 21, 28, *Jul:* 05, 12, 19, 26, *Aug:* 02, 09, 16, 23, 30, *Sep:* 06, 13, 20, 27, *Oct:* 04,
11, 18, 25, *Nov:* 01, 08, 15, 22, 29, *Dec:* 06, 13, 20, 27

2007 *Jan:* 03, 10, 17, 24, 31, *Feb:* 07, 14, 21, 28, *Mar:* 07, 14, 21, 28, *Apr:* 04, 11, 18, 25, *May:* 02, 09,
16, 23, 30, *Jun:* 06, 13, 20, 27, *Jul:* 04, 11, 18, 25, *Aug:* 01, 08, 15, 22, 29, *Sep:* 05, 12, 19, 26, *Oct:* 03,
10, 17, 24, 31, *Nov:* 07, 14, 21, 28, *Dec:* 05, 12, 19, 26

2008 *Jan:* 02, 09, 16, 23, 30, *Feb:* 06, 13, 20, 27, *Mar:* 05, 12, 19, 26, *Apr:* 02, 09, 16, 23, 30, *May:* 07,
14, 21, 28, *Jun:* 04, 11, 18, 25, *Jul:* 02, 09, 16, 23, 30, *Aug:* 06, 13, 20, 27, *Sep:* 03, 10, 17, 24, *Oct:* 01,
08, 15, 22, 29, *Nov:* 05, 12, 19, 26, *Dec:* 03, 10, 17, 24, 31

2009 *Jan:* 07, 14, 21, 28, *Feb:* 04, 11, 18, 25, *Mar:* 04, 11, 18, 25, *Apr:* 01, 08, 15, 22, 29, *May:* 06, 13,
20, 27, *Jun:* 03, 10, 17, 24, *Jul:* 01, 08, 15, 22, 29, *Aug:* 05, 12, 19, 26, *Sep:* 02, 09, 16, 23, 30, *Oct:* 07,
14, 21, 28, *Nov:* 04, 11, 18, 25, *Dec:* 02, 09, 16, 23, 30

2010 *Jan:* 06, 13, 20, 27, *Feb:* 03, 10, 17, 24, *Mar:* 03, 10, 17, 24, 31, *Apr:* 07, 14, 21, 28, *May:* 05, 12,
19, 26, *Jun:* 02, 09, 16, 23, 30, *Jul:* 07, 14, 21, 28, *Aug:* 04, 11, 18, 25, *Sep:* 01, 08, 15, 22, 29, *Oct:* 06,
13, 20, 27, *Nov:* 03, 10, 17, 24, *Dec:* 01, 08, 15, 22, 29

2011 *Jan:* 05, 12, 19, 26, *Feb:* 02, 09, 16, 23, *Mar:* 02, 09, 16, 23, 30, *Apr:* 06, 13, 20, 27, *May:* 04, 11,
18, 25, *Jun:* 01, 08, 15, 22, 29, *Jul:* 06, 13, 20, 27, *Aug:* 03, 10, 17, 24, 31, *Sep:* 07, 14, 21, 28, *Oct:* 05,
12, 19, 26, *Nov:* 02, 09, 16, 23, 30, *Dec:* 07, 14, 21, 28

2012 *Jan:* 04, 11, 18, 25, *Feb:* 01, 08, 15, 22, 29, *Mar:* 07, 14, 21, 28, *Apr:* 04, 11, 18, 25, *May:* 02, 09,
16, 23, 30, *Jun:* 06, 13, 20, 27, *Jul:* 04, 11, 18, 25, *Aug:* 01, 08, 15, 22, 29, *Sep:* 05, 12, 19, 26, *Oct:* 03,
10, 17, 24, 31, *Nov:* 07, 14, 21, 28, *Dec:* 05, 12, 19, 26

2013 *Jan:* 02, 09, 16, 23, 30, *Feb:* 06, 13, 20, 27, *Mar:* 06, 13, 20, 27, *Apr:* 03, 10, 17, 24, *May:* 01, 08,
15, 22, 29, *Jun:* 05, 12, 19, 26, *Jul:* 03, 10, 17, 24, 31, *Aug:* 07, 14, 21, 28, *Sep:* 04, 11, 18, 25, *Oct:* 02,
09, 16, 23, 30, *Nov:* 06, 13, 20, 27, *Dec:* 04, 11, 18, 25

Thursday: Zadkiel

IF YOUR DAY OF BIRTH IS THURSDAY: Zadkiel rules. His healing rays are turquoise and different shades of royal and indigo blue; his crystals are turquoise and lapis lazuli; his metal is tin. Attributes to focus on with Zadkiel are: abundance, wisdom, success with integrity.

♃ ♅ ♀ ♈

Zadkiel, whose name means 'Covering of God', is ruler of Thursday, the 6th of the Seven Heavens, the planet Jupiter and chief of the angelic order or group called Dominions. He holds the keys of wisdom and abundance (both spiritual and material) and can help us to expand our horizons in all sorts of ways. In terms of career development he supports us with knowledge and memory – two most useful assets. Zadkiel brings joy tempered with responsibility: the maintaining of ideals and integrity. There are many kinds of abundance, including money, loving kindness, health, happiness and spirituality. Be clear in what you seek.

When you receive your abundance he asks that you remember the spiritual law: 'Do as you would be done by'. Would you yourself like to be in receipt of the action you plan? Is the abundance you seek just for personal gain or are you going to share it? The law of Karma tells us that any actions we take which are good will result in manifold good deeds coming our way, while those of evil intent will rebound on us threefold (the threefold return) in this lifetime or the next.

Call on Zadkiel whenever you need abundance, and if he is the angel of the day of your birth, then he will also be one of your guardian angels. By practising the invocation, or carrying his crystal, you can learn to sense his energy around you.

Zadkiel, Zadkiel, Zadkiel, I ask for your aid to find the wisdom I need (or abundance or success that I will share with others), *in Love and Light, Love and Light, Love and Light.*

For abundance of success, wear or carry a Zadkiel crystal to remind you to invoke the angel when the time comes. Bear in mind that he will only help you if what you are asking is for your ultimate highest good.

Thursday birthdays

1940 *Jan:* 04, 11, 18, 25, *Feb:* 01, 08, 15, 22, 29, *Mar:* 07, 14, 21, 28, *Apr:* 04, 11, 18, 25, *May:* 02, 09, 16, 23, 30, *Jun:* 06, 13, 20, 27, *Jul:* 04, 11, 18, 25, *Aug:* 01, 08, 15, 22, 29, *Sep:* 05, 12, 19, 26, *Oct:* 03, 10, 17, 24, 31, *Nov:* 07, 14, 21, 28, *Dec:* 05, 12, 19, 26

1941 *Jan:* 02, 09, 16, 23, 30, *Feb:* 06, 13, 20, 27, *Mar:* 06, 13, 20, 27, *Apr:* 03, 10, 17, 24, *May:* 01, 08, 15, 22, 29, *Jun:* 05, 12, 19, 26, *Jul:* 03, 10, 17, 24, 31, *Aug:* 07, 14, 21, 28, *Sep:* 04, 11, 18, 25, *Oct:* 02, 09, 16, 23, 30, *Nov:* 06, 13, 20, 27, *Dec:* 04, 11, 18, 25

1942 *Jan:* 01, 08, 15, 22, 29, *Feb:* 05, 12, 19, 26, *Mar:* 05, 12, 19, 26, *Apr:* 02, 09, 16, 23, 30, *May:* 07, 14, 21, 28, *Jun:* 04, 11, 18, 25, *Jul:* 02, 09, 16, 23, 30, *Aug:* 06, 13, 20, 27, *Sep:* 03, 10, 17, 24, *Oct:* 01, 08, 15, 22, 29, *Nov:* 05, 12, 19, 26, *Dec:* 03, 10, 17, 24, 31

1943 *Jan:* 07, 14, 21, 28, *Feb:* 04, 11, 18, 25, *Mar:* 04, 11, 18, 25, *Apr:* 01, 08, 15, 22, 29, *May:* 06, 13, 20, 27, *Jun:* 03, 10, 17, 24, *Jul:* 01, 08, 15, 22, 29, *Aug:* 05, 12, 19, 26, *Sep:* 02, 09, 16, 23, 30, *Oct:* 07, 14, 21, 28, *Nov:* 04, 11, 18, 25, *Dec:* 02, 09, 16, 23, 30

1944 *Jan:* 06, 13, 20, 27, *Feb:* 03, 10, 17, 24, *Mar:* 02, 09, 16, 23, 30, *Apr:* 06, 13, 20, 27, *May:* 04, 11, 18, 25, *Jun:* 01, 08, 15, 22, 29, *Jul:* 06, 13, 20, 27, *Aug:* 03, 10, 17, 24, 31, *Sep:* 07, 14, 21, 28, *Oct:* 05, 12, 19, 26, *Nov:* 02, 09, 16, 23, 30, *Dec:* 07, 14, 21, 28

1945 *Jan:* 04, 11, 18, 25, *Feb:* 01, 08, 15, 22, *Mar:* 01, 08, 15, 22, 29, *Apr:* 05, 12, 19, 26, *May:* 03, 10, 17, 24, 31, *Jun:* 07, 14, 21, 28, *Jul:* 05, 12, 19, 26, *Aug:* 02, 09, 16, 23, 30, *Sep:* 06, 13, 20, 27, *Oct:* 04, 11, 18, 25, *Nov:* 01, 08, 15, 22, 29, *Dec:* 06, 13, 20, 27

1946 *Jan:* 03, 10, 17, 24, 31, *Feb:* 07, 14, 21, 28, *Mar:* 07, 14, 21, 28, *Apr:* 04, 11, 18, 25, *May:* 02, 09, 16, 23, 30, *Jun:* 06, 13, 20, 27, *Jul:* 04, 11, 18, 25, *Aug:* 01, 08, 15, 22, 29, *Sep:* 05, 12, 19, 26, *Oct:* 03, 10, 17, 24, 31, *Nov:* 07, 14, 21, 28, *Dec:* 05, 12, 19, 26

1947 *Jan:* 02, 09, 16, 23, 30, *Feb:* 06, 13, 20, 27, *Mar:* 06, 13, 20, 27, *Apr:* 03, 10, 17, 24, *May:* 01, 08, 15, 22, 29, *Jun:* 05, 12, 19, 26, *Jul:* 03, 10, 17, 24, 31, *Aug:* 07, 14, 21, 28, *Sep:* 04, 11, 18, 25, *Oct:* 02, 09, 16, 23, 30, *Nov:* 06, 13, 20, 27, *Dec:* 04, 11, 18, 25

1948 *Jan:* 01, 08, 15, 22, 29, *Feb:* 05, 12, 19, 26, *Mar:* 04, 11, 18, 25, *Apr:* 01, 08, 15, 22, 29, *May:* 06, 13, 20, 27, *Jun:* 03, 10, 17, 24, *Jul:* 01, 08, 15, 22, 29, *Aug:* 05, 12, 19, 26, *Sep:* 02, 09, 16, 23, 30, *Oct:* 07, 14, 21, 28, *Nov:* 04, 11, 18, 25, *Dec:* 02, 09, 16, 23, 30

1949 *Jan:* 06, 13, 20, 27, *Feb:* 03, 10, 17, 24, *Mar:* 03, 10, 17, 24, 31, *Apr:* 07, 14, 21, 28, *May:* 05, 12, 19, 26, *Jun:* 02, 09, 16, 23, 30, *Jul:* 07, 14, 21, 28, *Aug:* 04, 11, 18, 25, *Sep:* 01, 08, 15, 22, 29, *Oct:* 06, 13, 20, 27, *Nov:* 03, 10, 17, 24, *Dec:* 01, 08, 15, 22, 29

1950 *Jan:* 05, 12, 19, 26, *Feb:* 02, 09, 16, 23, *Mar:* 02, 09, 16, 23, 30, *Apr:* 06, 13, 20, 27, *May:* 04, 11, 18, 25, *Jun:* 01, 08, 15, 22, 29, *Jul:* 06, 13, 20, 27, *Aug:* 03, 10, 17, 24, 31, *Sep:* 07, 14, 21, 28, *Oct:* 05, 12, 19, 26, *Nov:* 02, 09, 16, 23, 30, *Dec:* 07, 14, 21, 28

1951 *Jan:* 04, 11, 18, 25, *Feb:* 01, 08, 15, 22, *Mar:* 01, 08, 15, 22, 29, *Apr:* 05, 12, 19, 26, *May:* 03, 10, 17, 24, 31, *Jun:* 07, 14, 21, 28, *Jul:* 05, 12, 19, 26, *Aug:* 02, 09, 16, 23, 30, *Sep:* 06, 13, 20, 27, *Oct:* 04, 11, 18, 25, *Nov:* 01, 08, 15, 22, 29, *Dec:* 06, 13, 20, 27

1952 *Jan:* 03, 10, 17, 24, 31, *Feb:* 07, 14, 21, 28, *Mar:* 06, 13, 20, 27, *Apr:* 03, 10, 17, 24, *May:* 01, 08, 15, 22, 29, *Jun:* 05, 12, 19, 26, *Jul:* 03, 10, 17, 24, 31, *Aug:* 07, 14, 21, 28, *Sep:* 04, 11, 18, 25, *Oct:* 02, 09, 16, 23, 30, *Nov:* 06, 13, 20, 27, *Dec:* 04, 11, 18, 25

1953 *Jan:* 01, 08, 15, 22, 29, *Feb:* 05, 12, 19, 26, *Mar:* 05, 12, 19, 26, *Apr:* 02, 09, 16, 23, 30, *May:* 07, 14, 21, 28, *Jun:* 04, 11, 18, 25, *Jul:* 02, 09, 16, 23, 30, *Aug:* 06, 13, 20, 27, *Sep:* 03, 10, 17, 24, *Oct:* 01, 08, 15, 22, 29, *Nov:* 05, 12, 19, 26, *Dec:* 03, 10, 17, 24, 31

1954 *Jan:* 07, 14, 21, 28, *Feb:* 04, 11, 18, 25, *Mar:* 04, 11, 18, 25, *Apr:* 01, 08, 15, 22, 29, *May:* 06, 13, 20, 27, *Jun:* 03, 10, 17, 24, *Jul:* 01, 08, 15, 22, 29, *Aug:* 05, 12, 19, 26, *Sep:* 02, 09, 16, 23, 30, *Oct:* 07, 14, 21, 28, *Nov:* 04, 11, 18, 25, *Dec:* 02, 09, 16, 23, 30

1955 *Jan:* 06, 13, 20, 27, *Feb:* 03, 10, 17, 24, *Mar:* 03, 10, 17, 24, 31, *Apr:* 07, 14, 21, 28, *May:* 05, 12, 19, 26, *Jun:* 02, 09, 16, 23, 30, *Jul:* 07, 14, 21, 28, *Aug:* 04, 11, 18, 25, *Sep:* 01, 08, 15, 22, 29, *Oct:* 06, 13, 20, 27, *Nov:* 03, 10, 17, 24, *Dec:* 01, 08, 15, 22, 29

1956 *Jan:* 05, 12, 19, 26, *Feb:* 02, 09, 16, 23, *Mar:* 01, 08, 15, 22, 29, *Apr:* 05, 12, 19, 26, *May:* 03, 10, 17, 24, 31, *Jun:* 07, 14, 21, 28, *Jul:* 05, 12, 19, 26, *Aug:* 02, 09, 16, 23, 30, *Sep:* 06, 13, 20, 27, *Oct:* 04, 11, 18, 25, *Nov:* 01, 08, 15, 22, 29, *Dec:* 06, 13, 20, 27

1957 *Jan:* 03, 10, 17, 24, 31, *Feb:* 07, 14, 21, 28, *Mar:* 07, 14, 21, 28, *Apr:* 04, 11, 18, 25, *May:* 02, 09, 16, 23, 30, *Jun:* 06, 13, 20, 27, *Jul:* 04, 11, 18, 25, *Aug:* 01, 08, 15, 22, 29, *Sep:* 05, 12, 19, 26, *Oct:* 03, 10, 17, 24, 31, *Nov:* 07, 14, 21, 28, *Dec:* 05, 12, 19, 26

1958 *Jan:* 02, 09, 16, 23, 30, *Feb:* 06, 13, 20, 27, *Mar:* 06, 13, 20, 27, *Apr:* 03, 10, 17, 24, *May:* 01, 08, 15, 22, 29, *Jun:* 05, 12, 19, 26, *Jul:* 03, 10, 17, 24, 31, *Aug:* 07, 14, 21, 28, *Sep:* 04, 11, 18, 25, *Oct:* 02, 09, 16, 23, 30, *Nov:* 06, 13, 20, 27, *Dec:* 04, 11, 18, 25

1959 *Jan:* 01, 08, 15, 22, 29, *Feb:* 05, 12, 19, 26, *Mar:* 05, 12, 19, 26, *Apr:* 02, 09, 16, 23, 30, *May:* 07, 14, 21, 28, *Jun:* 04, 11, 18, 25, *Jul:* 02, 09, 16, 23, 30, *Aug:* 06, 13, 20, 27, *Sep:* 03, 10, 17, 24, *Oct:* 01, 08, 15, 22, 29, *Nov:* 05, 12, 19, 26, *Dec:* 03, 10, 17, 24, 31

1960 *Jan:* 07, 14, 21, 28, *Feb:* 04, 11, 18, 25, *Mar:* 03, 10, 17, 24, 31, *Apr:* 07, 14, 21, 28, *May:* 05, 12, 19, 26, *Jun:* 02, 09, 16, 23, 30, *Jul:* 07, 14, 21, 28, *Aug:* 04, 11, 18, 25, *Sep:* 01, 08, 15, 22, 29, *Oct:* 06, 13, 20, 27, *Nov:* 03, 10, 17, 24, *Dec:* 01, 08, 15, 22, 29

1961 *Jan:* 05, 12, 19, 26, *Feb:* 02, 09, 16, 23, *Mar:* 02, 09, 16, 23, 30, *Apr:* 06, 13, 20, 27, *May:* 04, 11, 18, 25, *Jun:* 01, 08, 15, 22, 29, *Jul:* 06, 13, 20, 27, *Aug:* 03, 10, 17, 24, 31, *Sep:* 07, 14, 21, 28, *Oct:* 05, 12, 19, 26, *Nov:* 02, 09, 16, 23, 30, *Dec:* 07, 14, 21, 28

1962 *Jan:* 04, 11, 18, 25, *Feb:* 01, 08, 15, 22, *Mar:* 01, 08, 15, 22, 29, *Apr:* 05, 12, 19, 26, *May:* 03, 10, 17, 24, 31, *Jun:* 07, 14, 21, 28, *Jul:* 05, 12, 19, 26, *Aug:* 02, 09, 16, 23, 30, *Sep:* 06, 13, 20, 27, *Oct:* 04, 11, 18, 25, *Nov:* 01, 08, 15, 22, 29, *Dec:* 06, 13, 20, 27

1963 *Jan:* 03, 10, 17, 24, 31, *Feb:* 07, 14, 21, 28, *Mar:* 07, 14, 21, 28, *Apr:* 04, 11, 18, 25, *May:* 02, 09, 16, 23, 30, *Jun:* 06, 13, 20, 27, *Jul:* 04, 11, 18, 25, *Aug:* 01, 08, 15, 22, 29, *Sep:* 05, 12, 19, 26, *Oct:* 03, 10, 17, 24, 31, *Nov:* 07, 14, 21, 28, *Dec:* 05, 12, 19, 26

1964 *Jan:* 02, 09, 16, 23, 30, *Feb:* 06, 13, 20, 27, *Mar:* 05, 12, 19, 26, *Apr:* 02, 09, 16, 23, 30, *May:* 07, 14, 21, 28, *Jun:* 04, 11, 18, 25, *Jul:* 02, 09, 16, 23, 30, *Aug:* 06, 13, 20, 27, *Sep:* 03, 10, 17, 24, *Oct:* 01, 08, 15, 22, 29, *Nov:* 05, 12, 19, 26, *Dec:* 03, 10, 17, 24, 31

1965 *Jan:* 07, 14, 21, 28, *Feb:* 04, 11, 18, 25, *Mar:* 04, 11, 18, 25, *Apr:* 01, 08, 15, 22, 29, *May:* 06, 13, 20, 27, *Jun:* 03, 10, 17, 24, *Jul:* 01, 08, 15, 22, 29, *Aug:* 05, 12, 19, 26, *Sep:* 02, 09, 16, 23, 30, *Oct:* 07, 14, 21, 28, *Nov:* 04, 11, 18, 25, *Dec:* 02, 09, 16, 23, 30

1966 *Jan:* 06, 13, 20, 27, *Feb:* 03, 10, 17, 24, *Mar:* 03, 10, 17, 24, 31, *Apr:* 07, 14, 21, 28, *May:* 05, 12, 19, 26, *Jun:* 02, 09, 16, 23, 30, *Jul:* 07, 14, 21, 28, *Aug:* 04, 11, 18, 25, *Sep:* 01, 08, 15, 22, 29, *Oct:* 06, 13, 20, 27, *Nov:* 03, 10, 17, 24, *Dec:* 01, 08, 15, 22, 29

1967 *Jan:* 05, 12, 19, 26, *Feb:* 02, 09, 16, 23, *Mar:* 02, 09, 16, 23, 30, *Apr:* 06, 13, 20, 27, *May:* 04, 11, 18, 25, *Jun:* 01, 08, 15, 22, 29, *Jul:* 06, 13, 20, 27, *Aug:* 03, 10, 17, 24, 31, *Sep:* 07, 14, 21, 28, *Oct:* 05, 12, 19, 26, *Nov:* 02, 09, 16, 23, 30, *Dec:* 07, 14, 21, 28

1968 *Jan:* 04, 11, 18, 25, *Feb:* 01, 08, 15, 22, 29, *Mar:* 07, 14, 21, 28, *Apr:* 04, 11, 18, 25, *May:* 02, 09, 16, 23, 30, *Jun:* 06, 13, 20, 27, *Jul:* 04, 11, 18, 25, *Aug:* 01, 08, 15, 22, 29, *Sep:* 05, 12, 19, 26, *Oct:* 03, 10, 17, 24, 31, *Nov:* 07, 14, 21, 28, *Dec:* 05, 12, 19, 26

1969 *Jan:* 02, 09, 16, 23, 30, *Feb:* 06, 13, 20, 27, *Mar:* 06, 13, 20, 27, *Apr:* 03, 10, 17, 24, *May:* 01, 08, 15, 22, 29, *Jun:* 05, 12, 19, 26, *Jul:* 03, 10, 17, 24, 31, *Aug:* 07, 14, 21, 28, *Sep:* 04, 11, 18, 25, *Oct:* 02, 09, 16, 23, 30, *Nov:* 06, 13, 20, 27, *Dec:* 04, 11, 18, 25

1970 *Jan:* 01, 08, 15, 22, 29, *Feb:* 05, 12, 19, 26, *Mar:* 05, 12, 19, 26, *Apr:* 02, 09, 16, 23, 30, *May:* 07, 14, 21, 28, *Jun:* 04, 11, 18, 25, *Jul:* 02, 09, 16, 23, 30, *Aug:* 06, 13, 20, 27, *Sep:* 03, 10, 17, 24, *Oct:* 01, 08, 15, 22, 29, *Nov:* 05, 12, 19, 26, *Dec:* 03, 10, 17, 24, 31

1971 *Jan:* 07, 14, 21, 28, *Feb:* 04, 11, 18, 25, *Mar:* 04, 11, 18, 25, *Apr:* 01, 08, 15, 22, 29, *May:* 06, 13, 20, 27, *Jun:* 03, 10, 17, 24, *Jul:* 01, 08, 15, 22, 29, *Aug:* 05, 12, 19, 26, *Sep:* 02, 09, 16, 23, 30, *Oct:* 07, 14, 21, 28, *Nov:* 04, 11, 18, 25, *Dec:* 02, 09, 16, 23, 30

1972 *Jan:* 06, 13, 20, 27, *Feb:* 03, 10, 17, 24, *Mar:* 02, 09, 16, 23, 30, *Apr:* 06, 13, 20, 27, *May:* 04, 11, 18, 25, *Jun:* 01, 08, 15, 22, 29, *Jul:* 06, 13, 20, 27, *Aug:* 03, 10, 17, 24, 31, *Sep:* 07, 14, 21, 28, *Oct:* 05, 12, 19, 26, *Nov:* 02, 09, 16, 23, 30, *Dec:* 07, 14, 21, 28

1973 *Jan:* 04, 11, 18, 25, *Feb:* 01, 08, 15, 22, *Mar:* 01, 08, 15, 22, 29, *Apr:* 05, 12, 19, 26, *May:* 03, 10, 17, 24, 31, *Jun:* 07, 14, 21, 28, *Jul:* 05, 12, 19, 26, *Aug:* 02, 09, 16, 23, 30, *Sep:* 06, 13, 20, 27, *Oct:* 04, 11, 18, 25, *Nov:* 01, 08, 15, 22, 29, *Dec:* 06, 13, 20, 27

1974 *Jan:* 03, 10, 17, 24, 31, *Feb:* 07, 14, 21, 28, *Mar:* 07, 14, 21, 28, *Apr:* 04, 11, 18, 25, *May:* 02, 09, 16, 23, 30, *Jun:* 06, 13, 20, 27, *Jul:* 04, 11, 18, 25, *Aug:* 01, 08, 15, 22, 29, *Sep:* 05, 12, 19, 26, *Oct:* 03, 10, 17, 24, 31, *Nov:* 07, 14, 21, 28, *Dec:* 05, 12, 19, 26

1975 *Jan:* 02, 09, 16, 23, 30, *Feb:* 06, 13, 20, 27, *Mar:* 06, 13, 20, 27, *Apr:* 03, 10, 17, 24, *May:* 01, 08, 15, 22, 29, *Jun:* 05, 12, 19, 26, *Jul:* 03, 10, 17, 24, 31, *Aug:* 07, 14, 21, 28, *Sep:* 04, 11, 18, 25, *Oct:* 02, 09, 16, 23, 30, *Nov:* 06, 13, 20, 27, *Dec:* 04, 11, 18, 25

1976 *Jan:* 01, 08, 15, 22, 29, *Feb:* 05, 12, 19, 26, *Mar:* 04, 11, 18, 25, *Apr:* 01, 08, 15, 22, 29, *May:* 06, 13, 20, 27, *Jun:* 03, 10, 17, 24, *Jul:* 01, 08, 15, 22, 29, *Aug:* 05, 12, 19, 26, *Sep:* 02, 09, 16, 23, 30, *Oct:* 07, 14, 21, 28, *Nov:* 04, 11, 18, 25, *Dec:* 02, 09, 16, 23, 30

1977 *Jan:* 06, 13, 20, 27, *Feb:* 03, 10, 17, 24, *Mar:* 03, 10, 17, 24, 31, *Apr:* 07, 14, 21, 28, *May:* 05, 12, 19, 26, *Jun:* 02, 09, 16, 23, 30, *Jul:* 07, 14, 21, 28, *Aug:* 04, 11, 18, 25, *Sep:* 01, 08, 15, 22, 29, *Oct:* 06, 13, 20, 27, *Nov:* 03, 10, 17, 24, *Dec:* 01, 08, 15, 22, 29

1978 *Jan:* 05, 12, 19, 26, *Feb:* 02, 09, 16, 23, *Mar:* 02, 09, 16, 23, 30, *Apr:* 06, 13, 20, 27, *May:* 04, 11, 18, 25, *Jun:* 01, 08, 15, 22, 29, *Jul:* 06, 13, 20, 27, *Aug:* 03, 10, 17, 24, 31, *Sep:* 07, 14, 21, 28, *Oct:* 05, 12, 19, 26, *Nov:* 02, 09, 16, 23, 30, *Dec:* 07, 14, 21, 28

1979 *Jan:* 04, 11, 18, 25, *Feb:* 01, 08, 15, 22, *Mar:* 01, 08, 15, 22, 29, *Apr:* 05, 12, 19, 26, *May:* 03, 10, 17, 24, 31, *Jun:* 07, 14, 21, 28, *Jul:* 05, 12, 19, 26, *Aug:* 02, 09, 16, 23, 30, *Sep:* 06, 13, 20, 27, *Oct:* 04, 11, 18, 25, *Nov:* 01, 08, 15, 22, 29, *Dec:* 06, 13, 20, 27

1980 *Jan:* 03, 10, 17, 24, 31, *Feb:* 07, 14, 21, 28, *Mar:* 06, 13, 20, 27, *Apr:* 03, 10, 17, 24, *May:* 01, 08, 15, 22, 29, *Jun:* 05, 12, 19, 26, *Jul:* 03, 10, 17, 24, 31, *Aug:* 07, 14, 21, 28, *Sep:* 04, 11, 18, 25, *Oct:* 02, 09, 16, 23, 30, *Nov:* 06, 13, 20, 27, *Dec:* 04, 11, 18, 25

1981 *Jan:* 01, 08, 15, 22, 29, *Feb:* 05, 12, 19, 26, *Mar:* 05, 12, 19, 26, *Apr:* 02, 09, 16, 23, 30, *May:* 07, 14, 21, 28, *Jun:* 04, 11, 18, 25, *Jul:* 02, 09, 16, 23, 30, *Aug:* 06, 13, 20, 27, *Sep:* 03, 10, 17, 24, *Oct:* 01, 08, 15, 22, 29, *Nov:* 05, 12, 19, 26, *Dec:* 03, 10, 17, 24, 31

1982 *Jan:* 07, 14, 21, 28, *Feb:* 04, 11, 18, 25, *Mar:* 04, 11, 18, 25, *Apr:* 01, 08, 15, 22, 29, *May:* 06, 13, 20, 27, *Jun:* 03, 10, 17, 24, *Jul:* 01, 08, 15, 22, 29, *Aug:* 05, 12, 19, 26, *Sep:* 02, 09, 16, 23, 30, *Oct:* 07, 14, 21, 28, *Nov:* 04, 11, 18, 25, *Dec:* 02, 09, 16, 23, 30

1983 *Jan:* 06, 13, 20, 27, *Feb:* 03, 10, 17, 24, *Mar:* 03, 10, 17, 24, 31, *Apr:* 07, 14, 21, 28, *May:* 05, 12, 19, 26, *Jun:* 02, 09, 16, 23, 30, *Jul:* 07, 14, 21, 28, *Aug:* 04, 11, 18, 25, *Sep:* 01, 08, 15, 22, 29, *Oct:* 06, 13, 20, 27, *Nov:* 03, 10, 17, 24, *Dec:* 01, 08, 15, 22, 29

1984 *Jan:* 05, 12, 19, 26, *Feb:* 02, 09, 16, 23, *Mar:* 01, 08, 15, 22, 29, *Apr:* 05, 12, 19, 26, *May:* 03, 10, 17, 24, 31, *Jun:* 07, 14, 21, 28, *Jul:* 05, 12, 19, 26, *Aug:* 02, 09, 16, 23, 30, *Sep:* 06, 13, 20, 27, *Oct:* 04, 11, 18, 25, *Nov:* 01, 08, 15, 22, 29, *Dec:* 06, 13, 20, 27

1985 *Jan:* 03, 10, 17, 24, 31, *Feb:* 07, 14, 21, 28, *Mar:* 07, 14, 21, 28, *Apr:* 04, 11, 18, 25, *May:* 02, 09, 16, 23, 30, *Jun:* 06, 13, 20, 27, *Jul:* 04, 11, 18, 25, *Aug:* 01, 08, 15, 22, 29, *Sep:* 05, 12, 19, 26, *Oct:* 03, 10, 17, 24, 31, *Nov:* 07, 14, 21, 28, *Dec:* 05, 12, 19, 26

1986 *Jan:* 02, 09, 16, 23, 30, *Feb:* 06, 13, 20, 27, *Mar:* 06, 13, 20, 27, *Apr:* 03, 10, 17, 24, *May:* 01, 08, 15, 22, 29, *Jun:* 05, 12, 19, 26, *Jul:* 03, 10, 17, 24, 31, *Aug:* 07, 14, 21, 28, *Sep:* 04, 11, 18, 25, *Oct:* 02, 09, 16, 23, 30, *Nov:* 06, 13, 20, 27, *Dec:* 04, 11, 18, 25

1987 *Jan:* 01, 08, 15, 22, 29, *Feb:* 05, 12, 19, 26, *Mar:* 05, 12, 19, 26, *Apr:* 02, 09, 16, 23, 30, *May:* 07, 14, 21, 28, *Jun:* 04, 11, 18, 25, *Jul:* 02, 09, 16, 23, 30, *Aug:* 06, 13, 20, 27, *Sep:* 03, 10, 17, 24, *Oct:* 01, 08, 15, 22, 29, *Nov:* 05, 12, 19, 26, *Dec:* 03, 10, 17, 24, 31

1988 *Jan:* 07, 14, 21, 28, *Feb:* 04, 11, 18, 25, *Mar:* 03, 10, 17, 24, 31, *Apr:* 07, 14, 21, 28, *May:* 05, 12, 19, 26, *Jun:* 02, 09, 16, 23, 30, *Jul:* 07, 14, 21, 28, *Aug:* 04, 11, 18, 25, *Sep:* 01, 08, 15, 22, 29, *Oct:* 06, 13, 20, 27, *Nov:* 03, 10, 17, 24, *Dec:* 01, 08, 15, 22, 29

1989 *Jan:* 05, 12, 19, 26, *Feb:* 02, 09, 16, 23, *Mar:* 02, 09, 16, 23, 30, *Apr:* 06, 13, 20, 27, *May:* 04, 11, 18, 25, *Jun:* 01, 08, 15, 22, 29, *Jul:* 06, 13, 20, 27, *Aug:* 03, 10, 17, 24, 31, *Sep:* 07, 14, 21, 28, *Oct:* 05, 12, 19, 26, *Nov:* 02, 09, 16, 23, 30, *Dec:* 07, 14, 21, 28

1990 *Jan:* 04, 11, 18, 25, *Feb:* 01, 08, 15, 22, *Mar:* 01, 08, 15, 22, 29, *Apr:* 05, 12, 19, 26, *May:* 03, 10, 17, 24, 31, *Jun:* 07, 14, 21, 28, *Jul:* 05, 12, 19, 26, *Aug:* 02, 09, 16, 23, 30, *Sep:* 06, 13, 20, 27, *Oct:* 04, 11, 18, 25, *Nov:* 01, 08, 15, 22, 29, *Dec:* 06, 13, 20, 27

1991 *Jan:* 03, 10, 17, 24, 31, *Feb:* 07, 14, 21, 28, *Mar:* 07, 14, 21, 28, *Apr:* 04, 11, 18, 25, *May:* 02, 09, 16, 23, 30, *Jun:* 06, 13, 20, 27, *Jul:* 04, 11, 18, 25, *Aug:* 01, 08, 15, 22, 29, *Sep:* 05, 12, 19, 26, *Oct:* 03, 10, 17, 24, 31, *Nov:* 07, 14, 21, 28, *Dec:* 05, 12, 19, 26

1992 *Jan:* 02, 09, 16, 23, 30, *Feb:* 06, 13, 20, 27, *Mar:* 05, 12, 19, 26, *Apr:* 02, 09, 16, 23, 30, *May:* 07, 14, 21, 28, *Jun:* 04, 11, 18, 25, *Jul:* 02, 09, 16, 23, 30, *Aug:* 06, 13, 20, 27, *Sep:* 03, 10, 17, 24, *Oct:* 01, 08, 15, 22, 29, *Nov:* 05, 12, 19, 26, *Dec:* 03, 10, 17, 24, 31

1993 *Jan:* 07, 14, 21, 28, *Feb:* 04, 11, 18, 25, *Mar:* 04, 11, 18, 25, *Apr:* 01, 08, 15, 22, 29, *May:* 06, 13, 20, 27, *Jun:* 03, 10, 17, 24, *Jul:* 01, 08, 15, 22, 29, *Aug:* 05, 12, 19, 26, *Sep:* 02, 09, 16, 23, 30, *Oct:* 07, 14, 21, 28, *Nov:* 04, 11, 18, 25, *Dec:* 02, 09, 16, 23, 30

1994 *Jan:* 06, 13, 20, 27, *Feb:* 03, 10, 17, 24, *Mar:* 03, 10, 17, 24, 31, *Apr:* 07, 14, 21, 28, *May:* 05, 12, 19, 26, *Jun:* 02, 09, 16, 23, 30, *Jul:* 07, 14, 21, 28, *Aug:* 04, 11, 18, 25, *Sep:* 01, 08, 15, 22, 29, *Oct:* 06, 13, 20, 27, *Nov:* 03, 10, 17, 24, *Dec:* 01, 08, 15, 22, 29

1995 *Jan:* 05, 12, 19, 26, *Feb:* 02, 09, 16, 23, *Mar:* 02, 09, 16, 23, 30, *Apr:* 06, 13, 20, 27, *May:* 04, 11, 18, 25, *Jun:* 01, 08, 15, 22, 29, *Jul:* 06, 13, 20, 27, *Aug:* 03, 10, 17, 24, 31, *Sep:* 07, 14, 21, 28, *Oct:* 05, 12, 19, 26, *Nov:* 02, 09, 16, 23, 30, *Dec:* 07, 14, 21, 28

1996 *Jan:* 04, 11, 18, 25, *Feb:* 01, 08, 15, 22, 29, *Mar:* 07, 14, 21, 28, *Apr:* 04, 11, 18, 25, *May:* 02, 09, 16, 23, 30, *Jun:* 06, 13, 20, 27, *Jul:* 04, 11, 18, 25, *Aug:* 01, 08, 15, 22, 29, *Sep:* 05, 12, 19, 26, *Oct:* 03, 10, 17, 24, 31, *Nov:* 07, 14, 21, 28, *Dec:* 05, 12, 19, 26

1997 *Jan:* 02, 09, 16, 23, 30, *Feb:* 06, 13, 20, 27, *Mar:* 06, 13, 20, 27, *Apr:* 03, 10, 17, 24, *May:* 01, 08, 15, 22, 29, *Jun:* 05, 12, 19, 26, *Jul:* 03, 10, 17, 24, 31, *Aug:* 07, 14, 21, 28, *Sep:* 04, 11, 18, 25, *Oct:* 02, 09, 16, 23, 30, *Nov:* 06, 13, 20, 27, *Dec:* 04, 11, 18, 25

1998 *Jan:* 01, 08, 15, 22, 29, *Feb:* 05, 12, 19, 26, *Mar:* 05, 12, 19, 26, *Apr:* 02, 09, 16, 23, 30, *May:* 07, 14, 21, 28, *Jun:* 04, 11, 18, 25, *Jul:* 02, 09, 16, 23, 30, *Aug:* 06, 13, 20, 27, *Sep:* 03, 10, 17, 24, *Oct:* 01, 08, 15, 22, 29, *Nov:* 05, 12, 19, 26, *Dec:* 03, 10, 17, 24, 31

1999 *Jan:* 07, 14, 21, 28, *Feb:* 04, 11, 18, 25, *Mar:* 04, 11, 18, 25, *Apr:* 01, 08, 15, 22, 29, *May:* 06, 13, 20, 27, *Jun:* 03, 10, 17, 24, *Jul:* 01, 08, 15, 22, 29, *Aug:* 05, 12, 19, 26, *Sep:* 02, 09, 16, 23, 30, *Oct:* 07, 14, 21, 28, *Nov:* 04, 11, 18, 25, *Dec:* 02, 09, 16, 23, 30

2000 *Jan:* 06, 13, 20, 27, *Feb:* 03, 10, 17, 24, *Mar:* 02, 09, 16, 23, 30, *Apr:* 06, 13, 20, 27, *May:* 04, 11, 18, 25, *Jun:* 01, 08, 15, 22, 29, *Jul:* 06, 13, 20, 27, *Aug:* 03, 10, 17, 24, 31, *Sep:* 07, 14, 21, 28, *Oct:* 05, 12, 19, 26, *Nov:* 02, 09, 16, 23, 30, *Dec:* 07, 14, 21, 28

2001 *Jan:* 04, 11, 18, 25, *Feb:* 01, 08, 15, 22, *Mar:* 01, 08, 15, 22, 29, *Apr:* 05, 12, 19, 26, *May:* 03, 10, 17, 24, 31, *Jun:* 07, 14, 21, 28, *Jul:* 05, 12, 19, 26, *Aug:* 02, 09, 16, 23, 30, *Sep:* 06, 13, 20, 27, *Oct:* 04, 11, 18, 25, *Nov:* 01, 08, 15, 22, 29, *Dec:* 06, 13, 20, 27

2002 *Jan:* 03, 10, 17, 24, 31, *Feb:* 07, 14, 21, 28, *Mar:* 07, 14, 21, 28, *Apr:* 04, 11, 18, 25, *May:* 02, 09, 16, 23, 30, *Jun:* 06, 13, 20, 27, *Jul:* 04, 11, 18, 25, *Aug:* 01, 08, 15, 22, 29, *Sep:* 05, 12, 19, 26, *Oct:* 03, 10, 17, 24, 31, *Nov:* 07, 14, 21, 28, *Dec:* 05, 12, 19, 26

2003 *Jan:* 02, 09, 16, 23, 30, *Feb:* 06, 13, 20, 27, *Mar:* 06, 13, 20, 27, *Apr:* 03, 10, 17, 24, *May:* 01, 08, 15, 22, 29, *Jun:* 05, 12, 19, 26, *Jul:* 03, 10, 17, 24, 31, *Aug:* 07, 14, 21, 28, *Sep:* 04, 11, 18, 25, *Oct:* 02, 09, 16, 23, 30, *Nov:* 06, 13, 20, 27, *Dec:* 04, 11, 18, 25

2004 *Jan:* 01, 08, 15, 22, 29, *Feb:* 05, 12, 19, 26, *Mar:* 04, 11, 18, 25, *Apr:* 01, 08, 15, 22, 29, *May:* 06, 13, 20, 27, *Jun:* 03, 10, 17, 24, *Jul:* 01, 08, 15, 22, 29, *Aug:* 05, 12, 19, 26, *Sep:* 02, 09, 16, 23, 30, *Oct:* 07, 14, 21, 28, *Nov:* 04, 11, 18, 25, *Dec:* 02, 09, 16, 23, 30

2005 *Jan:* 06, 13, 20, 27, *Feb:* 03, 10, 17, 24, *Mar:* 03, 10, 17, 24, 31, *Apr:* 07, 14, 21, 28, *May:* 05, 12, 19, 26, *Jun:* 02, 09, 16, 23, 30, *Jul:* 07, 14, 21, 28, *Aug:* 04, 11, 18, 25, *Sep:* 01, 08, 15, 22, 29, *Oct:* 06, 13, 20, 27, *Nov:* 03, 10, 17, 24, *Dec:* 01, 08, 15, 22, 29

2006 *Jan:* 05, 12, 19, 26, *Feb:* 02, 09, 16, 23, *Mar:* 02, 09, 16, 23, 30, *Apr:* 06, 13, 20, 27, *May:* 04, 11, 18, 25, *Jun:* 01, 08, 15, 22, 29, *Jul:* 06, 13, 20, 27, *Aug:* 03, 10, 17, 24, 31, *Sep:* 07, 14, 21, 28, *Oct:* 05, 12, 19, 26, *Nov:* 02, 09, 16, 23, 30, *Dec:* 07, 14, 21, 28

2007 *Jan:* 04, 11, 18, 25, *Feb:* 01, 08, 15, 22, *Mar:* 01, 08, 15, 22, 29, *Apr:* 05, 12, 19, 26, *May:* 03, 10, 17, 24, 31, *Jun:* 07, 14, 21, 28, *Jul:* 05, 12, 19, 26, *Aug:* 02, 09, 16, 23, 30, *Sep:* 06, 13, 20, 27, *Oct:* 04, 11, 18, 25, *Nov:* 01, 08, 15, 22, 29, *Dec:* 06, 13, 20, 27

2008 *Jan:* 03, 10, 17, 24, 31, *Feb:* 07, 14, 21, 28, *Mar:* 06, 13, 20, 27, *Apr:* 03, 10, 17, 24, *May:* 01, 08, 15, 22, 29, *Jun:* 05, 12, 19, 26, *Jul:* 03, 10, 17, 24, 31, *Aug:* 07, 14, 21, 28, *Sep:* 04, 11, 18, 25, *Oct:* 02, 09, 16, 23, 30, *Nov:* 06, 13, 20, 27, *Dec:* 04, 11, 18, 25

2009 *Jan:* 01, 08, 15, 22, 29, *Feb:* 05, 12, 19, 26, *Mar:* 05, 12, 19, 26, *Apr:* 02, 09, 16, 23, 30, *May:* 07, 14, 21, 28, *Jun:* 04, 11, 18, 25, *Jul:* 02, 09, 16, 23, 30, *Aug:* 06, 13, 20, 27, *Sep:* 03, 10, 17, 24, *Oct:* 01, 08, 15, 22, 29, *Nov:* 05, 12, 19, 26, *Dec:* 03, 10, 17, 24, 31

2010 *Jan:* 07, 14, 21, 28, *Feb:* 04, 11, 18, 25, *Mar:* 04, 11, 18, 25, *Apr:* 01, 08, 15, 22, 29, *May:* 06, 13, 20, 27, *Jun:* 03, 10, 17, 24, *Jul:* 01, 08, 15, 22, 29, *Aug:* 05, 12, 19, 26, *Sep:* 02, 09, 16, 23, 30, *Oct:* 07, 14, 21, 28, *Nov:* 04, 11, 18, 25, *Dec:* 02, 09, 16, 23, 30

2011 *Jan:* 06, 13, 20, 27, *Feb:* 03, 10, 17, 24, *Mar:* 03, 10, 17, 24, 31, *Apr:* 07, 14, 21, 28, *May:* 05, 12, 19, 26, *Jun:* 02, 09, 16, 23, 30, *Jul:* 07, 14, 21, 28, *Aug:* 04, 11, 18, 25, *Sep:* 01, 08, 15, 22, 29, *Oct:* 06, 13, 20, 27, *Nov:* 03, 10, 17, 24, *Dec:* 01, 08, 15, 22, 29

2012 *Jan:* 05, 12, 19, 26, *Feb:* 02, 09, 16, 23, *Mar:* 01, 08, 15, 22, 29, *Apr:* 05, 12, 19, 26, *May:* 03, 10, 17, 24, 31, *Jun:* 07, 14, 21, 28, *Jul:* 05, 12, 19, 26, *Aug:* 02, 09, 16, 23, 30, *Sep:* 06, 13, 20, 27, *Oct:* 04, 11, 18, 25, *Nov:* 01, 08, 15, 22, 29, *Dec:* 06, 13, 20, 27

2013 *Jan:* 03, 10, 17, 24, 31, *Feb:* 07, 14, 21, 28, *Mar:* 07, 14, 21, 28, *Apr:* 04, 11, 18, 25, *May:* 02, 09, 16, 23, 30, *Jun:* 06, 13, 20, 27, *Jul:* 04, 11, 18, 25, *Aug:* 01, 08, 15, 22, 29, *Sep:* 05, 12, 19, 26, *Oct:* 03, 10, 17, 24, 31, *Nov:* 07, 14, 21, 28, *Dec:* 05, 12, 19, 26

Friday: Haniel

IF YOUR DAY OF BIRTH IS FRIDAY: Haniel rules. Haniel's healing rays are shades of green and pink, including pale rose and magenta. Her metal is copper; her crystals are emerald, rose quartz, kunzite and tourmaline. Attributes for Haniel on which to focus are: love, beauty and compassion, especially self-appreciation.

Haniel, whose name means 'Grace of God', rules Friday, Venus (the star of Love, morning or evening star) and 3rd Heaven. Again, generally considered as a feminine energy, she is primarily concerned with love, friendship, relationships and sexuality. She's chief of two angelic orders: Virtues, the healing angels, and Principalities. Virtues angels work miracles on earth and confer grace and bravery to those who are deserving of it. In the oldest recorded civilisation, Haniel was associated with the Chaldean deity Ishtar. For millennia her name has been engraved on good luck or love charms.

Haniel teaches that there are two kinds of love and therefore two heart chakras within your body. The first is love of a personal nature such as you feel for a partner, spouse, friend, family and especially for yourself; this is drawn from the emerald ray which powers the green chakra. Most of us are too judgemental about ourselves, perhaps through our past or upbringing and afraid to appreciate our own qualities. You must heal the green in order to move to the second kind of love.

This non-judgemental love has no limits: it is the magenta-pink ray of unconditional love and compassion for all sentient life on Mother Earth. It flows from the higher heart chakra or bridge between lower and higher self. This is like a water lily: the green leaves and bud are personal heart, while the magenta pink is the higher heart flower. Invoke Haniel as below for all kinds of relationship or heart healing issues, but especially on Fridays and if you are a Friday child:

Haniel, Haniel, Haniel, help me to open my heart to beauty of self and others (or love, or compassion), *in Love and Light, Love and Light, Love and Light.*

If your heart has been hurt, close your eyes and ask Haniel to help you visualise it as a water lily bud floating in emerald-green water. See the water supporting and nourishing it; if and when the pink flower begins to open this signifies that a level of heart healing is completed and your higher heart chakra is opening.

Friday birthdays

1940 *Jan:* 05, 12, 19, 26, *Feb:* 02, 09, 16, 23, *Mar:* 01, 08, 15, 22, 29, *Apr:* 05, 12, 19, 26, *May:* 03, 10, 17, 24, 31, *Jun:* 07, 14, 21, 28, *Jul:* 05, 12, 19, 26, *Aug:* 02, 09, 16, 23, 30, *Sep:* 06, 13, 20, 27, *Oct:* 04, 11, 18, 25, *Nov:* 01, 08, 15, 22, 29, *Dec:* 06, 13, 20, 27

1941 *Jan:* 03, 10, 17, 24, 31, *Feb:* 07, 14, 21, 28, *Mar:* 07, 14, 21, 28, *Apr:* 04, 11, 18, 25, *May:* 02, 09, 16, 23, 30, *Jun:* 06, 13, 20, 27, *Jul:* 04, 11, 18, 25, *Aug:* 01, 08, 15, 22, 29, *Sep:* 05, 12, 19, 26, *Oct:* 03, 10, 17, 24, 31, *Nov:* 07, 14, 21, 28, *Dec:* 05, 12, 19, 26

1942 *Jan:* 02, 09, 16, 23, 30, *Feb:* 06, 13, 20, 27, *Mar:* 06, 13, 20, 27, *Apr:* 03, 10, 17, 24, *May:* 01, 08, 15, 22, 29, *Jun:* 05, 12, 19, 26, *Jul:* 03, 10, 17, 24, 31, *Aug:* 07, 14, 21, 28, *Sep:* 04, 11, 18, 25, *Oct:* 02, 09, 16, 23, 30, *Nov:* 06, 13, 20, 27, *Dec:* 04, 11, 18, 25

1943 *Jan:* 01, 08, 15, 22, 29, *Feb:* 05, 12, 19, 26, *Mar:* 05, 12, 19, 26, *Apr:* 02, 09, 16, 23, 30, *May:* 07, 14, 21, 28, *Jun:* 04, 11, 18, 25, *Jul:* 02, 09, 16, 23, 30, *Aug:* 06, 13, 20, 27, *Sep:* 03, 10, 17, 24, *Oct:* 01, 08, 15, 22, 29, *Nov:* 05, 12, 19, 26, *Dec:* 03, 10, 17, 24, 31

1944 *Jan:* 07, 14, 21, 28, *Feb:* 04, 11, 18, 25, *Mar:* 03, 10, 17, 24, 31, *Apr:* 07, 14, 21, 28, *May:* 05, 12, 19, 26, *Jun:* 02, 09, 16, 23, 30, *Jul:* 07, 14, 21, 28, *Aug:* 04, 11, 18, 25, *Sep:* 01, 08, 15, 22, 29, *Oct:* 06, 13, 20, 27, *Nov:* 03, 10, 17, 24, *Dec:* 01, 08, 15, 22, 29

1945 *Jan:* 05, 12, 19, 26, *Feb:* 02, 09, 16, 23, *Mar:* 02, 09, 16, 23, 30, *Apr:* 06, 13, 20, 27, *May:* 04, 11, 18, 25, *Jun:* 01, 08, 15, 22, 29, *Jul:* 06, 13, 20, 27, *Aug:* 03, 10, 17, 24, 31, *Sep:* 07, 14, 21, 28, *Oct:* 05, 12, 19, 26, *Nov:* 02, 09, 16, 23, 30, *Dec:* 07, 14, 21, 28

1946 *Jan:* 04, 11, 18, 25, *Feb:* 01, 08, 15, 22, *Mar:* 01, 08, 15, 22, 29, *Apr:* 05, 12, 19, 26, *May:* 03, 10, 17, 24, 31, *Jun:* 07, 14, 21, 28, *Jul:* 05, 12, 19, 26, *Aug:* 02, 09, 16, 23, 30, *Sep:* 06, 13, 20, 27, *Oct:* 04, 11, 18, 25, *Nov:* 01, 08, 15, 22, 29, *Dec:* 06, 13, 20, 27

1947 *Jan:* 03, 10, 17, 24, 31, *Feb:* 07, 14, 21, 28, *Mar:* 07, 14, 21, 28, *Apr:* 04, 11, 18, 25, *May:* 02, 09, 16, 23, 30, *Jun:* 06, 13, 20, 27, *Jul:* 04, 11, 18, 25, *Aug:* 01, 08, 15, 22, 29, *Sep:* 05, 12, 19, 26, *Oct:* 03, 10, 17, 24, 31, *Nov:* 07, 14, 21, 28, *Dec:* 05, 12, 19, 26

1948 *Jan:* 02, 09, 16, 23, 30, *Feb:* 06, 13, 20, 27, *Mar:* 05, 12, 19, 26, *Apr:* 02, 09, 16, 23, 30, *May:* 07, 14, 21, 28, *Jun:* 04, 11, 18, 25, *Jul:* 02, 09, 16, 23, 30, *Aug:* 06, 13, 20, 27, *Sep:* 03, 10, 17, 24, *Oct:* 01, 08, 15, 22, 29, *Nov:* 05, 12, 19, 26, *Dec:* 03, 10, 17, 24, 31

1949 *Jan:* 07, 14, 21, 28, *Feb:* 04, 11, 18, 25, *Mar:* 04, 11, 18, 25, *Apr:* 01, 08, 15, 22, 29, *May:* 06, 13, 20, 27, *Jun:* 03, 10, 17, 24, *Jul:* 01, 08, 15, 22, 29, *Aug:* 05, 12, 19, 26, *Sep:* 02, 09, 16, 23, 30, *Oct:* 07, 14, 21, 28, *Nov:* 04, 11, 18, 25, *Dec:* 02, 09, 16, 23, 30

1950 *Jan:* 06, 13, 20, 27, *Feb:* 03, 10, 17, 24, *Mar:* 03, 10, 17, 24, 31, *Apr:* 07, 14, 21, 28, *May:* 05, 12, 19, 26, *Jun:* 02, 09, 16, 23, 30, *Jul:* 07, 14, 21, 28, *Aug:* 04, 11, 18, 25, *Sep:* 01, 08, 15, 22, 29, *Oct:* 06, 13, 20, 27, *Nov:* 03, 10, 17, 24, *Dec:* 01, 08, 15, 22, 29

1951 *Jan:* 05, 12, 19, 26, *Feb:* 02, 09, 16, 23, *Mar:* 02, 09, 16, 23, 30, *Apr:* 06, 13, 20, 27, *May:* 04, 11, 18, 25, *Jun:* 01, 08, 15, 22, 29, *Jul:* 06, 13, 20, 27, *Aug:* 03, 10, 17, 24, 31, *Sep:* 07, 14, 21, 28, *Oct:* 05, 12, 19, 26, *Nov:* 02, 09, 16, 23, 30, *Dec:* 07, 14, 21, 28

1952 *Jan:* 04, 11, 18, 25, *Feb:* 01, 08, 15, 22, 29, *Mar:* 07, 14, 21, 28, *Apr:* 04, 11, 18, 25, *May:* 02, 09, 16, 23, 30, *Jun:* 06, 13, 20, 27, *Jul:* 04, 11, 18, 25, *Aug:* 01, 08, 15, 22, 29, *Sep:* 05, 12, 19, 26, *Oct:* 03, 10, 17, 24, 31, *Nov:* 07, 14, 21, 28, *Dec:* 05, 12, 19, 26

1953 *Jan:* 02, 09, 16, 23, 30, *Feb:* 06, 13, 20, 27, *Mar:* 06, 13, 20, 27, *Apr:* 03, 10, 17, 24, *May:* 01, 08, 15, 22, 29, *Jun:* 05, 12, 19, 26, *Jul:* 03, 10, 17, 24, 31, *Aug:* 07, 14, 21, 28, *Sep:* 04, 11, 18, 25, *Oct:* 02, 09, 16, 23, 30, *Nov:* 06, 13, 20, 27, *Dec:* 04, 11, 18, 25

1954 *Jan:* 01, 08, 15, 22, 29, *Feb:* 05, 12, 19, 26, *Mar:* 05, 12, 19, 26, *Apr:* 02, 09, 16, 23, 30, *May:* 07, 14, 21, 28, *Jun:* 04, 11, 18, 25, *Jul:* 02, 09, 16, 23, 30, *Aug:* 06, 13, 20, 27, *Sep:* 03, 10, 17, 24, *Oct:* 01, 08, 15, 22, 29, *Nov:* 05, 12, 19, 26, *Dec:* 03, 10, 17, 24, 31

1955 *Jan:* 07, 14, 21, 28, *Feb:* 04, 11, 18, 25, *Mar:* 04, 11, 18, 25, *Apr:* 01, 08, 15, 22, 29, *May:* 06, 13, 20, 27, *Jun:* 03, 10, 17, 24, *Jul:* 01, 08, 15, 22, 29, *Aug:* 05, 12, 19, 26, *Sep:* 02, 09, 16, 23, 30, *Oct:* 07, 14, 21, 28, *Nov:* 04, 11, 18, 25, *Dec:* 02, 09, 16, 23, 30

1956 *Jan:* 06, 13, 20, 27, *Feb:* 03, 10, 17, 24, *Mar:* 02, 09, 16, 23, 30, *Apr:* 06, 13, 20, 27, *May:* 04, 11, 18, 25, *Jun:* 01, 08, 15, 22, 29, *Jul:* 06, 13, 20, 27, *Aug:* 03, 10, 17, 24, 31, *Sep:* 07, 14, 21, 28, *Oct:* 05, 12, 19, 26, *Nov:* 02, 09, 16, 23, 30, *Dec:* 07, 14, 21, 28

1957 *Jan:* 04, 11, 18, 25, *Feb:* 01, 08, 15, 22, *Mar:* 01, 08, 15, 22, 29, *Apr:* 05, 12, 19, 26, *May:* 03, 10, 17, 24, 31, *Jun:* 07, 14, 21, 28, *Jul:* 05, 12, 19, 26, *Aug:* 02, 09, 16, 23, 30, *Sep:* 06, 13, 20, 27, *Oct:* 04, 11, 18, 25, *Nov:* 01, 08, 15, 22, 29, *Dec:* 06, 13, 20, 27

1958 *Jan:* 03, 10, 17, 24, 31, *Feb:* 07, 14, 21, 28, *Mar:* 07, 14, 21, 28, *Apr:* 04, 11, 18, 25, *May:* 02, 09, 16, 23, 30, *Jun:* 06, 13, 20, 27, *Jul:* 04, 11, 18, 25, *Aug:* 01, 08, 15, 22, 29, *Sep:* 05, 12, 19, 26, *Oct:* 03, 10, 17, 24, 31, *Nov:* 07, 14, 21, 28, *Dec:* 05, 12, 19, 26

1959 *Jan:* 02, 09, 16, 23, 30, *Feb:* 06, 13, 20, 27, *Mar:* 06, 13, 20, 27, *Apr:* 03, 10, 17, 24, *May:* 01, 08, 15, 22, 29, *Jun:* 05, 12, 19, 26, *Jul:* 03, 10, 17, 24, 31, *Aug:* 07, 14, 21, 28, *Sep:* 04, 11, 18, 25, *Oct:* 02, 09, 16, 23, 30, *Nov:* 06, 13, 20, 27, *Dec:* 04, 11, 18, 25

1960 *Jan:* 01, 08, 15, 22, 29, *Feb:* 05, 12, 19, 26, *Mar:* 04, 11, 18, 25, *Apr:* 01, 08, 15, 22, 29, *May:* 06, 13, 20, 27, *Jun:* 03, 10, 17, 24, *Jul:* 01, 08, 15, 22, 29, *Aug:* 05, 12, 19, 26, *Sep:* 02, 09, 16, 23, 30, *Oct:* 07, 14, 21, 28, *Nov:* 04, 11, 18, 25, *Dec:* 02, 09, 16, 23, 30

1961 *Jan:* 06, 13, 20, 27, *Feb:* 03, 10, 17, 24, *Mar:* 03, 10, 17, 24, 31, *Apr:* 07, 14, 21, 28, *May:* 05, 12, 19, 26, *Jun:* 02, 09, 16, 23, 30, *Jul:* 07, 14, 21, 28, *Aug:* 04, 11, 18, 25, *Sep:* 01, 08, 15, 22, 29, *Oct:* 06, 13, 20, 27, *Nov:* 03, 10, 17, 24, *Dec:* 01, 08, 15, 22, 29

1962 *Jan:* 05, 12, 19, 26, *Feb:* 02, 09, 16, 23, *Mar:* 02, 09, 16, 23, 30, *Apr:* 06, 13, 20, 27, *May:* 04, 11, 18, 25, *Jun:* 01, 08, 15, 22, 29, *Jul:* 06, 13, 20, 27, *Aug:* 03, 10, 17, 24, 31, *Sep:* 07, 14, 21, 28, *Oct:* 05, 12, 19, 26, *Nov:* 02, 09, 16, 23, 30, *Dec:* 07, 14, 21, 28

1963 *Jan:* 04, 11, 18, 25, *Feb:* 01, 08, 15, 22, *Mar:* 01, 08, 15, 22, 29, *Apr:* 05, 12, 19, 26, *May:* 03, 10, 17, 24, 31, *Jun:* 07, 14, 21, 28, *Jul:* 05, 12, 19, 26, *Aug:* 02, 09, 16, 23, 30, *Sep:* 06, 13, 20, 27, *Oct:* 04, 11, 18, 25, *Nov:* 01, 08, 15, 22, 29, *Dec:* 06, 13, 20, 27

1964 *Jan:* 03, 10, 17, 24, 31, *Feb:* 07, 14, 21, 28, *Mar:* 06, 13, 20, 27, *Apr:* 03, 10, 17, 24, *May:* 01, 08, 15, 22, 29, *Jun:* 05, 12, 19, 26, *Jul:* 03, 10, 17, 24, 31, *Aug:* 07, 14, 21, 28, *Sep:* 04, 11, 18, 25, *Oct:* 02, 09, 16, 23, 30, *Nov:* 06, 13, 20, 27, *Dec:* 04, 11, 18, 25

1965 *Jan:* 01, 08, 15, 22, 29, *Feb:* 05, 12, 19, 26, *Mar:* 05, 12, 19, 26, *Apr:* 02, 09, 16, 23, 30, *May:* 07, 14, 21, 28, *Jun:* 04, 11, 18, 25, *Jul:* 02, 09, 16, 23, 30, *Aug:* 06, 13, 20, 27, *Sep:* 03, 10, 17, 24, *Oct:* 01, 08, 15, 22, 29, *Nov:* 05, 12, 19, 26, *Dec:* 03, 10, 17, 24, 31

1966 *Jan:* 07, 14, 21, 28, *Feb:* 04, 11, 18, 25, *Mar:* 04, 11, 18, 25, *Apr:* 01, 08, 15, 22, 29, *May:* 06, 13, 20, 27, *Jun:* 03, 10, 17, 24, *Jul:* 01, 08, 15, 22, 29, *Aug:* 05, 12, 19, 26, *Sep:* 02, 09, 16, 23, 30, *Oct:* 07, 14, 21, 28, *Nov:* 04, 11, 18, 25, *Dec:* 02, 09, 16, 23, 30

1967 *Jan:* 06, 13, 20, 27, *Feb:* 03, 10, 17, 24, *Mar:* 03, 10, 17, 24, 31, *Apr:* 07, 14, 21, 28, *May:* 05, 12, 19, 26, *Jun:* 02, 09, 16, 23, 30, *Jul:* 07, 14, 21, 28, *Aug:* 04, 11, 18, 25, *Sep:* 01, 08, 15, 22, 29, *Oct:* 06, 13, 20, 27, *Nov:* 03, 10, 17, 24, *Dec:* 01, 08, 15, 22, 29

1968 *Jan:* 05, 12, 19, 26, *Feb:* 02, 09, 16, 23, *Mar:* 01, 08, 15, 22, 29, *Apr:* 05, 12, 19, 26, *May:* 03, 10, 17, 24, 31, *Jun:* 07, 14, 21, 28, *Jul:* 05, 12, 19, 26, *Aug:* 02, 09, 16, 23, 30, *Sep:* 06, 13, 20, 27, *Oct:* 04, 11, 18, 25, *Nov:* 01, 08, 15, 22, 29, *Dec:* 06, 13, 20, 27

1969 *Jan:* 03, 10, 17, 24, 31, *Feb:* 07, 14, 21, 28, *Mar:* 07, 14, 21, 28, *Apr:* 04, 11, 18, 25, *May:* 02, 09, 16, 23, 30, *Jun:* 06, 13, 20, 27, *Jul:* 04, 11, 18, 25, *Aug:* 01, 08, 15, 22, 29, *Sep:* 05, 12, 19, 26, *Oct:* 03, 10, 17, 24, 31, *Nov:* 07, 14, 21, 28, *Dec:* 05, 12, 19, 26

1970 *Jan:* 02, 09, 16, 23, 30, *Feb:* 06, 13, 20, 27, *Mar:* 06, 13, 20, 27, *Apr:* 03, 10, 17, 24, *May:* 01, 08, 15, 22, 29, *Jun:* 05, 12, 19, 26, *Jul:* 03, 10, 17, 24, 31, *Aug:* 07, 14, 21, 28, *Sep:* 04, 11, 18, 25, *Oct:* 02, 09, 16, 23, 30, *Nov:* 06, 13, 20, 27, *Dec:* 04, 11, 18, 25

1971 *Jan:* 01, 08, 15, 22, 29, *Feb:* 05, 12, 19, 26, *Mar:* 05, 12, 19, 26, *Apr:* 02, 09, 16, 23, 30, *May:* 07, 14, 21, 28, *Jun:* 04, 11, 18, 25, *Jul:* 02, 09, 16, 23, 30, *Aug:* 06, 13, 20, 27, *Sep:* 03, 10, 17, 24, *Oct:* 01, 08, 15, 22, 29, *Nov:* 05, 12, 19, 26, *Dec:* 03, 10, 17, 24, 31

1972 *Jan:* 07, 14, 21, 28, *Feb:* 04, 11, 18, 25, *Mar:* 03, 10, 17, 24, 31, *Apr:* 07, 14, 21, 28, *May:* 05, 12, 19, 26, *Jun:* 02, 09, 16, 23, 30, *Jul:* 07, 14, 21, 28, *Aug:* 04, 11, 18, 25, *Sep:* 01, 08, 15, 22, 29, *Oct:* 06, 13, 20, 27, *Nov:* 03, 10, 17, 24, *Dec:* 01, 08, 15, 22, 29

1973 *Jan:* 05, 12, 19, 26, *Feb:* 02, 09, 16, 23, *Mar:* 02, 09, 16, 23, 30, *Apr:* 06, 13, 20, 27, *May:* 04, 11, 18, 25, *Jun:* 01, 08, 15, 22, 29, *Jul:* 06, 13, 20, 27, *Aug:* 03, 10, 17, 24, 31, *Sep:* 07, 14, 21, 28, *Oct:* 05, 12, 19, 26, *Nov:* 02, 09, 16, 23, 30, *Dec:* 07, 14, 21, 28

1974 *Jan:* 04, 11, 18, 25, *Feb:* 01, 08, 15, 22, *Mar:* 01, 08, 15, 22, 29, *Apr:* 05, 12, 19, 26, *May:* 03, 10, 17, 24, 31, *Jun:* 07, 14, 21, 28, *Jul:* 05, 12, 19, 26, *Aug:* 02, 09, 16, 23, 30, *Sep:* 06, 13, 20, 27, *Oct:* 04, 11, 18, 25, *Nov:* 01, 08, 15, 22, 29, *Dec:* 06, 13, 20, 27

1975 *Jan:* 03, 10, 17, 24, 31, *Feb:* 07, 14, 21, 28, *Mar:* 07, 14, 21, 28, *Apr:* 04, 11, 18, 25, *May:* 02, 09, 16, 23, 30, *Jun:* 06, 13, 20, 27, *Jul:* 04, 11, 18, 25, *Aug:* 01, 08, 15, 22, 29, *Sep:* 05, 12, 19, 26, *Oct:* 03, 10, 17, 24, 31, *Nov:* 07, 14, 21, 28, *Dec:* 05, 12, 19, 26

1976 *Jan:* 02, 09, 16, 23, 30, *Feb:* 06, 13, 20, 27, *Mar:* 05, 12, 19, 26, *Apr:* 02, 09, 16, 23, 30, *May:* 07, 14, 21, 28, *Jun:* 04, 11, 18, 25, *Jul:* 02, 09, 16, 23, 30, *Aug:* 06, 13, 20, 27, *Sep:* 03, 10, 17, 24, *Oct:* 01, 08, 15, 22, 29, *Nov:* 05, 12, 19, 26, *Dec:* 03, 10, 17, 24, 31

1977 *Jan:* 07, 14, 21, 28, *Feb:* 04, 11, 18, 25, *Mar:* 04, 11, 18, 25, *Apr:* 01, 08, 15, 22, 29, *May:* 06, 13, 20, 27, *Jun:* 03, 10, 17, 24, *Jul:* 01, 08, 15, 22, 29, *Aug:* 05, 12, 19, 26, *Sep:* 02, 09, 16, 23, 30, *Oct:* 07, 14, 21, 28, *Nov:* 04, 11, 18, 25, *Dec:* 02, 09, 16, 23, 30

1978 *Jan:* 06, 13, 20, 27, *Feb:* 03, 10, 17, 24, *Mar:* 03, 10, 17, 24, 31, *Apr:* 07, 14, 21, 28, *May:* 05, 12, 19, 26, *Jun:* 02, 09, 16, 23, 30, *Jul:* 07, 14, 21, 28, *Aug:* 04, 11, 18, 25, *Sep:* 01, 08, 15, 22, 29, *Oct:* 06, 13, 20, 27, *Nov:* 03, 10, 17, 24, *Dec:* 01, 08, 15, 22, 29

1979 *Jan:* 05, 12, 19, 26, *Feb:* 02, 09, 16, 23, *Mar:* 02, 09, 16, 23, 30, *Apr:* 06, 13, 20, 27, *May:* 04, 11, 18, 25, *Jun:* 01, 08, 15, 22, 29, *Jul:* 06, 13, 20, 27, *Aug:* 03, 10, 17, 24, 31, *Sep:* 07, 14, 21, 28, *Oct:* 05, 12, 19, 26, *Nov:* 02, 09, 16, 23, 30, *Dec:* 07, 14, 21, 28

1980 *Jan:* 04, 11, 18, 25, *Feb:* 01, 08, 15, 22, 29, *Mar:* 07, 14, 21, 28, *Apr:* 04, 11, 18, 25, *May:* 02, 09, 16, 23, 30, *Jun:* 06, 13, 20, 27, *Jul:* 04, 11, 18, 25, *Aug:* 01, 08, 15, 22, 29, *Sep:* 05, 12, 19, 26, *Oct:* 03, 10, 17, 24, 31, *Nov:* 07, 14, 21, 28, *Dec:* 05, 12, 19, 26

1981 *Jan:* 02, 09, 16, 23, 30, *Feb:* 06, 13, 20, 27, *Mar:* 06, 13, 20, 27, *Apr:* 03, 10, 17, 24, *May:* 01, 08, 15, 22, 29, *Jun:* 05, 12, 19, 26, *Jul:* 03, 10, 17, 24, 31, *Aug:* 07, 14, 21, 28, *Sep:* 04, 11, 18, 25, *Oct:* 02, 09, 16, 23, 30, *Nov:* 06, 13, 20, 27, *Dec:* 04, 11, 18, 25

1982 *Jan:* 01, 08, 15, 22, 29, *Feb:* 05, 12, 19, 26, *Mar:* 05, 12, 19, 26, *Apr:* 02, 09, 16, 23, 30, *May:* 07, 14, 21, 28, *Jun:* 04, 11, 18, 25, *Jul:* 02, 09, 16, 23, 30, *Aug:* 06, 13, 20, 27, *Sep:* 03, 10, 17, 24, *Oct:* 01, 08, 15, 22, 29, *Nov:* 05, 12, 19, 26, *Dec:* 03, 10, 17, 24, 31

1983 *Jan:* 07, 14, 21, 28, *Feb:* 04, 11, 18, 25, *Mar:* 04, 11, 18, 25, *Apr:* 01, 08, 15, 22, 29, *May:* 06, 13, 20, 27, *Jun:* 03, 10, 17, 24, *Jul:* 01, 08, 15, 22, 29, *Aug:* 05, 12, 19, 26, *Sep:* 02, 09, 16, 23, 30, *Oct:* 07, 14, 21, 28, *Nov:* 04, 11, 18, 25, *Dec:* 02, 09, 16, 23, 30

1984 *Jan:* 06, 13, 20, 27, *Feb:* 03, 10, 17, 24, *Mar:* 02, 09, 16, 23, 30, *Apr:* 06, 13, 20, 27, *May:* 04, 11, 18, 25, *Jun:* 01, 08, 15, 22, 29, *Jul:* 06, 13, 20, 27, *Aug:* 03, 10, 17, 24, 31, *Sep:* 07, 14, 21, 28, *Oct:* 05, 12, 19, 26, *Nov:* 02, 09, 16, 23, 30, *Dec:* 07, 14, 21, 28

1985 *Jan:* 04, 11, 18, 25, *Feb:* 01, 08, 15, 22, *Mar:* 01, 08, 15, 22, 29, *Apr:* 05, 12, 19, 26, *May:* 03, 10, 17, 24, 31, *Jun:* 07, 14, 21, 28, *Jul:* 05, 12, 19, 26, *Aug:* 02, 09, 16, 23, 30, *Sep:* 06, 13, 20, 27, *Oct:* 04, 11, 18, 25, *Nov:* 01, 08, 15, 22, 29, *Dec:* 06, 13, 20, 27

1986 *Jan:* 03, 10, 17, 24, 31, *Feb:* 07, 14, 21, 28, *Mar:* 07, 14, 21, 28, *Apr:* 04, 11, 18, 25, *May:* 02, 09, 16, 23, 30, *Jun:* 06, 13, 20, 27, *Jul:* 04, 11, 18, 25, *Aug:* 01, 08, 15, 22, 29, *Sep:* 05, 12, 19, 26, *Oct:* 03, 10, 17, 24, 31, *Nov:* 07, 14, 21, 28, *Dec:* 05, 12, 19, 26

1987 *Jan:* 02, 09, 16, 23, 30, *Feb:* 06, 13, 20, 27, *Mar:* 06, 13, 20, 27, *Apr:* 03, 10, 17, 24, *May:* 01, 08, 15, 22, 29, *Jun:* 05, 12, 19, 26, *Jul:* 03, 10, 17, 24, 31, *Aug:* 07, 14, 21, 28, *Sep:* 04, 11, 18, 25, *Oct:* 02, 09, 16, 23, 30, *Nov:* 06, 13, 20, 27, *Dec:* 04, 11, 18, 25

1988 *Jan:* 01, 08, 15, 22, 29, *Feb:* 05, 12, 19, 26, *Mar:* 04, 11, 18, 25, *Apr:* 01, 08, 15, 22, 29, *May:* 06, 13, 20, 27, *Jun:* 03, 10, 17, 24, *Jul:* 01, 08, 15, 22, 29, *Aug:* 05, 12, 19, 26, *Sep:* 02, 09, 16, 23, 30, *Oct:* 07, 14, 21, 28, *Nov:* 04, 11, 18, 25, *Dec:* 02, 09, 16, 23, 30

1989 *Jan:* 06, 13, 20, 27, *Feb:* 03, 10, 17, 24, *Mar:* 03, 10, 17, 24, 31, *Apr:* 07, 14, 21, 28, *May:* 05, 12, 19, 26, *Jun:* 02, 09, 16, 23, 30, *Jul:* 07, 14, 21, 28, *Aug:* 04, 11, 18, 25, *Sep:* 01, 08, 15, 22, 29, *Oct:* 06, 13, 20, 27, *Nov:* 03, 10, 17, 24, *Dec:* 01, 08, 15, 22, 29

1990 *Jan:* 05, 12, 19, 26, *Feb:* 02, 09, 16, 23, *Mar:* 02, 09, 16, 23, 30, *Apr:* 06, 13, 20, 27, *May:* 04, 11, 18, 25, *Jun:* 01, 08, 15, 22, 29, *Jul:* 06, 13, 20, 27, *Aug:* 03, 10, 17, 24, 31, *Sep:* 07, 14, 21, 28, *Oct:* 05, 12, 19, 26, *Nov:* 02, 09, 16, 23, 30, *Dec:* 07, 14, 21, 28

1991 *Jan:* 04, 11, 18, 25, *Feb:* 01, 08, 15, 22, *Mar:* 01, 08, 15, 22, 29, *Apr:* 05, 12, 19, 26, *May:* 03, 10, 17, 24, 31, *Jun:* 07, 14, 21, 28, *Jul:* 05, 12, 19, 26, *Aug:* 02, 09, 16, 23, 30, *Sep:* 06, 13, 20, 27, *Oct:* 04, 11, 18, 25, *Nov:* 01, 08, 15, 22, 29, *Dec:* 06, 13, 20, 27

1992 *Jan:* 03, 10, 17, 24, 31, *Feb:* 07, 14, 21, 28, *Mar:* 06, 13, 20, 27, *Apr:* 03, 10, 17, 24, *May:* 01, 08, 15, 22, 29, *Jun:* 05, 12, 19, 26, *Jul:* 03, 10, 17, 24, 31, *Aug:* 07, 14, 21, 28, *Sep:* 04, 11, 18, 25, *Oct:* 02, 09, 16, 23, 30, *Nov:* 06, 13, 20, 27, *Dec:* 04, 11, 18, 25

1993 *Jan:* 01, 08, 15, 22, 29, *Feb:* 05, 12, 19, 26, *Mar:* 05, 12, 19, 26, *Apr:* 02, 09, 16, 23, 30, *May:* 07, 14, 21, 28, *Jun:* 04, 11, 18, 25, *Jul:* 02, 09, 16, 23, 30, *Aug:* 06, 13, 20, 27, *Sep:* 03, 10, 17, 24, *Oct:* 01, 08, 15, 22, 29, *Nov:* 05, 12, 19, 26, *Dec:* 03, 10, 17, 24, 31

1994 *Jan:* 07, 14, 21, 28, *Feb:* 04, 11, 18, 25, *Mar:* 04, 11, 18, 25, *Apr:* 01, 08, 15, 22, 29, *May:* 06, 13, 20, 27, *Jun:* 03, 10, 17, 24, *Jul:* 01, 08, 15, 22, 29, *Aug:* 05, 12, 19, 26, *Sep:* 02, 09, 16, 23, 30, *Oct:* 07, 14, 21, 28, *Nov:* 04, 11, 18, 25, *Dec:* 02, 09, 16, 23, 30

1995 *Jan:* 06, 13, 20, 27, *Feb:* 03, 10, 17, 24, *Mar:* 03, 10, 17, 24, 31, *Apr:* 07, 14, 21, 28, *May:* 05, 12, 19, 26, *Jun:* 02, 09, 16, 23, 30, *Jul:* 07, 14, 21, 28, *Aug:* 04, 11, 18, 25, *Sep:* 01, 08, 15, 22, 29, *Oct:* 06, 13, 20, 27, *Nov:* 03, 10, 17, 24, *Dec:* 01, 08, 15, 22, 29

1996 *Jan:* 05, 12, 19, 26, *Feb:* 02, 09, 16, 23, *Mar:* 01, 08, 15, 22, 29, *Apr:* 05, 12, 19, 26, *May:* 03, 10, 17, 24, 31, *Jun:* 07, 14, 21, 28, *Jul:* 05, 12, 19, 26, *Aug:* 02, 09, 16, 23, 30, *Sep:* 06, 13, 20, 27, *Oct:* 04, 11, 18, 25, *Nov:* 01, 08, 15, 22, 29, *Dec:* 06, 13, 20, 27

1997 *Jan:* 03, 10, 17, 24, 31, *Feb:* 07, 14, 21, 28, *Mar:* 07, 14, 21, 28, *Apr:* 04, 11, 18, 25, *May:* 02, 09, 16, 23, 30, *Jun:* 06, 13, 20, 27, *Jul:* 04, 11, 18, 25, *Aug:* 01, 08, 15, 22, 29, *Sep:* 05, 12, 19, 26, *Oct:* 03, 10, 17, 24, 31, *Nov:* 07, 14, 21, 28, *Dec:* 05, 12, 19, 26

1998 *Jan:* 02, 09, 16, 23, 30, *Feb:* 06, 13, 20, 27, *Mar:* 06, 13, 20, 27, *Apr:* 03, 10, 17, 24, *May:* 01, 08, 15, 22, 29, *Jun:* 05, 12, 19, 26, *Jul:* 03, 10, 17, 24, 31, *Aug:* 07, 14, 21, 28, *Sep:* 04, 11, 18, 25, *Oct:* 02, 09, 16, 23, 30, *Nov:* 06, 13, 20, 27, *Dec:* 04, 11, 18, 25

1999 *Jan:* 01, 08, 15, 22, 29, *Feb:* 05, 12, 19, 26, *Mar:* 05, 12, 19, 26, *Apr:* 02, 09, 16, 23, 30, *May:* 07, 14, 21, 28, *Jun:* 04, 11, 18, 25, *Jul:* 02, 09, 16, 23, 30, *Aug:* 06, 13, 20, 27, *Sep:* 03, 10, 17, 24, *Oct:* 01, 08, 15, 22, 29, *Nov:* 05, 12, 19, 26, *Dec:* 03, 10, 17, 24, 31

2000 *Jan:* 07, 14, 21, 28, *Feb:* 04, 11, 18, 25, *Mar:* 03, 10, 17, 24, 31, *Apr:* 07, 14, 21, 28, *May:* 05, 12, 19, 26, *Jun:* 02, 09, 16, 23, 30, *Jul:* 07, 14, 21, 28, *Aug:* 04, 11, 18, 25, *Sep:* 01, 08, 15, 22, 29, *Oct:* 06, 13, 20, 27, *Nov:* 03, 10, 17, 24, *Dec:* 01, 08, 15, 22, 29

2001 *Jan:* 05, 12, 19, 26, *Feb:* 02, 09, 16, 23, *Mar:* 02, 09, 16, 23, 30, *Apr:* 06, 13, 20, 27, *May:* 04, 11, 18, 25, *Jun:* 01, 08, 15, 22, 29, *Jul:* 06, 13, 20, 27, *Aug:* 03, 10, 17, 24, 31, *Sep:* 07, 14, 21, 28, *Oct:* 05, 12, 19, 26, *Nov:* 02, 09, 16, 23, 30, *Dec:* 07, 14, 21, 28

2002 *Jan:* 04, 11, 18, 25, *Feb:* 01, 08, 15, 22, *Mar:* 01, 08, 15, 22, 29, *Apr:* 05, 12, 19, 26, *May:* 03, 10, 17, 24, 31, *Jun:* 07, 14, 21, 28, *Jul:* 05, 12, 19, 26, *Aug:* 02, 09, 16, 23, 30, *Sep:* 06, 13, 20, 27, *Oct:* 04, 11, 18, 25, *Nov:* 01, 08, 15, 22, 29, *Dec:* 06, 13, 20, 27

2003 *Jan:* 03, 10, 17, 24, 31, *Feb:* 07, 14, 21, 28, *Mar:* 07, 14, 21, 28, *Apr:* 04, 11, 18, 25, *May:* 02, 09, 16, 23, 30, *Jun:* 06, 13, 20, 27, *Jul:* 04, 11, 18, 25, *Aug:* 01, 08, 15, 22, 29, *Sep:* 05, 12, 19, 26, *Oct:* 03, 10, 17, 24, 31, *Nov:* 07, 14, 21, 28, *Dec:* 05, 12, 19, 26

2004 *Jan:* 02, 09, 16, 23, 30, *Feb:* 06, 13, 20, 27, *Mar:* 05, 12, 19, 26, *Apr:* 02, 09, 16, 23, 30, *May:* 07, 14, 21, 28, *Jun:* 04, 11, 18, 25, *Jul:* 02, 09, 16, 23, 30, *Aug:* 06, 13, 20, 27, *Sep:* 03, 10, 17, 24, *Oct:* 01, 08, 15, 22, 29, *Nov:* 05, 12, 19, 26, *Dec:* 03, 10, 17, 24, 31

2005 *Jan:* 07, 14, 21, 28, *Feb:* 04, 11, 18, 25, *Mar:* 04, 11, 18, 25, *Apr:* 01, 08, 15, 22, 29, *May:* 06, 13, 20, 27, *Jun:* 03, 10, 17, 24, *Jul:* 01, 08, 15, 22, 29, *Aug:* 05, 12, 19, 26, *Sep:* 02, 09, 16, 23, 30, *Oct:* 07, 14, 21, 28, *Nov:* 04, 11, 18, 25, *Dec:* 02, 09, 16, 23, 30

2006 *Jan:* 06, 13, 20, 27, *Feb:* 03, 10, 17, 24, *Mar:* 03, 10, 17, 24, 31, *Apr:* 07, 14, 21, 28, *May:* 05, 12, 19, 26, *Jun:* 02, 09, 16, 23, 30, *Jul:* 07, 14, 21, 28, *Aug:* 04, 11, 18, 25, *Sep:* 01, 08, 15, 22, 29, *Oct:* 06, 13, 20, 27, *Nov:* 03, 10, 17, 24, *Dec:* 01, 08, 15, 22, 29

2007 *Jan:* 05, 12, 19, 26, *Feb:* 02, 09, 16, 23, *Mar:* 02, 09, 16, 23, 30, *Apr:* 06, 13, 20, 27, *May:* 04, 11, 18, 25, *Jun:* 01, 08, 15, 22, 29, *Jul:* 06, 13, 20, 27, *Aug:* 03, 10, 17, 24, 31, *Sep:* 07, 14, 21, 28, *Oct:* 05, 12, 19, 26, *Nov:* 02, 09, 16, 23, 30, *Dec:* 07, 14, 21, 28

2008 *Jan:* 04, 11, 18, 25, *Feb:* 01, 08, 15, 22, 29, *Mar:* 07, 14, 21, 28, *Apr:* 04, 11, 18, 25, *May:* 02, 09, 16, 23, 30, *Jun:* 06, 13, 20, 27, *Jul:* 04, 11, 18, 25, *Aug:* 01, 08, 15, 22, 29, *Sep:* 05, 12, 19, 26, *Oct:* 03, 10, 17, 24, 31, *Nov:* 07, 14, 21, 28, *Dec:* 05, 12, 19, 26

2009 *Jan:* 02, 09, 16, 23, 30, *Feb:* 06, 13, 20, 27, *Mar:* 06, 13, 20, 27, *Apr:* 03, 10, 17, 24, *May:* 01, 08, 15, 22, 29, *Jun:* 05, 12, 19, 26, *Jul:* 03, 10, 17, 24, 31, *Aug:* 07, 14, 21, 28, *Sep:* 04, 11, 18, 25, *Oct:* 02, 09, 16, 23, 30, *Nov:* 06, 13, 20, 27, *Dec:* 04, 11, 18, 25

2010 *Jan:* 01, 08, 15, 22, 29, *Feb:* 05, 12, 19, 26, *Mar:* 05, 12, 19, 26, *Apr:* 02, 09, 16, 23, 30, *May:* 07, 14, 21, 28, *Jun:* 04, 11, 18, 25, *Jul:* 02, 09, 16, 23, 30, *Aug:* 06, 13, 20, 27, *Sep:* 03, 10, 17, 24, *Oct:* 01, 08, 15, 22, 29, *Nov:* 05, 12, 19, 26, *Dec:* 03, 10, 17, 24, 31

2011 *Jan:* 07, 14, 21, 28, *Feb:* 04, 11, 18, 25, *Mar:* 04, 11, 18, 25, *Apr:* 01, 08, 15, 22, 29, *May:* 06, 13, 20, 27, *Jun:* 03, 10, 17, 24, *Jul:* 01, 08, 15, 22, 29, *Aug:* 05, 12, 19, 26, *Sep:* 02, 09, 16, 23, 30, *Oct:* 07, 14, 21, 28, *Nov:* 04, 11, 18, 25, *Dec:* 02, 09, 16, 23, 30

2012 *Jan:* 06, 13, 20, 27, *Feb:* 03, 10, 17, 24, *Mar:* 02, 09, 16, 23, 30, *Apr:* 06, 13, 20, 27, *May:* 04, 11, 18, 25, *Jun:* 01, 08, 15, 22, 29, *Jul:* 06, 13, 20, 27, *Aug:* 03, 10, 17, 24, 31, *Sep:* 07, 14, 21, 28, *Oct:* 05, 12, 19, 26, *Nov:* 02, 09, 16, 23, 30, *Dec:* 07, 14, 21, 28

2013 *Jan:* 04, 11, 18, 25, *Feb:* 01, 08, 15, 22, *Mar:* 01, 08, 15, 22, 29, *Apr:* 05, 12, 19, 26, *May:* 03, 10, 17, 24, 31, *Jun:* 07, 14, 21, 28, *Jul:* 05, 12, 19, 26, *Aug:* 02, 09, 16, 23, 30, *Sep:* 06, 13, 20, 27, *Oct:* 04, 11, 18, 25, *Nov:* 01, 08, 15, 22, 29, *Dec:* 06, 13, 20, 27

Saturday: Cassiel

IF YOUR DAY OF BIRTH IS SATURDAY: Cassiel rules. Cassiel's healing rays are white and black (or brown), showing the contrast and balance needed between the two. His metal is lead (or pewter), his crystals are black-and-white agate, Apache's Tears, and gold sheen obsidian. Attributes for Cassiel: harmony, peace and serenity.

Cassiel, whose name means 'Knowledge of God', is the angel of solitude and tears, ruler of the order of Cherabim, Saturday and the planet Saturn. He's gatekeeper of 7th Heaven (the abode of the Creator). Cassiel used to be called the 'angel of temperance', meaning seeking to live as harmonious a life as possible. Is your life tranquil, balanced and unified, or are you overcome by stress or distracted by something negative that you need to overcome? Perhaps you are coming to terms with sorrow. The point is whether you make enough time for yourself to calmly consider where you go from here to find inner peace and serenity.

If you are dealing with bereavement, sorrow or rejection, you may feel alone and surrounded by darkness. But with Cassiel you will never be alone; he invites you to let go of this feeling (without diminishing its importance). He reminds you that the (Divine) spark of Light is always within us, even though we may have forgotten about it, and if we will and intend it we can ignite this once again as part of our Soul Quest to rejoin All in Unity Consciousness.

Man mirrors nature's sacred geometric perfection of form, which is in turn a galactic fragment of the universe itself. Therefore we are a Microcosm of All – the Macrocosm. By understanding this, respecting Mother Earth and by working with Cassiel, we regain equilibrium and re-harmonise with All. The first meditation on the CD (*The Cosmic Web*) aids you with this important spiritual step.

Remember that we can all call on Cassiel any day (especially Saturday) and work with his crystals. If he is the angel of the day you were born (and he is my angel!), he is one of your guardian angels:

Cassiel, Cassiel, Cassiel, please help me regain harmony (or peace or serenity), *in Love and Light, Love and Light, Love and Light.*

Place a Cassiel crystal (or, say, Gabriel's selenite and Cassiel's obsidian) near you as a constant reminder that all dark things pass, life will return to Light, and hope will be re-awakened.

Saturday birthdays

1940 *Jan:* 06, 13, 20, 27, *Feb:* 03, 10, 17, 24, *Mar:* 02, 09, 16, 23, 30, *Apr:* 06, 13, 20, 27, *May:* 04, 11, 18, 25, *Jun:* 01, 08, 15, 22, 29, *Jul:* 06, 13, 20, 27, *Aug:* 03, 10, 17, 24, 31, *Sep:* 07, 14, 21, 28, *Oct:* 05, 12, 19, 26, *Nov:* 02, 09, 16, 23, 30, *Dec:* 07, 14, 21, 28

1941 *Jan:* 04, 11, 18, 25, *Feb:* 01, 08, 15, 22, *Mar:* 01, 08, 15, 22, 29, *Apr:* 05, 12, 19, 26, *May:* 03, 10, 17, 24, 31, *Jun:* 07, 14, 21, 28, *Jul:* 05, 12, 19, 26, *Aug:* 02, 09, 16, 23, 30, *Sep:* 06, 13, 20, 27, *Oct:* 04, 11, 18, 25, *Nov:* 01, 08, 15, 22, 29, *Dec:* 06, 13, 20, 27

1942 *Jan:* 03, 10, 17, 24, 31, *Feb:* 07, 14, 21, 28, *Mar:* 07, 14, 21, 28, *Apr:* 04, 11, 18, 25, *May:* 02, 09, 16, 23, 30, *Jun:* 06, 13, 20, 27, *Jul:* 04, 11, 18, 25, *Aug:* 01, 08, 15, 22, 29, *Sep:* 05, 12, 19, 26, *Oct:* 03, 10, 17, 24, 31, *Nov:* 07, 14, 21, 28, *Dec:* 05, 12, 19, 26

1943 *Jan:* 02, 09, 16, 23, 30, *Feb:* 06, 13, 20, 27, *Mar:* 06, 13, 20, 27, *Apr:* 03, 10, 17, 24, *May:* 01, 08, 15, 22, 29, *Jun:* 05, 12, 19, 26, *Jul:* 03, 10, 17, 24, 31, *Aug:* 07, 14, 21, 28, *Sep:* 04, 11, 18, 25, *Oct:* 02, 09, 16, 23, 30, *Nov:* 06, 13, 20, 27, *Dec:* 04, 11, 18, 25

1944 *Jan:* 01, 08, 15, 22, 29, *Feb:* 05, 12, 19, 26, *Mar:* 04, 11, 18, 25, *Apr:* 01, 08, 15, 22, 29, *May:* 06, 13, 20, 27, *Jun:* 03, 10, 17, 24, *Jul:* 01, 08, 15, 22, 29, *Aug:* 05, 12, 19, 26, *Sep:* 02, 09, 16, 23, 30, *Oct:* 07, 14, 21, 28, *Nov:* 04, 11, 18, 25, *Dec:* 02, 09, 16, 23, 30

1945 *Jan:* 06, 13, 20, 27, *Feb:* 03, 10, 17, 24, *Mar:* 03, 10, 17, 24, 31, *Apr:* 07, 14, 21, 28, *May:* 05, 12, 19, 26, *Jun:* 02, 09, 16, 23, 30, *Jul:* 07, 14, 21, 28, *Aug:* 04, 11, 18, 25, *Sep:* 01, 08, 15, 22, 29, *Oct:* 06, 13, 20, 27, *Nov:* 03, 10, 17, 24, *Dec:* 01, 08, 15, 22, 29

1946 *Jan:* 05, 12, 19, 26, *Feb:* 02, 09, 16, 23, *Mar:* 02, 09, 16, 23, 30, *Apr:* 06, 13, 20, 27, *May:* 04, 11, 18, 25, *Jun:* 01, 08, 15, 22, 29, *Jul:* 06, 13, 20, 27, *Aug:* 03, 10, 17, 24, 31, *Sep:* 07, 14, 21, 28, *Oct:* 05, 12, 19, 26, *Nov:* 02, 09, 16, 23, 30, *Dec:* 07, 14, 21, 28

1947 *Jan:* 04, 11, 18, 25, *Feb:* 01, 08, 15, 22, *Mar:* 01, 08, 15, 22, 29, *Apr:* 05, 12, 19, 26, *May:* 03, 10, 17, 24, 31, *Jun:* 07, 14, 21, 28, *Jul:* 05, 12, 19, 26, *Aug:* 02, 09, 16, 23, 30, *Sep:* 06, 13, 20, 27, *Oct:* 04, 11, 18, 25, *Nov:* 01, 08, 15, 22, 29, *Dec:* 06, 13, 20, 27

1948 *Jan:* 03, 10, 17, 24, 31, *Feb:* 07, 14, 21, 28, *Mar:* 06, 13, 20, 27, *Apr:* 03, 10, 17, 24, *May:* 01, 08, 15, 22, 29, *Jun:* 05, 12, 19, 26, *Jul:* 03, 10, 17, 24, 31, *Aug:* 07, 14, 21, 28, *Sep:* 04, 11, 18, 25, *Oct:* 02, 09, 16, 23, 30, *Nov:* 06, 13, 20, 27, *Dec:* 04, 11, 18, 25

1949 *Jan:* 01, 08, 15, 22, 29, *Feb:* 05, 12, 19, 26, *Mar:* 05, 12, 19, 26, *Apr:* 02, 09, 16, 23, 30, *May:* 07, 14, 21, 28, *Jun:* 04, 11, 18, 25, *Jul:* 02, 09, 16, 23, 30, *Aug:* 06, 13, 20, 27, *Sep:* 03, 10, 17, 24, *Oct:* 01, 08, 15, 22, 29, *Nov:* 05, 12, 19, 26, *Dec:* 03, 10, 17, 24, 31

1950 *Jan:* 07, 14, 21, 28, *Feb:* 04, 11, 18, 25, *Mar:* 04, 11, 18, 25, *Apr:* 01, 08, 15, 22, 29, *May:* 06, 13, 20, 27, *Jun:* 03, 10, 17, 24, *Jul:* 01, 08, 15, 22, 29, *Aug:* 05, 12, 19, 26, *Sep:* 02, 09, 16, 23, 30, *Oct:* 07, 14, 21, 28, *Nov:* 04, 11, 18, 25, *Dec:* 02, 09, 16, 23, 30

1951 *Jan:* 06, 13, 20, 27, *Feb:* 03, 10, 17, 24, *Mar:* 03, 10, 17, 24, 31, *Apr:* 07, 14, 21, 28, *May:* 05, 12, 19, 26, *Jun:* 02, 09, 16, 23, 30, *Jul:* 07, 14, 21, 28, *Aug:* 04, 11, 18, 25, *Sep:* 01, 08, 15, 22, 29, *Oct:* 06, 13, 20, 27, *Nov:* 03, 10, 17, 24, *Dec:* 01, 08, 15, 22, 29

1952 *Jan:* 05, 12, 19, 26, *Feb:* 02, 09, 16, 23, *Mar:* 01, 08, 15, 22, 29, *Apr:* 05, 12, 19, 26, *May:* 03, 10, 17, 24, 31, *Jun:* 07, 14, 21, 28, *Jul:* 05, 12, 19, 26, *Aug:* 02, 09, 16, 23, 30, *Sep:* 06, 13, 20, 27, *Oct:* 04, 11, 18, 25, *Nov:* 01, 08, 15, 22, 29, *Dec:* 06, 13, 20, 27

1953 *Jan:* 03, 10, 17, 24, 31, *Feb:* 07, 14, 21, 28, *Mar:* 07, 14, 21, 28, *Apr:* 04, 11, 18, 25, *May:* 02, 09, 16, 23, 30, *Jun:* 06, 13, 20, 27, *Jul:* 04, 11, 18, 25, *Aug:* 01, 08, 15, 22, 29, *Sep:* 05, 12, 19, 26, *Oct:* 03, 10, 17, 24, 31, *Nov:* 07, 14, 21, 28, *Dec:* 05, 12, 19, 26

1954 *Jan:* 02, 09, 16, 23, 30, *Feb:* 06, 13, 20, 27, *Mar:* 06, 13, 20, 27, *Apr:* 03, 10, 17, 24, *May:* 01, 08, 15, 22, 29, *Jun:* 05, 12, 19, 26, *Jul:* 03, 10, 17, 24, 31, *Aug:* 07, 14, 21, 28, *Sep:* 04, 11, 18, 25, *Oct:* 02, 09, 16, 23, 30, *Nov:* 06, 13, 20, 27, *Dec:* 04, 11, 18, 25

1955 *Jan:* 01, 08, 15, 22, 29, *Feb:* 05, 12, 19, 26, *Mar:* 05, 12, 19, 26, *Apr:* 02, 09, 16, 23, 30, *May:* 07, 14, 21, 28, *Jun:* 04, 11, 18, 25, *Jul:* 02, 09, 16, 23, 30, *Aug:* 06, 13, 20, 27, *Sep:* 03, 10, 17, 24, *Oct:* 01, 08, 15, 22, 29, *Nov:* 05, 12, 19, 26, *Dec:* 03, 10, 17, 24, 31

1956 *Jan:* 07, 14, 21, 28, *Feb:* 04, 11, 18, 25, *Mar:* 03, 10, 17, 24, 31, *Apr:* 07, 14, 21, 28, *May:* 05, 12, 19, 26, *Jun:* 02, 09, 16, 23, 30, *Jul:* 07, 14, 21, 28, *Aug:* 04, 11, 18, 25, *Sep:* 01, 08, 15, 22, 29, *Oct:* 06, 13, 20, 27, *Nov:* 03, 10, 17, 24, *Dec:* 01, 08, 15, 22, 29

1957 *Jan:* 05, 12, 19, 26, *Feb:* 02, 09, 16, 23, *Mar:* 02, 09, 16, 23, 30, *Apr:* 06, 13, 20, 27, *May:* 04, 11, 18, 25, *Jun:* 01, 08, 15, 22, 29, *Jul:* 06, 13, 20, 27, *Aug:* 03, 10, 17, 24, 31, *Sep:* 07, 14, 21, 28, *Oct:* 05, 12, 19, 26, *Nov:* 02, 09, 16, 23, 30, *Dec:* 07, 14, 21, 28

1958 *Jan:* 04, 11, 18, 25, *Feb:* 01, 08, 15, 22, *Mar:* 01, 08, 15, 22, 29, *Apr:* 05, 12, 19, 26, *May:* 03, 10, 17, 24, 31, *Jun:* 07, 14, 21, 28, *Jul:* 05, 12, 19, 26, *Aug:* 02, 09, 16, 23, 30, *Sep:* 06, 13, 20, 27, *Oct:* 04, 11, 18, 25, *Nov:* 01, 08, 15, 22, 29, *Dec:* 06, 13, 20, 27

1959 *Jan:* 03, 10, 17, 24, 31, *Feb:* 07, 14, 21, 28, *Mar:* 07, 14, 21, 28, *Apr:* 04, 11, 18, 25, *May:* 02, 09, 16, 23, 30, *Jun:* 06, 13, 20, 27, *Jul:* 04, 11, 18, 25, *Aug:* 01, 08, 15, 22, 29, *Sep:* 05, 12, 19, 26, *Oct:* 03, 10, 17, 24, 31, *Nov:* 07, 14, 21, 28, *Dec:* 05, 12, 19, 26

1960 *Jan:* 02, 09, 16, 23, 30, *Feb:* 06, 13, 20, 27, *Mar:* 05, 12, 19, 26, *Apr:* 02, 09, 16, 23, 30, *May:* 07, 14, 21, 28, *Jun:* 04, 11, 18, 25, *Jul:* 02, 09, 16, 23, 30, *Aug:* 06, 13, 20, 27, *Sep:* 03, 10, 17, 24, *Oct:* 01, 08, 15, 22, 29, *Nov:* 05, 12, 19, 26, *Dec:* 03, 10, 17, 24, 31

1961 *Jan:* 07, 14, 21, 28, *Feb:* 04, 11, 18, 25, *Mar:* 04, 11, 18, 25, *Apr:* 01, 08, 15, 22, 29, *May:* 06, 13, 20, 27, *Jun:* 03, 10, 17, 24, *Jul:* 01, 08, 15, 22, 29, *Aug:* 05, 12, 19, 26, *Sep:* 02, 09, 16, 23, 30, *Oct:* 07, 14, 21, 28, *Nov:* 04, 11, 18, 25, *Dec:* 02, 09, 16, 23, 30

1962 *Jan:* 06, 13, 20, 27, *Feb:* 03, 10, 17, 24, *Mar:* 03, 10, 17, 24, 31, *Apr:* 07, 14, 21, 28, *May:* 05, 12, 19, 26, *Jun:* 02, 09, 16, 23, 30, *Jul:* 07, 14, 21, 28, *Aug:* 04, 11, 18, 25, *Sep:* 01, 08, 15, 22, 29, *Oct:* 06, 13, 20, 27, *Nov:* 03, 10, 17, 24, *Dec:* 01, 08, 15, 22, 29

1963 *Jan:* 05, 12, 19, 26, *Feb:* 02, 09, 16, 23, *Mar:* 02, 09, 16, 23, 30, *Apr:* 06, 13, 20, 27, *May:* 04, 11, 18, 25, *Jun:* 01, 08, 15, 22, 29, *Jul:* 06, 13, 20, 27, *Aug:* 03, 10, 17, 24, 31, *Sep:* 07, 14, 21, 28, *Oct:* 05, 12, 19, 26, *Nov:* 02, 09, 16, 23, 30, *Dec:* 07, 14, 21, 28

1964 *Jan:* 04, 11, 18, 25, *Feb:* 01, 08, 15, 22, 29, *Mar:* 07, 14, 21, 28, *Apr:* 04, 11, 18, 25, *May:* 02, 09, 16, 23, 30, *Jun:* 06, 13, 20, 27, *Jul:* 04, 11, 18, 25, *Aug:* 01, 08, 15, 22, 29, *Sep:* 05, 12, 19, 26, *Oct:* 03, 10, 17, 24, 31, *Nov:* 07, 14, 21, 28, *Dec:* 05, 12, 19, 26

1965 *Jan:* 02, 09, 16, 23, 30, *Feb:* 06, 13, 20, 27, *Mar:* 06, 13, 20, 27, *Apr:* 03, 10, 17, 24, *May:* 01, 08, 15, 22, 29, *Jun:* 05, 12, 19, 26, *Jul:* 03, 10, 17, 24, 31, *Aug:* 07, 14, 21, 28, *Sep:* 04, 11, 18, 25, *Oct:* 02, 09, 16, 23, 30, *Nov:* 06, 13, 20, 27, *Dec:* 04, 11, 18, 25

1966 *Jan:* 01, 08, 15, 22, 29, *Feb:* 05, 12, 19, 26, *Mar:* 05, 12, 19, 26, *Apr:* 02, 09, 16, 23, 30, *May:* 07, 14, 21, 28, *Jun:* 04, 11, 18, 25, *Jul:* 02, 09, 16, 23, 30, *Aug:* 06, 13, 20, 27, *Sep:* 03, 10, 17, 24, *Oct:* 01, 08, 15, 22, 29, *Nov:* 05, 12, 19, 26, *Dec:* 03, 10, 17, 24, 31

1967 *Jan:* 07, 14, 21, 28, *Feb:* 04, 11, 18, 25, *Mar:* 04, 11, 18, 25, *Apr:* 01, 08, 15, 22, 29, *May:* 06, 13, 20, 27, *Jun:* 03, 10, 17, 24, *Jul:* 01, 08, 15, 22, 29, *Aug:* 05, 12, 19, 26, *Sep:* 02, 09, 16, 23, 30, *Oct:* 07, 14, 21, 28, *Nov:* 04, 11, 18, 25, *Dec:* 02, 09, 16, 23, 30

1968 *Jan:* 06, 13, 20, 27, *Feb:* 03, 10, 17, 24, *Mar:* 02, 09, 16, 23, 30, *Apr:* 06, 13, 20, 27, *May:* 04, 11, 18, 25, *Jun:* 01, 08, 15, 22, 29, *Jul:* 06, 13, 20, 27, *Aug:* 03, 10, 17, 24, 31, *Sep:* 07, 14, 21, 28, *Oct:* 05, 12, 19, 26, *Nov:* 02, 09, 16, 23, 30, *Dec:* 07, 14, 21, 28

1969 *Jan:* 04, 11, 18, 25, *Feb:* 01, 08, 15, 22, *Mar:* 01, 08, 15, 22, 29, *Apr:* 05, 12, 19, 26, *May:* 03, 10, 17, 24, 31, *Jun:* 07, 14, 21, 28, *Jul:* 05, 12, 19, 26, *Aug:* 02, 09, 16, 23, 30, *Sep:* 06, 13, 20, 27, *Oct:* 04, 11, 18, 25, *Nov:* 01, 08, 15, 22, 29, *Dec:* 06, 13, 20, 27

1970 *Jan:* 03, 10, 17, 24, 31, *Feb:* 07, 14, 21, 28, *Mar:* 07, 14, 21, 28, *Apr:* 04, 11, 18, 25, *May:* 02, 09, 16, 23, 30, *Jun:* 06, 13, 20, 27, *Jul:* 04, 11, 18, 25, *Aug:* 01, 08, 15, 22, 29, *Sep:* 05, 12, 19, 26, *Oct:* 03, 10, 17, 24, 31, *Nov:* 07, 14, 21, 28, *Dec:* 05, 12, 19, 26

1971 *Jan:* 02, 09, 16, 23, 30, *Feb:* 06, 13, 20, 27, *Mar:* 06, 13, 20, 27, *Apr:* 03, 10, 17, 24, *May:* 01, 08, 15, 22, 29, *Jun:* 05, 12, 19, 26, *Jul:* 03, 10, 17, 24, 31, *Aug:* 07, 14, 21, 28, *Sep:* 04, 11, 18, 25, *Oct:* 02, 09, 16, 23, 30, *Nov:* 06, 13, 20, 27, *Dec:* 04, 11, 18, 25

1972 *Jan:* 01, 08, 15, 22, 29, *Feb:* 05, 12, 19, 26, *Mar:* 04, 11, 18, 25, *Apr:* 01, 08, 15, 22, 29, *May:* 06, 13, 20, 27, *Jun:* 03, 10, 17, 24, *Jul:* 01, 08, 15, 22, 29, *Aug:* 05, 12, 19, 26, *Sep:* 02, 09, 16, 23, 30, *Oct:* 07, 14, 21, 28, *Nov:* 04, 11, 18, 25, *Dec:* 02, 09, 16, 23, 30

1973 *Jan:* 06, 13, 20, 27, *Feb:* 03, 10, 17, 24, *Mar:* 03, 10, 17, 24, 31, *Apr:* 07, 14, 21, 28, *May:* 05, 12, 19, 26, *Jun:* 02, 09, 16, 23, 30, *Jul:* 07, 14, 21, 28, *Aug:* 04, 11, 18, 25, *Sep:* 01, 08, 15, 22, 29, *Oct:* 06, 13, 20, 27, *Nov:* 03, 10, 17, 24, *Dec:* 01, 08, 15, 22, 29

1974 *Jan:* 05, 12, 19, 26, *Feb:* 02, 09, 16, 23, *Mar:* 02, 09, 16, 23, 30, *Apr:* 06, 13, 20, 27, *May:* 04, 11, 18, 25, *Jun:* 01, 08, 15, 22, 29, *Jul:* 06, 13, 20, 27, *Aug:* 03, 10, 17, 24, 31, *Sep:* 07, 14, 21, 28, *Oct:* 05, 12, 19, 26, *Nov:* 02, 09, 16, 23, 30, *Dec:* 07, 14, 21, 28

1975 *Jan:* 04, 11, 18, 25, *Feb:* 01, 08, 15, 22, *Mar:* 01, 08, 15, 22, 29, *Apr:* 05, 12, 19, 26, *May:* 03, 10, 17, 24, 31, *Jun:* 07, 14, 21, 28, *Jul:* 05, 12, 19, 26, *Aug:* 02, 09, 16, 23, 30, *Sep:* 06, 13, 20, 27, *Oct:* 04, 11, 18, 25, *Nov:* 01, 08, 15, 22, 29, *Dec:* 06, 13, 20, 27

1976 *Jan:* 03, 10, 17, 24, 31, *Feb:* 07, 14, 21, 28, *Mar:* 06, 13, 20, 27, *Apr:* 03, 10, 17, 24, *May:* 01, 08, 15, 22, 29, *Jun:* 05, 12, 19, 26, *Jul:* 03, 10, 17, 24, 31, *Aug:* 07, 14, 21, 28, *Sep:* 04, 11, 18, 25, *Oct:* 02, 09, 16, 23, 30, *Nov:* 06, 13, 20, 27, *Dec:* 04, 11, 18, 25

1977 *Jan:* 01, 08, 15, 22, 29, *Feb:* 05, 12, 19, 26, *Mar:* 05, 12, 19, 26, *Apr:* 02, 09, 16, 23, 30, *May:* 07, 14, 21, 28, *Jun:* 04, 11, 18, 25, *Jul:* 02, 09, 16, 23, 30, *Aug:* 06, 13, 20, 27, *Sep:* 03, 10, 17, 24, *Oct:* 01, 08, 15, 22, 29, *Nov:* 05, 12, 19, 26, *Dec:* 03, 10, 17, 24, 31

1978 Jan: 07, 14, 21, 28, Feb: 04, 11, 18, 25, Mar: 04, 11, 18, 25, Apr: 01, 08, 15, 22, 29, May: 06, 13,
20, 27, Jun: 03, 10, 17, 24, Jul: 01, 08, 15, 22, 29, Aug: 05, 12, 19, 26, Sep: 02, 09, 16, 23, 30, Oct: 07,
14, 21, 28, Nov: 04, 11, 18, 25, Dec: 02, 09, 16, 23, 30

1979 Jan: 06, 13, 20, 27, Feb: 03, 10, 17, 24, Mar: 03, 10, 17, 24, 31, Apr: 07, 14, 21, 28, May: 05, 12,
19, 26, Jun: 02, 09, 16, 23, 30, Jul: 07, 14, 21, 28, Aug: 04, 11, 18, 25, Sep: 01, 08, 15, 22, 29, Oct: 06,
13, 20, 27, Nov: 03, 10, 17, 24, Dec: 01, 08, 15, 22, 29

1980 Jan: 05, 12, 19, 26, Feb: 02, 09, 16, 23, Mar: 01, 08, 15, 22, 29, Apr: 05, 12, 19, 26, May: 03, 10,
17, 24, 31, Jun: 07, 14, 21, 28, Jul: 05, 12, 19, 26, Aug: 02, 09, 16, 23, 30, Sep: 06, 13, 20, 27, Oct: 04,
11, 18, 25, Nov: 01, 08, 15, 22, 29, Dec: 06, 13, 20, 27

1981 Jan: 03, 10, 17, 24, 31, Feb: 07, 14, 21, 28, Mar: 07, 14, 21, 28, Apr: 04, 11, 18, 25, May: 02, 09,
16, 23, 30, Jun: 06, 13, 20, 27, Jul: 04, 11, 18, 25, Aug: 01, 08, 15, 22, 29, Sep: 05, 12, 19, 26, Oct: 03,
10, 17, 24, 31, Nov: 07, 14, 21, 28, Dec: 05, 12, 19, 26

1982 Jan: 02, 09, 16, 23, 30, Feb: 06, 13, 20, 27, Mar: 06, 13, 20, 27, Apr: 03, 10, 17, 24, May: 01, 08,
15, 22, 29, Jun: 05, 12, 19, 26, Jul: 03, 10, 17, 24, 31, Aug: 07, 14, 21, 28, Sep: 04, 11, 18, 25, Oct: 02,
09, 16, 23, 30, Nov: 06, 13, 20, 27, Dec: 04, 11, 18, 25

1983 Jan: 01, 08, 15, 22, 29, Feb: 05, 12, 19, 26, Mar: 05, 12, 19, 26, Apr: 02, 09, 16, 23, 30, May: 07,
14, 21, 28, Jun: 04, 11, 18, 25, Jul: 02, 09, 16, 23, 30, Aug: 06, 13, 20, 27, Sep: 03, 10, 17, 24, Oct: 01,
08, 15, 22, 29, Nov: 05, 12, 19, 26, Dec: 03, 10, 17, 24, 31

1984 Jan: 07, 14, 21, 28, Feb: 04, 11, 18, 25, Mar: 03, 10, 17, 24, 31, Apr: 07, 14, 21, 28, May: 05, 12,
19, 26, Jun: 02, 09, 16, 23, 30, Jul: 07, 14, 21, 28, Aug: 04, 11, 18, 25, Sep: 01, 08, 15, 22, 29, Oct: 06,
13, 20, 27, Nov: 03, 10, 17, 24, Dec: 01, 08, 15, 22, 29

1985 Jan: 05, 12, 19, 26, Feb: 02, 09, 16, 23, Mar: 02, 09, 16, 23, 30, Apr: 06, 13, 20, 27, May: 04, 11,
18, 25, Jun: 01, 08, 15, 22, 29, Jul: 06, 13, 20, 27, Aug: 03, 10, 17, 24, 31, Sep: 07, 14, 21, 28, Oct: 05,
12, 19, 26, Nov: 02, 09, 16, 23, 30, Dec: 07, 14, 21, 28

1986 Jan: 04, 11, 18, 25, Feb: 01, 08, 15, 22, Mar: 01, 08, 15, 22, 29, Apr: 05, 12, 19, 26, May: 03, 10,
17, 24, 31, Jun: 07, 14, 21, 28, Jul: 05, 12, 19, 26, Aug: 02, 09, 16, 23, 30, Sep: 06, 13, 20, 27, Oct: 04,
11, 18, 25, Nov: 01, 08, 15, 22, 29, Dec: 06, 13, 20, 27

1987 Jan: 03, 10, 17, 24, 31, Feb: 07, 14, 21, 28, Mar: 29, 07, 14, 21, 28, Apr: 04, 11, 18, 25, May: 02,
09, 16, 23, 30, Jun: 06, 13, 20, 27, Jul: 04, 11, 18, 25, Aug: 01, 08, 15, 22, 29, Sep: 05, 12, 19, 26, Oct:
03, 10, 17, 24, 31, Nov: 07, 14, 21, 28, Dec: 05, 12, 19, 26

1988 Jan: 02, 09, 16, 23, 30, Feb: 06, 13, 20, 27, Mar: 05, 12, 19, 26, Apr: 02, 09, 16, 23, 30, May: 07,
14, 21, 28, Jun: 04, 11, 18, 25, Jul: 02, 09, 16, 23, 30, Aug: 06, 13, 20, 27, Sep: 03, 10, 17, 24, Oct: 01,
08, 15, 22, 29, Nov: 05, 12, 19, 26, Dec: 03, 10, 17, 24, 31

1989 Jan: 07, 14, 21, 28, Feb: 04, 11, 18, 25, Mar: 04, 11, 18, 25, Apr: 01, 08, 15, 22, 29, May: 06, 13,
20, 27, Jun: 03, 10, 17, 24, Jul: 01, 08, 15, 22, 29, Aug: 05, 12, 19, 26, Sep: 02, 09, 16, 23, 30, Oct: 07,
14, 21, 28, Nov: 04, 11, 18, 25, Dec: 02, 09, 16, 23, 30

1990 Jan: 06, 13, 20, 27, Feb: 03, 10, 17, 24, Mar: 03, 10, 17, 24, 31, Apr: 07, 14, 21, 28, May: 05, 12,
19, 26, Jun: 02, 09, 16, 23, 30, Jul: 07, 14, 21, 28, Aug: 04, 11, 18, 25, Sep: 01, 08, 15, 22, 29, Oct: 06,
13, 20, 27, Nov: 03, 10, 17, 24, Dec: 01, 08, 15, 22, 29

1991 *Jan:* 05, 12, 19, 26, *Feb:* 02, 09, 16, 23, *Mar:* 02, 09, 16, 23, 30, *Apr:* 06, 13, 20, 27, *May:* 04, 11, 18, 25, *Jun:* 01, 08, 15, 22, 29, *Jul:* 06, 13, 20, 27, *Aug:* 03, 10, 17, 24, 31, *Sep:* 07, 14, 21, 28, *Oct:* 05, 12, 19, 26, *Nov:* 02, 09, 16, 23, 30, *Dec:* 07, 14, 21, 28

1992 *Jan:* 04, 11, 18, 25, *Feb:* 01, 08, 15, 22, 29, *Mar:* 07, 14, 21, 28, *Apr:* 04, 11, 18, 25, *May:* 02, 09, 16, 23, 30, *Jun:* 06, 13, 20, 27, *Jul:* 04, 11, 18, 25, *Aug:* 01, 08, 15, 22, 29, *Sep:* 05, 12, 19, 26, *Oct:* 03, 10, 17, 24, 31, *Nov:* 07, 14, 21, 28, *Dec:* 05, 12, 19, 26

1993 *Jan:* 02, 09, 16, 23, 30, *Feb:* 06, 13, 20, 27, *Mar:* 06, 13, 20, 27, *Apr:* 03, 10, 17, 24, *May:* 01, 08, 15, 22, 29, *Jun:* 05, 12, 19, 26, *Jul:* 03, 10, 17, 24, 31, *Aug:* 07, 14, 21, 28, *Sep:* 04, 11, 18, 25, *Oct:* 02, 09, 16, 23, 30, *Nov:* 06, 13, 20, 27, *Dec:* 04, 11, 18, 25

1994 *Jan:* 01, 08, 15, 22, 29, *Feb:* 05, 12, 19, 26, *Mar:* 05, 12, 19, 26, *Apr:* 02, 09, 16, 23, 30, *May:* 07, 14, 21, 28, *Jun:* 04, 11, 18, 25, *Jul:* 02, 09, 16, 23, 30, *Aug:* 06, 13, 20, 27, *Sep:* 03, 10, 17, 24, *Oct:* 01, 08, 15, 22, 29, *Nov:* 05, 12, 19, 26, *Dec:* 03, 10, 17, 24, 31

1995 *Jan:* 07, 14, 21, 28, *Feb:* 04, 11, 18, 25, *Mar:* 04, 11, 18, 25, *Apr:* 01, 08, 15, 22, 29, *May:* 06, 13, 20, 27, *Jun:* 03, 10, 17, 24, *Jul:* 01, 08, 15, 22, 29, *Aug:* 05, 12, 19, 26, *Sep:* 02, 09, 16, 23, 30, *Oct:* 07, 14, 21, 28, *Nov:* 04, 11, 18, 25, *Dec:* 02, 09, 16, 23, 30

1996 *Jan:* 06, 13, 20, 27, *Feb:* 03, 10, 17, 24, *Mar:* 02, 09, 16, 23, 30, *Apr:* 06, 13, 20, 27, *May:* 04, 11, 18, 25, *Jun:* 01, 08, 15, 22, 29, *Jul:* 06, 13, 20, 27, *Aug:* 03, 10, 17, 24, 31, *Sep:* 07, 14, 21, 28, *Oct:* 05, 12, 19, 26, *Nov:* 02, 09, 16, 23, 30, *Dec:* 07, 14, 21, 28

1997 *Jan:* 04, 11, 18, 25, *Feb:* 01, 08, 15, 22, *Mar:* 01, 08, 15, 22, 29, *Apr:* 05, 12, 19, 26, *May:* 03, 10, 17, 24, 31, *Jun:* 07, 14, 21, 28, *Jul:* 05, 12, 19, 26, *Aug:* 02, 09, 16, 23, 30, *Sep:* 06, 13, 20, 27, *Oct:* 04, 11, 18, 25, *Nov:* 01, 08, 15, 22, 29, *Dec:* 06, 13, 20, 27

1998 *Jan:* 03, 10, 17, 24, 31, *Feb:* 07, 14, 21, 28, *Mar:* 07, 14, 21, 28, *Apr:* 04, 11, 18, 25, *May:* 02, 09, 16, 23, 30, *Jun:* 06, 13, 20, 27, *Jul:* 04, 11, 18, 25, *Aug:* 01, 08, 15, 22, 29, *Sep:* 05, 12, 19, 26, *Oct:* 03, 10, 17, 24, 31, *Nov:* 07, 14, 21, 28, *Dec:* 05, 12, 19, 26

1999 *Jan:* 02, 09, 16, 23, 30, *Feb:* 06, 13, 20, 27, *Mar:* 06, 13, 20, 27, *Apr:* 03, 10, 17, 24, *May:* 01, 08, 15, 22, 29, *Jun:* 05, 12, 19, 26, *Jul:* 03, 10, 17, 24, 31, *Aug:* 07, 14, 21, 28, *Sep:* 04, 11, 18, 25, *Oct:* 02, 09, 16, 23, 30, *Nov:* 06, 13, 20, 27, *Dec:* 04, 11, 18, 25

2000 *Jan:* 01, 08, 15, 22, 29, *Feb:* 05, 12, 19, 26, *Mar:* 04, 11, 18, 25, *Apr:* 01, 08, 15, 22, 29, *May:* 06, 13, 20, 27, *Jun:* 03, 10, 17, 24, *Jul:* 01, 08, 15, 22, 29, *Aug:* 05, 12, 19, 26, *Sep:* 02, 09, 16, 23, 30, *Oct:* 07, 14, 21, 28, *Nov:* 04, 11, 18, 25, *Dec:* 02, 09, 16, 23, 30

2001 *Jan:* 06, 13, 20, 27, *Feb:* 03, 10, 17, 24, *Mar:* 03, 10, 17, 24, 31, *Apr:* 07, 14, 21, 28, *May:* 05, 12, 19, 26, *Jun:* 02, 09, 16, 23, 30, *Jul:* 07, 14, 21, 28, *Aug:* 04, 11, 18, 25, *Sep:* 01, 08, 15, 22, 29, *Oct:* 06, 13, 20, 27, *Nov:* 03, 10, 17, 24, *Dec:* 01, 08, 15, 22, 29

2002 *Jan:* 05, 12, 19, 26, *Feb:* 02, 09, 16, 23, *Mar:* 02, 09, 16, 23, 30, *Apr:* 06, 13, 20, 27, *May:* 04, 11, 18, 25, *Jun:* 01, 08, 15, 22, 29, *Jul:* 06, 13, 20, 27, *Aug:* 03, 10, 17, 24, 31, *Sep:* 07, 14, 21, 28, *Oct:* 05, 12, 19, 26, *Nov:* 02, 09, 16, 23, 30, *Dec:* 07, 14, 21, 28

2003 *Jan:* 04, 11, 18, 25, *Feb:* 01, 08, 15, 22, *Mar:* 01, 08, 15, 22, 29, *Apr:* 05, 12, 19, 26, *May:* 03, 10, 17, 24, 31, *Jun:* 07, 14, 21, 28, *Jul:* 05, 12, 19, 26, *Aug:* 02, 09, 16, 23, 30, *Sep:* 06, 13, 20, 27, *Oct:* 04, 11, 18, 25, *Nov:* 01, 08, 15, 22, 29, *Dec:* 06, 13, 20, 27

2004 *Jan:* 03, 10, 17, 24, 31, *Feb:* 07, 14, 21, 28, *Mar:* 06, 13, 20, 27, *Apr:* 03, 10, 17, 24, *May:* 01, 08, 15, 22, 29, *Jun:* 05, 12, 19, 26, *Jul:* 03, 10, 17, 24, 31, *Aug:* 07, 14, 21, 28, *Sep:* 04, 11, 18, 25, *Oct:* 02, 09, 16, 23, 30, *Nov:* 06, 13, 20, 27, *Dec:* 04, 11, 18, 25

2005 *Jan:* 01, 08, 15, 22, 29, *Feb:* 05, 12, 19, 26, *Mar:* 05, 12, 19, 26, *Apr:* 02, 09, 16, 23, 30, *May:* 07, 14, 21, 28, *Jun:* 04, 11, 18, 25, *Jul:* 02, 09, 16, 23, 30, *Aug:* 06, 13, 20, 27, *Sep:* 03, 10, 17, 24, *Oct:* 01, 08, 15, 22, 29, *Nov:* 05, 12, 19, 26, *Dec:* 03, 10, 17, 24, 31

2006 *Jan:* 07, 14, 21, 28, *Feb:* 04, 11, 18, 25, *Mar:* 04, 11, 18, 25, *Apr:* 01, 08, 15, 22, 29, *May:* 06, 13, 20, 27, *Jun:* 03, 10, 17, 24, *Jul:* 01, 08, 15, 22, 29, *Aug:* 05, 12, 19, 26, *Sep:* 02, 09, 16, 23, 30, *Oct:* 07, 14, 21, 28, *Nov:* 04, 11, 18, 25, *Dec:* 02, 09, 16, 23, 30

2007 *Jan:* 06, 13, 20, 27, *Feb:* 03, 10, 17, 24, *Mar:* 03, 10, 17, 24, 31, *Apr:* 07, 14, 21, 28, *May:* 05, 12, 19, 26, *Jun:* 02, 09, 16, 23, 30, *Jul:* 07, 14, 21, 28, *Aug:* 04, 11, 18, 25, *Sep:* 01, 08, 15, 22, 29, *Oct:* 06, 13, 20, 27, *Nov:* 03, 10, 17, 24, *Dec:* 01, 08, 15, 22, 29

2008 *Jan:* 05, 12, 19, 26, *Feb:* 02, 09, 16, 23, *Mar:* 01, 08, 15, 22, 29, *Apr:* 05, 12, 19, 26, *May:* 03, 10, 17, 24, 31, *Jun:* 07, 14, 21, 28, *Jul:* 05, 12, 19, 26, *Aug:* 02, 09, 16, 23, 30, *Sep:* 06, 13, 20, 27, *Oct:* 04, 11, 18, 25, *Nov:* 01, 08, 15, 22, 29, *Dec:* 06, 13, 20, 27

2009 *Jan:* 03, 10, 17, 24, 31, *Feb:* 07, 14, 21, 28, *Mar:* 07, 14, 21, 28, *Apr:* 04, 11, 18, 25, *May:* 02, 09, 16, 23, 30, *Jun:* 06, 13, 20, 27, *Jul:* 04, 11, 18, 25, *Aug:* 01, 08, 15, 22, 29, *Sep:* 05, 12, 19, 26, *Oct:* 03, 10, 17, 24, 31, *Nov:* 07, 14, 21, 28, *Dec:* 05, 12, 19, 26

2010 *Jan:* 02, 09, 16, 23, 30, *Feb:* 06, 13, 20, 27, *Mar:* 06, 13, 20, 27, *Apr:* 03, 10, 17, 24, *May:* 01, 08, 15, 22, 29, *Jun:* 05, 12, 19, 26, *Jul:* 03, 10, 17, 24, 31, *Aug:* 07, 14, 21, 28, *Sep:* 04, 11, 18, 25, *Oct:* 02, 09, 16, 23, 30, *Nov:* 06, 13, 20, 27, *Dec:* 04, 11, 18, 25

2011 *Jan:* 01, 08, 15, 22, 29, *Feb:* 05, 12, 19, 26, *Mar:* 05, 12, 19, 26, *Apr:* 02, 09, 16, 23, 30, *May:* 07, 14, 21, 28, *Jun:* 04, 11, 18, 25, *Jul:* 02, 09, 16, 23, 30, *Aug:* 06, 13, 20, 27, *Sep:* 03, 10, 17, 24, *Oct:* 01, 08, 15, 22, 29, *Nov:* 05, 12, 19, 26, *Dec:* 03, 10, 17, 24, 31

2012 *Jan:* 07, 14, 21, 28, *Feb:* 04, 11, 18, 25, *Mar:* 03, 10, 17, 24, 31, *Apr:* 07, 14, 21, 28, *May:* 05, 12, 19, 26, *Jun:* 02, 09, 16, 23, 30, *Jul:* 07, 14, 21, 28, *Aug:* 04, 11, 18, 25, *Sep:* 01, 08, 15, 22, 29, *Oct:* 06, 13, 20, 27, *Nov:* 03, 10, 17, 24, *Dec:* 01, 08, 15, 22, 29

2013 *Jan:* 05, 12, 19, 26, *Feb:* 02, 09, 16, 23, *Mar:* 02, 09, 16, 23, 30, *Apr:* 06, 13, 20, 27, *May:* 04, 11, 18, 25, *Jun:* 01, 08, 15, 22, 29, *Jul:* 06, 13, 20, 27, *Aug:* 03, 10, 17, 24, 31, *Sep:* 07, 14, 21, 28, *Oct:* 05, 12, 19, 26, *Nov:* 02, 09, 16, 23, 30, *Dec:* 07, 14, 21, 28

Sunday: Raphael

IF YOUR DAY OF BIRTH IS SUNDAY: Raphael rules. His healing rays are golden or yellow – although from the sun come all rainbow colours. His metal is gold; his crystals are clear quartz or diamond, as these refract the entire spectrum. Attributes for Raphael are: healing, energy science and knowledge, plus masculine balance.

Of ancient origin (Ra in Egypt), Raphael's name means 'God has healed'. Sacred texts record that through him the earth is made a suitable dwelling place for man, whom he also helps to heal of all maladies. He is ruler of the sun (source of life), Sunday, 2nd Heaven and the west wind. Legends about him say he assisted Solomon with the building of his famous temple, bringing him a ring to subdue demons, so they built the temple for him! His main crystals of quartz and diamond (if you are lucky enough) aid energy at every level as well as encouraging development of hidden talents.

Raphael is the most important angel who can be invoked for healing – the gift of Spirit. We are all surrounded by this energy; it's formed of Love and Light, the most powerful forces in the cosmos. Spiritual healers act as a clear channel (conduit) to direct this energy through themselves and into others, but anyone is capable of accessing healing energy given loving will and intention. Absorbing healing rays can strengthen energy chakras and lift the immune system, facilitating the body's ability to self-heal in future.

Please remember that to be an effective healer you must first heal yourself. Raphael also brings balance to masculine aspects of personality, while Gabriel does the same for feminine aspects.

We can all call on Raphael any time for support and guidance on healing self or loved ones. If you are a Sunday child Raphael is one of your guardians and Sunday will always special for you. Here are an invocation and a healing idea:

Raphael, Raphael, Raphael, I ask for your help with knowledge of what I need for healing and wholeness in mind, body and spirit; in Love and Light, Love and Light, Love and Light.

Focus on Raphael on any day, whatever the weather, and invoke him, asking for his sunrays to flow into your solar plexus and out from there around your body. This dispels dark self-doubt and uncertainty, heals at all levels and can also (if you will and intend it) energise willpower.

Sunday birthdays

1940 Jan: 07, 14, 21, 28, Feb: 04, 11, 18, 25, Mar: 03, 10, 17, 24, 31, Apr: 07, 14, 21, 28, May: 05, 12, 19, 26, Jun: 02, 09, 16, 23, 30, Jul: 07, 14, 21, 28, Aug: 04, 11, 18, 25, Sep: 01, 08, 15, 22, 29, Oct: 06, 13, 20, 27, Nov: 03, 10, 17, 24, Dec: 01, 08, 15, 22, 29

1941 Jan: 05, 12, 19, 26, Feb: 02, 09, 16, 23, Mar: 02, 09, 16, 23, 30, Apr: 06, 13, 20, 27, May: 04, 11, 18, 25, Jun: 01, 08, 15, 22, 29, Jul: 06, 13, 20, 27, Aug: 03, 10, 17, 24, 31, Sep: 07, 14, 21, 28, Oct: 05, 12, 19, 26, Nov: 02, 09, 16, 23, 30, Dec: 07, 14, 21, 28

1942 Jan: 04, 11, 18, 25, Feb: 01, 08, 15, 22, Mar: 01, 08, 15, 22, 29, Apr: 05, 12, 19, 26, May: 03, 10, 17, 24, 31, Jun: 07, 14, 21, 28, Jul: 05, 12, 19, 26, Aug: 02, 09, 16, 23, 30, Sep: 06, 13, 20, 27, Oct: 04, 11, 18, 25, Nov: 01, 08, 15, 22, 29, Dec: 06, 13, 20, 27

1943 Jan: 03, 10, 17, 24, 31, Feb: 07, 14, 21, 28, Mar: 07, 14, 21, 28, Apr: 04, 11, 18, 25, May: 02, 09, 16, 23, 30, Jun: 06, 13, 20, 27, Jul: 04, 11, 18, 25, Aug: 01, 08, 15, 22, 29, Sep: 05, 12, 19, 26, Oct: 03, 10, 17, 24, 31, Nov: 07, 14, 21, 28, Dec: 05, 12, 19, 26

1944 Jan: 02, 09, 16, 23, 30, Feb: 06, 13, 20, 27, Mar: 05, 12, 19, 26, Apr: 02, 09, 16, 23, 30, May: 07, 14, 21, 28, Jun: 04, 11, 18, 25, Jul: 02, 09, 16, 23, 30, Aug: 06, 13, 20, 27, Sep: 03, 10, 17, 24, Oct: 01, 08, 15, 22, 29, Nov: 05, 12, 19, 26, Dec: 03, 10, 17, 24, 31

1945 Jan: 07, 14, 21, 28, Feb: 04, 11, 18, 25, Mar: 04, 11, 18, 25, Apr: 01, 08, 15, 22, 29, May: 06, 13, 20, 27, Jun: 03, 10, 17, 24, Jul: 01, 08, 15, 22, 29, Aug: 05, 12, 19, 26, Sep: 02, 09, 16, 23, 30, Oct: 07, 14, 21, 28, Nov: 04, 11, 18, 25, Dec: 02, 09, 16, 23, 30

1946 Jan: 06, 13, 20, 27, Feb: 03, 10, 17, 24, Mar: 03, 10, 17, 24, 31, Apr: 07, 14, 21, 28, May: 05, 12, 19, 26, Jun: 02, 09, 16, 23, 30, Jul: 07, 14, 21, 28, Aug: 04, 11, 18, 25, Sep: 01, 08, 15, 22, 29, Oct: 06, 13, 20, 27, Nov: 03, 10, 17, 24, Dec: 01, 08, 15, 22, 29

1947 Jan: 05, 12, 19, 26, Feb: 02, 09, 16, 23, Mar: 02, 09, 16, 23, 30, Apr: 06, 13, 20, 27, May: 04, 11, 18, 25, Jun: 01, 08, 15, 22, 29, Jul: 06, 13, 20, 27, Aug: 03, 10, 17, 24, 31, Sep: 07, 14, 21, 28, Oct: 05, 12, 19, 26, Nov: 02, 09, 16, 23, 30, Dec: 07, 14, 21, 28

1948 Jan: 04, 11, 18, 25, Feb: 01, 08, 15, 22, 29, Mar: 07, 14, 21, 28, Apr: 04, 11, 18, 25, May: 02, 09, 16, 23, 30, Jun: 06, 13, 20, 27, Jul: 04, 11, 18, 25, Aug: 01, 08, 15, 22, 29, Sep: 05, 12, 19, 26, Oct: 03, 10, 17, 24, 31, Nov: 07, 14, 21, 28, Dec: 05, 12, 19, 26

1949 Jan: 02, 09, 16, 23, 30, Feb: 06, 13, 20, 27, Mar: 06, 13, 20, 27, Apr: 03, 10, 17, 24, May: 01, 08, 15, 22, 29, Jun: 05, 12, 19, 26, Jul: 03, 10, 17, 24, 31, Aug: 07, 14, 21, 28, Sep: 04, 11, 18, 25, Oct: 02, 09, 16, 23, 30, Nov: 06, 13, 20, 27, Dec: 04, 11, 18, 25

1950 Jan: 01, 08, 15, 22, 29, Feb: 05, 12, 19, 26, Mar: 05, 12, 19, 26, Apr: 02, 09, 16, 23, 30, May: 07, 14, 21, 28, Jun: 04, 11, 18, 25, Jul: 02, 09, 16, 23, 30, Aug: 06, 13, 20, 27, Sep: 03, 10, 17, 24, Oct: 01, 08, 15, 22, 29, Nov: 05, 12, 19, 26, Dec: 03, 10, 17, 24, 31

1951 Jan: 07, 14, 21, 28, Feb: 04, 11, 18, 25, Mar: 04, 11, 18, 25, Apr: 01, 08, 15, 22, 29, May: 06, 13, 20, 27, Jun: 03, 10, 17, 24, Jul: 01, 08, 15, 22, 29, Aug: 05, 12, 19, 26, Sep: 02, 09, 16, 23, 30, Oct: 07, 14, 21, 28, Nov: 04, 11, 18, 25, Dec: 02, 09, 16, 23, 30

1952 Jan: 06, 13, 20, 27, Feb: 03, 10, 17, 24, Mar: 02, 09, 16, 23, 30, Apr: 06, 13, 20, 27, May: 04, 11, 18, 25, Jun: 01, 08, 15, 22, 29, Jul: 06, 13, 20, 27, Aug: 03, 10, 17, 24, 31, Sep: 07, 14, 21, 28, Oct: 05, 12, 19, 26, Nov: 02, 09, 16, 23, 30, Dec: 07, 14, 21, 28

1953 Jan: 04, 11, 18, 25, Feb: 01, 08, 15, 22, Mar: 01, 08, 15, 22, 29, Apr: 05, 12, 19, 26, May: 03, 10, 17, 24, 31, Jun: 07, 14, 21, 28, Jul: 05, 12, 19, 26, Aug: 02, 09, 16, 23, 30, Sep: 06, 13, 20, 27, Oct: 04, 11, 18, 25, Nov: 01, 08, 15, 22, 29, Dec: 06, 13, 20, 27

1954 Jan: 03, 10, 17, 24, 31, Feb: 07, 14, 21, 28, Mar: 07, 14, 21, 28, Apr: 04, 11, 18, 25, May: 02, 09, 16, 23, 30, Jun: 06, 13, 20, 27, Jul: 04, 11, 18, 25, Aug: 01, 08, 15, 22, 29, Sep: 05, 12, 19, 26, Oct: 03, 10, 17, 24, 31, Nov: 07, 14, 21, 28, Dec: 05, 12, 19, 26

1955 Jan: 02, 09, 16, 23, 30, Feb: 06, 13, 20, 27, Mar: 06, 13, 20, 27, Apr: 03, 10, 17, 24, May: 01, 08, 15, 22, 29, Jun: 05, 12, 19, 26, Jul: 03, 10, 17, 24, 31, Aug: 07, 14, 21, 28, Sep: 04, 11, 18, 25, Oct: 02, 09, 16, 23, 30, Nov: 06, 13, 20, 27, Dec: 04, 11, 18, 25

1956 Jan: 01, 08, 15, 22, 29, Feb: 05, 12, 19, 26, Mar: 04, 11, 18, 25, Apr: 01, 08, 15, 22, 29, May: 06, 13, 20, 27, Jun: 03, 10, 17, 24, Jul: 01, 08, 15, 22, 29, Aug: 05, 12, 19, 26, Sep: 02, 09, 16, 23, 30, Oct: 07, 14, 21, 28, Nov: 04, 11, 18, 25, Dec: 02, 09, 16, 23, 30

1957 Jan: 06, 13, 20, 27, Feb: 03, 10, 17, 24, Mar: 03, 10, 17, 24, 31, Apr: 07, 14, 21, 28, May: 05, 12, 19, 26, Jun: 02, 09, 16, 23, 30, Jul: 07, 14, 21, 28, Aug: 04, 11, 18, 25, Sep: 01, 08, 15, 22, 29, Oct: 06, 13, 20, 27, Nov: 03, 10, 17, 24, Dec: 01, 08, 15, 22, 29

1958 Jan: 05, 12, 19, 26, Feb: 02, 09, 16, 23, Mar: 02, 09, 16, 23, 30, Apr: 06, 13, 20, 27, May: 04, 11, 18, 25, Jun: 01, 08, 15, 22, 29, Jul: 06, 13, 20, 27, Aug: 03, 10, 17, 24, 31, Sep: 07, 14, 21, 28, Oct: 05, 12, 19, 26, Nov: 02, 09, 16, 23, 30, Dec: 07, 14, 21, 28

1959 Jan: 04, 11, 18, 25, Feb: 01, 08, 15, 22, Mar: 01, 08, 15, 22, 29, Apr: 05, 12, 19, 26, May: 03, 10, 17, 24, 31, Jun: 07, 14, 21, 28, Jul: 05, 12, 19, 26, Aug: 02, 09, 16, 23, 30, Sep: 06, 13, 20, 27, Oct: 04, 11, 18, 25, Nov: 01, 08, 15, 22, 29, Dec: 06, 13, 20, 27

1960 Jan: 03, 10, 17, 24, 31, Feb: 07, 14, 21, 28, Mar: 06, 13, 20, 27, Apr: 03, 10, 17, 24, May: 01, 08, 15, 22, 29, Jun: 05, 12, 19, 26, Jul: 03, 10, 17, 24, 31, Aug: 07, 14, 21, 28, Sep: 04, 11, 18, 25, Oct: 02, 09, 16, 23, 30, Nov: 06, 13, 20, 27, Dec: 04, 11, 18, 25

1961 Jan: 01, 08, 15, 22, 29, Feb: 05, 12, 19, 26, Mar: 05, 12, 19, 26, Apr: 02, 09, 16, 23, 30, May: 07, 14, 21, 28, Jun: 04, 11, 18, 25, Jul: 02, 09, 16, 23, 30, Aug: 06, 13, 20, 27, Sep: 03, 10, 17, 24, Oct: 01, 08, 15, 22, 29, Nov: 05, 12, 19, 26, Dec: 03, 10, 17, 24, 31

1962 Jan: 07, 14, 21, 28, Feb: 04, 11, 18, 25, Mar: 04, 11, 18, 25, Apr: 01, 08, 15, 22, 29, May: 06, 13, 20, 27, Jun: 03, 10, 17, 24, Jul: 01, 08, 15, 22, 29, Aug: 05, 12, 19, 26, Sep: 02, 09, 16, 23, 30, Oct: 07, 14, 21, 28, Nov: 04, 11, 18, 25, Dec: 02, 09, 16, 23, 30

1963 Jan: 06, 13, 20, 27, Feb: 03, 10, 17, 24, Mar: 03, 10, 17, 24, 31, Apr: 07, 14, 21, 28, May: 05, 12, 19, 26, Jun: 02, 09, 16, 23, 30, Jul: 07, 14, 21, 28, Aug: 04, 11, 18, 25, Sep: 01, 08, 15, 22, 29, Oct: 06, 13, 20, 27, Nov: 03, 10, 17, 24, Dec: 01, 08, 15, 22, 29

1964 Jan: 05, 12, 19, 26, Feb: 02, 09, 16, 23, Mar: 01, 08, 15, 22, 29, Apr: 05, 12, 19, 26, May: 03, 10, 17, 24, 31, Jun: 07, 14, 21, 28, Jul: 05, 12, 19, 26, Aug: 02, 09, 16, 23, 30, Sep: 06, 13, 20, 27, Oct: 04, 11, 18, 25, Nov: 01, 08, 15, 22, 29, Dec: 06, 13, 20, 27

1965 *Jan:* 03, 10, 17, 24, 31, *Feb:* 07, 14, 21, 28, *Mar:* 07, 14, 21, 28, *Apr:* 04, 11, 18, 25, *May:* 02, 09, 16, 23, 30, *Jun:* 06, 13, 20, 27, *Jul:* 04, 11, 18, 25, *Aug:* 01, 08, 15, 22, 29, *Sep:* 05, 12, 19, 26, *Oct:* 03, 10, 17, 24, 31, *Nov:* 07, 14, 21, 28, *Dec:* 05, 12, 19, 26

1966 *Jan:* 02, 09, 16, 23, 30, *Feb:* 06, 13, 20, 27, *Mar:* 06, 13, 20, 27, *Apr:* 03, 10, 17, 24, *May:* 01, 08, 15, 22, 29, *Jun:* 05, 12, 19, 26, *Jul:* 03, 10, 17, 24, 31, *Aug:* 07, 14, 21, 28, *Sep:* 04, 11, 18, 25, *Oct:* 02, 09, 16, 23, 30, *Nov:* 06, 13, 20, 27, *Dec:* 04, 11, 18, 25

1967 *Jan:* 01, 08, 15, 22, 29, *Feb:* 05, 12, 19, 26, *Mar:* 05, 12, 19, 26, *Apr:* 02, 09, 16, 23, 30, *May:* 07, 14, 21, 28, *Jun:* 04, 11, 18, 25, *Jul:* 02, 09, 16, 23, 30, *Aug:* 06, 13, 20, 27, *Sep:* 03, 10, 17, 24, *Oct:* 01, 08, 15, 22, 29, *Nov:* 05, 12, 19, 26, *Dec:* 03, 10, 17, 24, 31

1968 *Jan:* 07, 14, 21, 28, *Feb:* 04, 11, 18, 25, *Mar:* 03, 10, 17, 24, 31, *Apr:* 07, 14, 21, 28, *May:* 05, 12, 19, 26, *Jun:* 02, 09, 16, 23, 30, *Jul:* 07, 14, 21, 28, *Aug:* 04, 11, 18, 25, *Sep:* 01, 08, 15, 22, 29, *Oct:* 06, 13, 20, 27, *Nov:* 03, 10, 17, 24, *Dec:* 01, 08, 15, 22, 29

1969 *Jan:* 05, 12, 19, 26, *Feb:* 02, 09, 16, 23, *Mar:* 02, 09, 16, 23, 30, *Apr:* 06, 13, 20, 27, *May:* 04, 11, 18, 25, *Jun:* 01, 08, 15, 22, 29, *Jul:* 06, 13, 20, 27, *Aug:* 03, 10, 17, 24, 31, *Sep:* 07, 14, 21, 28, *Oct:* 05, 12, 19, 26, *Nov:* 02, 09, 16, 23, 30, *Dec:* 07, 14, 21, 28

1970 *Jan:* 04, 11, 18, 25, *Feb:* 01, 08, 15, 22, *Mar:* 01, 08, 15, 22, 29, *Apr:* 05, 12, 19, 26, *May:* 03, 10, 17, 24, 31, *Jun:* 07, 14, 21, 28, *Jul:* 05, 12, 19, 26, *Aug:* 02, 09, 16, 23, 30, *Sep:* 06, 13, 20, 27, *Oct:* 04, 11, 18, 25, *Nov:* 01, 08, 15, 22, 29, *Dec:* 06, 13, 20, 27

1971 *Jan:* 03, 10, 17, 24, 31, *Feb:* 07, 14, 21, 28, *Mar:* 07, 14, 21, 28, *Apr:* 04, 11, 18, 25, *May:* 02, 09, 16, 23, 30, *Jun:* 06, 13, 20, 27, *Jul:* 04, 11, 18, 25, *Aug:* 01, 08, 15, 22, 29, *Sep:* 05, 12, 19, 26, *Oct:* 03, 10, 17, 24, 31, *Nov:* 07, 14, 21, 28, *Dec:* 05, 12, 19, 26

1972 *Jan:* 02, 09, 16, 23, 30, *Feb:* 06, 13, 20, 27, *Mar:* 05, 12, 19, 26, *Apr:* 02, 09, 16, 23, 30, *May:* 07, 14, 21, 28, *Jun:* 04, 11, 18, 25, *Jul:* 02, 09, 16, 23, 30, *Aug:* 06, 13, 20, 27, *Sep:* 03, 10, 17, 24, *Oct:* 01, 08, 15, 22, 29, *Nov:* 05, 12, 19, 26, *Dec:* 03, 10, 17, 24, 31

1973 *Jan:* 07, 14, 21, 28, *Feb:* 04, 11, 18, 25, *Mar:* 04, 11, 18, 25, *Apr:* 01, 08, 15, 22, 29, *May:* 06, 13, 20, 27, *Jun:* 03, 10, 17, 24, *Jul:* 01, 08, 15, 22, 29, *Aug:* 05, 12, 19, 26, *Sep:* 02, 09, 16, 23, 30, *Oct:* 07, 14, 21, 28, *Nov:* 04, 11, 18, 25, *Dec:* 02, 09, 16, 23, 30

1974 *Jan:* 06, 13, 20, 27, *Feb:* 03, 10, 17, 24, *Mar:* 03, 10, 17, 24, 31, *Apr:* 07, 14, 21, 28, *May:* 05, 12, 19, 26, *Jun:* 02, 09, 16, 23, 30, *Jul:* 07, 14, 21, 28, *Aug:* 04, 11, 18, 25, *Sep:* 01, 08, 15, 22, 29, *Oct:* 06, 13, 20, 27, *Nov:* 03, 10, 17, 24, *Dec:* 01, 08, 15, 22, 29

1975 *Jan:* 05, 12, 19, 26, *Feb:* 02, 09, 16, 23, *Mar:* 02, 09, 16, 23, 30, *Apr:* 06, 13, 20, 27, *May:* 04, 11, 18, 25, *Jun:* 01, 08, 15, 22, 29, *Jul:* 06, 13, 20, 27, *Aug:* 03, 10, 17, 24, 31, *Sep:* 07, 14, 21, 28, *Oct:* 05, 12, 19, 26, *Nov:* 02, 09, 16, 23, 30, *Dec:* 07, 14, 21, 28

1976 *Jan:* 04, 11, 18, 25, *Feb:* 01, 08, 15, 22, 29, *Mar:* 07, 14, 21, 28, *Apr:* 04, 11, 18, 25, *May:* 02, 09, 16, 23, 30, *Jun:* 06, 13, 20, 27, *Jul:* 04, 11, 18, 25, *Aug:* 01, 08, 15, 22, 29, *Sep:* 05, 12, 19, 26, *Oct:* 03, 10, 17, 24, 31, *Nov:* 07, 14, 21, 28, *Dec:* 05, 12, 19, 26

1977 *Jan:* 02, 09, 16, 23, 30, *Feb:* 06, 13, 20, 27, *Mar:* 06, 13, 20, 27, *Apr:* 03, 10, 17, 24, *May:* 01, 08, 15, 22, 29, *Jun:* 05, 12, 19, 26, *Jul:* 03, 10, 17, 24, 31, *Aug:* 07, 14, 21, 28, *Sep:* 04, 11, 18, 25, *Oct:* 02, 09, 16, 23, 30, *Nov:* 06, 13, 20, 27, *Dec:* 04, 11, 18, 25

1978 *Jan:* 01, 08, 15, 22, 29, *Feb:* 05, 12, 19, 26, *Mar:* 05, 12, 19, 26, *Apr:* 02, 09, 16, 23, 30, *May:* 07, 14, 21, 28, *Jun:* 04, 11, 18, 25, *Jul:* 02, 09, 16, 23, 30, *Aug:* 06, 13, 20, 27, *Sep:* 03, 10, 17, 24, *Oct:* 01, 08, 15, 22, 29, *Nov:* 05, 12, 19, 26, *Dec:* 03, 10, 17, 24, 31

1979 *Jan:* 07, 14, 21, 28, *Feb:* 04, 11, 18, 25, *Mar:* 04, 11, 18, 25, *Apr:* 01, 08, 15, 22, 29, *May:* 06, 13, 20, 27, *Jun:* 03, 10, 17, 24, *Jul:* 01, 08, 15, 22, 29, *Aug:* 05, 12, 19, 26, *Sep:* 02, 09, 16, 23, 30, *Oct:* 07, 14, 21, 28, *Nov:* 04, 11, 18, 25, *Dec:* 02, 09, 16, 23, 30

1980 *Jan:* 06, 13, 20, 27, *Feb:* 03, 10, 17, 24, *Mar:* 02, 09, 16, 23, 30, *Apr:* 06, 13, 20, 27, *May:* 04, 11, 18, 25, *Jun:* 01, 08, 15, 22, 29, *Jul:* 06, 13, 20, 27, *Aug:* 03, 10, 17, 24, 31, *Sep:* 07, 14, 21, 28, *Oct:* 05, 12, 19, 26, *Nov:* 02, 09, 16, 23, 30, *Dec:* 07, 14, 21, 28

1981 *Jan:* 04, 11, 18, 25, *Feb:* 01, 08, 15, 22, *Mar:* 01, 08, 15, 22, 29, *Apr:* 05, 12, 19, 26, *May:* 03, 10, 17, 24, 31, *Jun:* 07, 14, 21, 28, *Jul:* 05, 12, 19, 26, *Aug:* 02, 09, 16, 23, 30, *Sep:* 06, 13, 20, 27, *Oct:* 04, 11, 18, 25, *Nov:* 01, 08, 15, 22, 29, *Dec:* 06, 13, 20, 27

1982 *Jan:* 03, 10, 17, 24, 31, *Feb:* 07, 14, 21, 28, *Mar:* 07, 14, 21, 28, *Apr:* 04, 11, 18, 25, *May:* 02, 09, 16, 23, 30, *Jun:* 06, 13, 20, 27, *Jul:* 04, 11, 18, 25, *Aug:* 01, 08, 15, 22, 29, *Sep:* 05, 12, 19, 26, *Oct:* 03, 10, 17, 24, 31, *Nov:* 07, 14, 21, 28, *Dec:* 05, 12, 19, 26

1983 *Jan:* 02, 09, 16, 23, 30, *Feb:* 06, 13, 20, 27, *Mar:* 06, 13, 20, 27, *Apr:* 03, 10, 17, 24, *May:* 01, 08, 15, 22, 29, *Jun:* 05, 12, 19, 26, *Jul:* 03, 10, 17, 24, 31, *Aug:* 07, 14, 21, 28, *Sep:* 04, 11, 18, 25, *Oct:* 02, 09, 16, 23, 30, *Nov:* 06, 13, 20, 27, *Dec:* 04, 11, 18, 25

1984 *Jan:* 01, 08, 15, 22, 29, *Feb:* 05, 12, 19, 26, *Mar:* 04, 11, 18, 25, *Apr:* 01, 08, 15, 22, 29, *May:* 06, 13, 20, 27, *Jun:* 03, 10, 17, 24, *Jul:* 01, 08, 15, 22, 29, *Aug:* 05, 12, 19, 26, *Sep:* 02, 09, 16, 23, 30, *Oct:* 07, 14, 21, 28, *Nov:* 04, 11, 18, 25, *Dec:* 02, 09, 16, 23, 30

1985 *Jan:* 06, 13, 20, 27, *Feb:* 03, 10, 17, 24, *Mar:* 03, 10, 17, 24, 31, *Apr:* 07, 14, 21, 28, *May:* 05, 12, 19, 26, *Jun:* 02, 09, 16, 23, 30, *Jul:* 07, 14, 21, 28, *Aug:* 04, 11, 18, 25, *Sep:* 01, 08, 15, 22, 29, *Oct:* 06, 13, 20, 27, *Nov:* 03, 10, 17, 24, *Dec:* 01, 08, 15, 22, 29

1986 *Jan:* 05, 12, 19, 26, *Feb:* 02, 09, 16, 23, *Mar:* 02, 09, 16, 23, 30, *Apr:* 06, 13, 20, 27, *May:* 04, 11, 18, 25, *Jun:* 01, 08, 15, 22, 29, *Jul:* 06, 13, 20, 27, *Aug:* 03, 10, 17, 24, 31, *Sep:* 07, 14, 21, 28, *Oct:* 05, 12, 19, 26, *Nov:* 02, 09, 16, 23, 30, *Dec:* 07, 14, 21, 28

1987 *Jan:* 04, 11, 18, 25, *Feb:* 01, 08, 15, 22, *Mar:* 01, 08, 15, 22, 29, *Apr:* 05, 12, 19, 26, *May:* 03, 10, 17, 24, 31, *Jun:* 07, 14, 21, 28, *Jul:* 05, 12, 19, 26, *Aug:* 02, 09, 16, 23, 30, *Sep:* 06, 13, 20, 27, *Oct:* 04, 11, 18, 25, *Nov:* 01, 08, 15, 22, 29, *Dec:* 06, 13, 20, 27

1988 *Jan:* 03, 10, 17, 24, 31, *Feb:* 07, 14, 21, 28, *Mar:* 06, 13, 20, 27, *Apr:* 03, 10, 17, 24, *May:* 01, 08, 15, 22, 29, *Jun:* 05, 12, 19, 26, *Jul:* 03, 10, 17, 24, 31, *Aug:* 07, 14, 21, 28, *Sep:* 04, 11, 18, 25, *Oct:* 02, 09, 16, 23, 30, *Nov:* 06, 13, 20, 27, *Dec:* 04, 11, 18, 25

1989 *Jan:* 01, 08, 15, 22, 29, *Feb:* 05, 12, 19, 26, *Mar:* 05, 12, 19, 26, *Apr:* 02, 09, 16, 23, 30, *May:* 07, 14, 21, 28, *Jun:* 04, 11, 18, 25, *Jul:* 02, 09, 16, 23, 30, *Aug:* 06, 13, 20, 27, *Sep:* 03, 10, 17, 24, *Oct:* 01, 08, 15, 22, 29, *Nov:* 05, 12, 19, 26, *Dec:* 03, 10, 17, 24, 31

1990 *Jan:* 07, 14, 21, 28, *Feb:* 04, 11, 18, 25, *Mar:* 04, 11, 18, 25, *Apr:* 01, 08, 15, 22, 29, *May:* 06, 13, 20, 27, *Jun:* 03, 10, 17, 24, *Jul:* 01, 08, 15, 22, 29, *Aug:* 05, 12, 19, 26, *Sep:* 02, 09, 16, 23, 30, *Oct:* 07, 14, 21, 28, *Nov:* 04, 11, 18, 25, *Dec:* 02, 09, 16, 23, 30

1991 Jan: 06, 13, 20, 27, Feb: 03, 10, 17, 24, Mar: 03, 10, 17, 24, 31, Apr: 07, 14, 21, 28, May: 05, 12, 19, 26, Jun: 02, 09, 16, 23, 30, Jul: 07, 14, 21, 28, Aug: 4, 11, 18, 25, Sep: 01, 08, 15, 22, 29, Oct: 06, 13, 20, 27, Nov: 03, 10, 17, 24, Dec: 01, 08, 15, 22, 29

1992 Jan: 05, 12, 19, 26, Feb: 02, 09, 16, 23, Mar: 01, 08, 15, 22, 29, Apr: 05, 12, 19, 26, May: 03, 10, 17, 24, 31, Jun: 07, 14, 21, 28, Jul: 05, 12, 19, 26, Aug: 2, 9, 16, 23, 30, Sep: 06, 13, 20, 27, Oct: 04, 11, 18, 25, Nov: 01, 08, 15, 22, 29, Dec: 06, 13, 20, 27

1993 Jan: 03, 10, 17, 24, 31, Feb: 07, 14, 21, 28, Mar: 07, 14, 21, 28, Apr: 04, 11, 18, 25, May: 02, 09, 16, 23, 30, Jun: 06, 13, 20, 27, Jul: 04, 11, 18, 25, Aug: 1, 8, 15, 22, 29, Sep: 05, 12, 19, 26, Oct: 03, 10, 17, 24, 31, Nov: 07, 14, 21, 28, Dec: 05, 12, 19, 26

1994 Jan: 02, 09, 16, 23, 30, Feb: 06, 13, 20, 27, Mar: 06, 13, 20, 27, Apr: 03, 10, 17, 24, May: 01, 08, 15, 22, 29, Jun: 05, 12, 19, 26, Jul: 03, 10, 17, 24, 31, Aug: 7, 14, 21, 28, Sep: 04, 11, 18, 25, Oct: 02, 09, 16, 23, 30, Nov: 06, 13, 20, 27, Dec: 04, 11, 18, 25

1995 Jan: 01, 08, 15, 22, 29, Feb: 05, 12, 19, 26, Mar: 05, 12, 19, 26, Apr: 02, 09, 16, 23, 30, May: 07, 14, 21, 28, Jun: 04, 11, 18, 25, Jul: 02, 09, 16, 23, 30, Aug: 6, 13, 20, 27, Sep: 03, 10, 17, 24, Oct: 01, 08, 15, 22, 29, Nov: 05, 12, 19, 26, Dec: 03, 10, 17, 24, 31

1996 Jan: 07, 14, 21, 28, Feb: 04, 11, 18, 25, Mar: 03, 10, 17, 24, 31, Apr: 07, 14, 21, 28, May: 05, 12, 19, 26, Jun: 02, 09, 16, 23, 30, Jul: 07, 14, 21, 28, Aug: 4, 11, 18, 25, Sep: 01, 08, 15, 22, 29, Oct: 06, 13, 20, 27, Nov: 03, 10, 17, 24, Dec: 01, 08, 15, 22, 29

1997 Jan: 05, 12, 19, 26, Feb: 02, 09, 16, 23, Mar: 02, 09, 16, 23, 30, Apr: 06, 13, 20, 27, May: 04, 11, 18, 25, Jun: 01, 08, 15, 22, 29, Jul: 06, 13, 20, 27, Aug: 3, 10, 17, 24, 31, Sep: 07, 14, 21, 28, Oct: 05, 12, 19, 26, Nov: 02, 09, 16, 23, 30, Dec: 07, 14, 21, 28

1998 Jan: 04, 11, 18, 25, Feb: 01, 08, 15, 22, Mar: 01, 08, 15, 22, 29, Apr: 05, 12, 19, 26, May: 03, 10, 17, 24, 31, Jun: 07, 14, 21, 28, Jul: 05, 12, 19, 26, Aug: 2, 9, 16, 23, 30, Sep: 06, 13, 20, 27, Oct: 04, 11, 18, 25, Nov: 01, 08, 15, 22, 29, Dec: 06, 13, 20, 27

1999 Jan: 03, 10, 17, 24, 31, Feb: 07, 14, 21, 28, Mar: 07, 14, 21, 28, Apr: 04, 11, 18, 25, May: 02, 09, 16, 23, 30, Jun: 06, 13, 20, 27, Jul: 04, 11, 18, 25, Aug: 1, 8, 15, 22, 29, Sep: 05, 12, 19, 26, Oct: 03, 10, 17, 24, 31, Nov: 07, 14, 21, 28, Dec: 05, 12, 19, 26

2000 Jan: 02, 09, 16, 23, 30, Feb: 06, 13, 20, 27, Mar: 05, 12, 19, 26, Apr: 02, 09, 16, 23, 30, May: 07, 14, 21, 28, Jun: 04, 11, 18, 25, Jul: 02, 09, 16, 23, 30, Aug: 6, 13, 20, 27, Sep: 03, 10, 17, 24, Oct: 01, 08, 15, 22, 29, Nov: 05, 12, 19, 26, Dec: 03, 10, 17, 24, 31

2001 Jan: 07, 14, 21, 28, Feb: 04, 11, 18, 25, Mar: 04, 11, 18, 25, Apr: 01, 08, 15, 22, 29, May: 06, 13, 20, 27, Jun: 03, 10, 17, 24, Jul: 01, 08, 15, 22, 29, Aug: 5, 12, 19, 26, Sep: 02, 09, 16, 23, 30, Oct: 07, 14, 21, 28, Nov: 04, 11, 18, 25, Dec: 02, 09, 16, 23, 30

2002 Jan: 06, 13, 20, 27, Feb: 03, 10, 17, 24, Mar: 03, 10, 17, 24, 31, Apr: 07, 14, 21, 28, May: 05, 12, 19, 26, Jun: 02, 09, 16, 23, 30, Jul: 07, 14, 21, 28, Aug: 4, 11, 18, 25, Sep: 01, 08, 15, 22, 29, Oct: 06, 13, 20, 27, Nov: 03, 10, 17, 24, Dec: 01, 08, 15, 22, 29

2003 Jan: 05, 12, 19, 26, Feb: 02, 09, 16, 23, Mar: 02, 09, 16, 23, 30, Apr: 06, 13, 20, 27, May: 04, 11, 18, 25, Jun: 01, 08, 15, 22, 29, Jul: 06, 13, 20, 27, Aug: 3, 10, 17, 24, 31, Sep: 07, 14, 21, 28, Oct: 05, 12, 19, 26, Nov: 02, 09, 16, 23, 30, Dec: 07, 14, 21, 28

2004 *Jan:* 04, 11, 18, 25, *Feb:* 01, 08, 15, 22, 29, *Mar:* 07, 14, 21, 28, *Apr:* 04, 11, 18, 25, *May:* 02, 09, 16, 23, 30, *Jun:* 06, 13, 20, 27, *Jul:* 04, 11, 18, 25, *Aug:* 1, 8, 15, 22, 29, *Sep:* 05, 12, 19, 26, *Oct:* 03, 10, 17, 24, 31, *Nov:* 07, 14, 21, 28, *Dec:* 05, 12, 19, 26

2005 *Jan:* 02, 09, 16, 23, 30, *Feb:* 06, 13, 20, 27, *Mar:* 06, 13, 20, 27, *Apr:* 03, 10, 17, 24, *May:* 01, 08, 15, 22, 29, *Jun:* 05, 12, 19, 26, *Jul:* 03, 10, 17, 24, 31, *Aug:* 7, 14, 21, 28, *Sep:* 04, 11, 18, 25, *Oct:* 02, 09, 16, 23, 30, *Nov:* 06, 13, 20, 27, *Dec:* 04, 11, 18, 25

2006 *Jan:* 01, 08, 15, 22, 29, *Feb:* 05, 12, 19, 26, *Mar:* 05, 12, 19, 26, *Apr:* 02, 09, 16, 23, 30, *May:* 07, 14, 21, 28, *Jun:* 04, 11, 18, 25, *Jul:* 02, 09, 16, 23, 30, *Aug:* 6, 13, 20, 27, *Sep:* 03, 10, 17, 24, *Oct:* 01, 08, 15, 22, 29, *Nov:* 05, 12, 19, 26, *Dec:* 03, 10, 17, 24, 31

2007 *Jan:* 07, 14, 21, 28, *Feb:* 04, 11, 18, 25, *Mar:* 04, 11, 18, 25, *Apr:* 01, 08, 15, 22, 29, *May:* 06, 13, 20, 27, *Jun:* 03, 10, 17, 24, *Jul:* 01, 08, 15, 22, 29, *Aug:* 5, 12, 19, 26, *Sep:* 02, 09, 16, 23, 30, *Oct:* 07, 14, 21, 28, *Nov:* 04, 11, 18, 25, *Dec:* 02, 09, 16, 23, 30

2008 *Jan:* 06, 13, 20, 27, *Feb:* 03, 10, 17, 24, *Mar:* 02, 09, 16, 23, 30, *Apr:* 06, 13, 20, 27, *May:* 04, 11, 18, 25, *Jun:* 01, 08, 15, 22, 29, *Jul:* 06, 13, 20, 27, *Aug:* 4, 11, 18, 25, *Sep:* 07, 14, 21, 28, *Oct:* 05, 12, 19, 26, *Nov:* 02, 09, 16, 23, 30, *Dec:* 07, 14, 21, 28

2009 *Jan:* 04, 11, 18, 25, *Feb:* 01, 08, 15, 22, *Mar:* 01, 08, 15, 22, 29, *Apr:* 05, 12, 19, 26, *May:* 03, 10, 17, 24, 31, *Jun:* 07, 14, 21, 28, *Jul:* 05, 12, 19, 26, *Aug:* 2, 9, 16, 23, 30, *Sep:* 06, 13, 20, 27, *Oct:* 04, 11, 18, 25, *Nov:* 01, 08, 15, 22, 29, *Dec:* 06, 13, 20, 27

2010 *Jan:* 03, 10, 17, 24, 31, *Feb:* 07, 14, 21, 28, *Mar:* 07, 14, 21, 28, *Apr:* 04, 11, 18, 25, *May:* 02, 09, 16, 23, 30, *Jun:* 06, 13, 20, 27, *Jul:* 04, 11, 18, 25, *Aug:* 1, 8, 15, 22, 29, *Sep:* 05, 12, 19, 26, *Oct:* 03, 10, 17, 24, 31, *Nov:* 07, 14, 21, 28, *Dec:* 05, 12, 19, 26

2011 *Jan:* 02, 09, 16, 23, 30, *Feb:* 06, 13, 20, 27, *Mar:* 06, 13, 20, 27, *Apr:* 03, 10, 17, 24, *May:* 01, 08, 15, 22, 29, *Jun:* 05, 12, 19, 26, *Jul:* 03, 10, 17, 24, 31, *Aug:* 7, 14, 21, 28, *Sep:* 04, 11, 18, 25, *Oct:* 02, 09, 16, 23, 30, *Nov:* 06, 13, 20, 27, *Dec:* 04, 11, 18, 25

2012 *Jan:* 01, 08, 15, 22, 29, *Feb:* 05, 12, 19, 26, *Mar:* 04, 11, 18, 25, *Apr:* 01, 08, 15, 22, 29, *May* 06, 13, 20, 27, *Jun:* 03, 10, 17, 24, *Jul:* 01, 08, 15, 22, 29, *Aug:* 5, 12, 19, 26, *Sep:* 02, 09, 16, 23, 30, *Oct:* 07, 14, 21, 28, *Nov:* 04, 11, 18, 25, *Dec:* 02, 09, 16, 23, 30

2013 *Jan:* 06, 13, 20, 27, *Feb:* 03, 10, 17, 24, *Mar:* 03, 10, 17, 24, 31, *Apr:* 07, 14, 21, 28, *May:* 05, 12, 19, 26, *Jun:* 02, 09, 16, 23, 30, *Jul:* 07, 14, 21, 28, *Aug:* 4, 11, 18, 25, *Sep:* 01, 08, 15, 22, 29, *Oct:* 06, 13, 20, 27, *Nov:* 03, 10, 17, 24, *Dec:* 01, 08, 15, 22, 29

PISTIS SOPHIA: Heavenly Mother of Mankind

Pistis Sophia, ruler of the Zodiac Angels, says:

As heavenly mother to my zodiac angel family, and earthly mother to mankind, I hold a watching brief for all that you do. I rejoice at your achievements, and descend at troublesome times to comfort you, reminding you that whatever happens is Divine Order and all things pass.

I offer you my twelve zodiac angels to aid your Heart Quest and urge you to resolve karma by self-healing, for the opening of your higher heart is the way to Oneness. You can work with any of my twelve, but your own zodiac sign will reveal three further guardians – zodiac, elemental and planetary ruler – to guide your future.

With eight of eternity I extend to you golden celestial star fire, entwined with sacred blue earth flame, enfolding you with veils of pure Love and Light. Try my joining exercise to really feel my loving energy: this supports you through life's many challenges towards finding your own true worth.

The first Joining to All: Heart Quest

This exercise with Pistis Sophia joins you to All through her shining energy veils. It takes only a few moments and can bring powerful healing. (In Part Three you can also add Seraphiel's Joining Exercise for your Soul Quest.)

Sit quietly, close your eyes, hold your hands up in front of you, palms facing away from you, and say:
Pistis Sophia, Pistis Sophia, Pistis Sophia, please join my right hand through All Above with celestial star fire to my left hand. Feel energy travel from one hand to the other.
And my right foot through All Below with sacred and eternal earth flame to my left foot. Feel energy travel from one foot to the other.
Through my heart, and the heart of Mother Earth, I am so joined. Feel the energy travel in a figure of eight centred through your higher heart.

The general principle, in energy terms, is that the right hand/foot gives to the universe and the left hand/foot takes from the universe. Sometimes, particularly in left-handed people, the flow is reversed. Follow what feels right for you. Using sacred breathing (on the Meditation CD) adds even more power to this exercise.

Aries: Machidiel

IF YOUR ZODIAC SIGN IS ARIES: your zodiac guardian angel is
Machidiel. Machidiel helps you to balance your assertiveness, energy
and individuality with caution and open-mindedness, and urges you to
accept guidance from others. Machidiel's link to a part of the human
body is the head.

Machidiel says:

*I am ruler of Aries. As your guardian angel (as well as to anyone
who invokes me with my particular guardianship qualities), I praise
your confidence, self-belief, enthusiasm and passion for what you
believe is right. For I also carry the influence and ruby-red energy of
Camael as well as Uriel's orange transformational Fire of Life;
together we can help empower you to achieve your true heart's
desires. But be sure they are true, and you understand that which is
worth winning takes time. Whatever you've decided is right for you,
whether projects, relationships, career or even your future, I counsel
caution when making your decisions, and ask you always to take
enough time for proper consideration and consultation.*

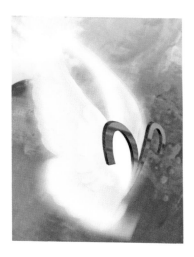

The part of the body with which I assist is your head, but it is for you to choose to involve your heart as well. Your assertiveness and individuality will take you far, so long as when setting your goal you allow yourself to be suitably guided by others and make your decisions using both head and heart, for that is the only way to find peace and contentment.

DAILY AFFIRMATION WITH MACHIDIEL UNTIL YOUR GOAL IS ACHIEVED:
Machidiel, Machidiel, Machidiel, I have carefully determined my true heart's desire, using both head and heart, and I am confident of achieving it. My goal is to allow others also to guide me in this for my highest good. Please help me to strengthen my strengths and overcome my weaknesses until my goal is achieved, in Love and Light, Love and Light, Love and Light.

Taurus: Tual

IF YOUR ZODIAC SIGN IS TAURUS: your zodiac guardian angel is Tual. Tual enhances your patient, steadfast and dependable nature with knowing when to let go and say 'no' to people, for their sake as well as yours. Tual's links to the human body: shoulders, neck and throat.

Tual says:

As ruler of Taurus, if I am one of your guardians I support your strength of character and reliability, as well as your steadfast nature and dependability for friends and loved ones. I bring with my sign the power of Ariel's earth, to help ground you as well as to provide the firm foundations to enhance that security you hold so dear. Also linked to me is the planet Venus, whose ruler is Haniel. As we three combine our green, rose and earth energies, we anchor, fill and surround you with deep love and compassion. For this is the time for you to say 'no', especially if your shoulders ache with the pressures of all the responsibilities you have taken on and keep accepting for self and others.

If you are going to achieve your true heart's desire, then you must make some time in your life for yourself, being fair but firm in your dealings with others. Only then, when you can focus fully on your goal, will you see the way to achieve it. The parts of the body that I assist are shoulders, neck and throat, as these are the areas where you hold stress and tension. Be prepared to let go and speak out, creating space in life to achieve the heart's desire that you truly seek.

DAILY AFFIRMATION WITH TUAL UNTIL YOUR GOAL IS ACHIEVED:
Tual, Tual, Tual, my goal is to release stress and relax my shoulders, letting go of what I must to make space in my life. This is not to be selfish, but to enable pursuit of my true heart's desire for my highest good. Please help me to strengthen my strengths and overcome my weaknesses until my goal is achieved, in Love and Light, Love and Light, Love and Light.

Gemini: Ambriel

IF YOUR ZODIAC SIGN IS GEMINI: your zodiac guardian angel is Ambriel. Ambriel aids you to remain focused on heart's desire, and helps your intelligent, enthusiastic and versatile approach to life and loved ones not to go too far and become 'burnt out'. Ambriel's link to a part of the human body: arms and fingers.

Ambriel says:

I rule the sign of Gemini, and if I am one of your guardians I recognise your great qualities of listening, applying intelligence and versatility in approaching problems, so that you and those you care about can surmount them successfully. I praise your immense loyalty, yet at the same time I see that sometimes this is an obstacle to your determining your own true heart's desires, rather than spending your life aiding others to find theirs.

In my role as ruler of the sign I am assisted by Michael, great angel of communication, whose cobalt-blue cloak protects you from negativity, as well as by Ariel's violet-blue Air, Breath of Life. Between us we aid you to find the thoughts and words you need, plus the strength and opportunity to air them when necessary. Also we aid your focus, for you are inclined to be mercurial in your pursuits, and need to stay on course if you are to achieve your true heart's desire.

The part of the body that I assist incorporates your arms and fingers and, when you've decided on one true goal I can help you to hold onto this until you can rejoice in the achievement that you richly deserve in life.

DAILY AFFIRMATION WITH AMBRIEL UNTIL YOUR GOAL IS ACHIEVED:
Ambriel, Ambriel, Ambriel, I have set a goal to focus fully on one true heart's desire, instead of dispersing my energy over many. I shall hold onto this, and keep pursuing it until I have achieved what I want for my highest good. Please help me to strengthen my strengths and overcome my weaknesses until my goal is achieved, in Love and Light, Love and Light, Love and Light.

Cancer: Muriel

IF YOUR ZODIAC SIGN IS CANCER: your zodiac guardian angel is Muriel. Muriel is the voice of your heart that you sometimes fail to listen to, because of your introspection and desire for a peaceful and quiet existence. Muriel's link to a part of the human body is between neck and abdomen.

Muriel says:

To assist mankind, and especially as a guardian angel, I see so clearly what perhaps you fail to see, and this is that your true heart's desire will not be won until you have the determination to speak your innermost feelings by moving out of your comfort zone. You know about this desire, for it resides deep in your heart, together with your most passionate emotions, and it is time to let it all emerge for your own highest good. I respect your qualities of self-possession and self-reliance, and your love of hearth and home, but you must spread your wings for there is much more that you can achieve in this life path towards which I, together with my fellow angels of this sign, will aid you.

The part of the body with which we help is that part from neck to abdomen enclosing your thymus, personal and higher heart chakras. While I bring you the opportunity of more balance to your life and work, Gabriel offers silvery moon energy to boost your ambitions and fill you with fresh hope as well as the intuition you need.

Let your inner voice be heard. Phuel's green and aquamarine rays of Water of Life soothe your heart with calm assurance that will, if you allow it, result in an ability to pursue confident action. Don't you think you should set a goal to speak out from your heart? We counsel that you owe it to yourself to do this before it's too late.

DAILY AFFIRMATION WITH MURIEL UNTIL YOUR GOAL IS ACHIEVED: *Muriel, Muriel, Muriel, deep down I know my true heart's desire, but to date I have failed to let it emerge. Now I have set a goal to calmly speak my truth for my highest good. I am ready to do this immediately I intuit that the time is right, knowing it must be soon. Please help me to strengthen my strengths and overcome my weaknesses until my goal is achieved, in Love and Light, Love and Light, Love and Light.*

Leo: Verchiel

IF YOUR ZODIAC SIGN IS LEO: your zodiac guardian angel is Verchiel. Verchiel is your champion; you are a leader, who inspires, is courageous and really helps others to achieve their potential. What holds you back sometimes is an inner lack of confidence. Verchiel's link to the human body is the back and spine.

Verchiel says:

As guardian of Leo and if I am one of your own guardians, I salute the Lion's courage in you, for I know you deserve this accolade. You have many of the qualities of leadership: you perceive what others need and you inspire them onwards. But should you not also apply these qualities to yourself to win your own heart's desire? For in fact there is very little you could not achieve if you set your heart on it – you just need that inner knowing that confirms your self-belief and underpins faith in your own immense ability. It is there if you can but find it.

I bring tawny golden colours to uplift you. With my sign come also Raphael, the healer, with the power of the sun. He offers rainbows to aid your bodily strength and balance; also empowering the thought processes and decision-making powers you need. Also, Uriel brings alchemy of Fire of Life, to purify and cleanse away obstacles to your progress, such as that lack of confidence.

All that then remains is for you to set a goal to remove the blocks you have to achieving your chosen heart's desire, and as the sun's fire flows through your will, you can make it all happen. The part of the body with which I help you is your spine – your very backbone, which when straight and strong supports that Lion's heart within your energy system. If you choose to call on me, with Raphael and Uriel, we will aid you to step into your own power at last.

DAILY AFFIRMATION WITH VERCHIEL UNTIL YOUR GOAL IS ACHIEVED:
Verchiel, Verchiel, Verchiel, I have identified a true heart's desire and deserve to let go of anything that holds me back. My goal is to strengthen my willpower and self-belief, to truly know I can achieve my heart's desire for my highest good. Please help me to strengthen my strengths and overcome my weaknesses until my goal is achieved, in Love and Light, Love and Light, Love and Light.

Virgo: Hamaliel

IF YOUR ZODIAC SIGN IS VIRGO: your zodiac guardian angel is Hamaliel. Hamaliel strengthens your considerable social and administrative skills and conscientiousness, while also enhancing your ability to take a more global view of issues. Hamaliel's link to the human body is the belly and digestive system.

Hamaliel says:

In my glorious Virgo month, to all that call me, and as a guardian angel to those born at this time, I urge you to feast your eyes on emerald green and lift them to the blue sky to enjoy life as much as possible. Perhaps you are too fond of getting right up close to issues and situations to see these wonders? You are so able when it comes to managing, controlling, communicating and solving problems, but life is also about freedom, letting go of worry, leaving details below and taking a bird's eye view of your own heart's desires!

For with me come Ariel, with his grounding element of earth, and you can be sure that he will bring you back down when necessary, ensuring your roots are firmly planted. From this base you can grow in strength and sturdiness with my supporting abundance of green energy rays. Then Michael's sky blue flows down to meet you, further empowering your throat chakra and your skills in networking and interacting with others.

The part of the body I associate with is your stomach. I offer advice about maintaining balance between Ariel's earth and Michael's sky, leading to greater calmness within. Between us we can help dispel digestive disorders, caused through stress or worry, that prevent you enjoying life as you should.

DAILY AFFIRMATION WITH HAMALIEL UNTIL YOUR GOAL IS ACHIEVED: *Hamaliel, Hamaliel, Hamaliel, I know that I need to let go of some immediate concerns, and find vision, time and space to determine my own true heart's desire. My goal is to define and follow a plan to achieve this desire, for my own highest good. Please help me to strengthen my strengths and overcome my weaknesses until my goal is achieved, in Love and Light, Love and Light, Love and Light.*

Libra: Zuriel

IF YOUR ZODIAC SIGN IS LIBRA: your zodiac guardian angel is Zuriel. Zuriel rejoices in your straightforward dealings with others, and enhances your decisiveness while guiding and integrating life/work balance. Zuriel's links to the human body are the hips and coccyx.

♎

Zuriel says:

If I am one of your guardian angels I ask you to stop and consider your own considerable ability, as occasionally you seem to doubt this. You have admirable qualities of organisation, of following instructions, and of impressive straightforwardness in your dealings with others, once you have made up your mind about them. Sometimes, however, you deliberate far too long on these and other things, and the balance of your life may become a little skewed. This is where I, together with Haniel, ruler of Venus, bring rose and emerald rays of love to boost your self-appreciation and even up the scales for you.

You may also be locked into patterns of behavioural conformity that you would dearly like to eradicate. Ariel brings power of Air, Breath of Life, to blow away these mindsets, setting you free to start again with how you want to be as well as how you would like others to perceive you.

You can choose to change, and work towards a heart's desire that you identified but felt was too far beyond you. The part of the body with which Haniel, Ariel and I aid you is hips, as well as coccyx, the joining of your root chakra down to earth and upwards to air. If you firm up your foundations, and build from there, you will find your heart's desire no longer seems unachievable – the choice is yours.

DAILY AFFIRMATION WITH ZURIEL UNTIL YOUR GOAL IS ACHIEVED:
Zuriel, Zuriel, Zuriel, my goal is to let go of mindsets that prevent me moving out of my conformity to achieve a new and exciting heart's desire. With you I will blow these mindsets away, fully believe in myself, and be decisive enough to find greater harmony and balance. Please help me to strengthen my strengths and overcome my weaknesses until my goal is achieved, in Love and Light, Love and Light, Love and Light.

Scorpio: Barakiel

IF YOUR ZODIAC SIGN IS SCORPIO: your zodiac guardian angel is Barakiel (also ruler of Pisces). Barakiel values your ambition, astuteness and passion for life, and supports your undoubted ability to manage and conclude exciting new ventures by helping you to evaluate risk and chance. Barakiel's link (in Scorpio) to the body is the pelvis.

Barakiel says:

As one of your guardians I admire your undoubted acumen, as you apply your intelligence and huge ability to achieve your ambitions and aspirations. Your enthusiasm and energy take you far, for you are also one who is prepared to gamble on the game of life. But do not do this without allowing the time to evaluate properly the people involved, or the risks in the venture. This is where I come to support you with my unconditional love, and counsel you to be sure to verify all these aspects with both heart and head.

With my sign I bring Phuel, whose aquamarine Water of Life can be cool and soothing, but also steamy and powerful. Whichever you need you can ask for, so long as you wish to have it for your highest good. Ariel and the ruling planet Pluto guide and build your psychic skills, with mauve and violet rays, so that you start to see beyond the obvious, bringing a rounded physical and spiritual approach to your self-development.

The part of the body with which I assist is the pelvis, from which creative passion drives you to new heart's desires or enterprises as the game of your life rolls ever onwards.

DAILY AFFIRMATION WITH BARAKIEL UNTIL YOUR GOAL IS ACHIEVED: *Barakiel, Barakiel, Barakiel, I know that I thrive on taking gambles in my life, but my goal is to ensure that I ask for your support in firstly evaluating them before making commitments. I need to direct my passion towards a true heart's desire and to accept necessary guidance. Please help me to strengthen my strengths and overcome my weaknesses until my goal is achieved, in Love and Light, Love and Light, Love and Light.*

Sagittarius: Adnachiel

IF YOUR ZODIAC SIGN IS SAGITTARIUS: your zodiac guardian angel is Adnachiel. Adnachiel widens your whole power of vision, expands your horizons, increases optimism and aids you to make your dreams actual reality. Adnachiel's link to the human body is the thighs and legs.

Adnachiel says:

As one of your guardians I am aware that you have the breadth of vision to perceive brand new ideas, concepts and ambitions, yet sometimes you lack the optimism or self-belief actually to carry these through to fruition. You may persuade yourself that a project is not even worth starting! But I come to reassure you that you are perfectly capable of all that you desire, it is you who is placing the limitations on yourself and, if you so choose, I will help you release yourself from these fetters.

With me I bring Zadkiel, mighty ruler of Jupiter, and all his deep blue abundance; this may be of opportunity, of health, of wisdom, of success. It is all there in your sign. Also Uriel's Fire of Life, to infuse you with glorious energy of fulfilment. Let Uriel aid you to burn away self-doubt, while Zadkiel's wisdom shows the opportunity this creates within you, then allow Uriel to return with passion's fire to drive you forwards.

The part of the body with which I aid you is your thighs and legs. What better way to move on with conviction than to accept our loving support – to really achieve that heart's desire that you can see in your mind's eye and that you know is for your future happiness?

DAILY AFFIRMATION WITH ADNACHIEL UNTIL YOUR GOAL IS ACHIEVED: *Adnachiel, Adnachiel, Adnachiel, my goal is that I have the vision of what I want, but I must truly believe that I can make this happen for me. With your loving support I fill myself with the abundance I need, and with Fire of Life to power me on towards realising my heart's desire. Please help me strengthen my strengths and overcome my weaknesses until my goal is achieved, in Love and Light, Love and Light, Love and Light.*

Capricorn: Nadiel

IF YOUR ZODIAC SIGN IS CAPRICORN: its ruler is Nadiel, who is your zodiac guardian angel. Nadiel supports your confidence, practicality, thoroughness and determination to make life changes towards greater harmony. Nadiel's link to a physical part of the human body is the knees.

Nadiel says:

I am ruler of Capricorn, but my directives from the Creator also cover your major life changes, such as new job, new house, new country, new you. If I am one of your guardians I assure you my remit is wide and encompasses all the loving support you need to add to your own practicality, thoroughness and determination. Together, we can transform any aspects within yourself that prevent you from finding greater fulfilment.

With green rays I offer these possibilities for change and growth, especially at the start of a new year, and I bring Ariel, ruler of earth with my sign. Since civilisation was young, this has been the traditional time of earth and re-birth. Your years pass quickly – have you enough to show for them? There will be things you wish were different, and so we bring supporting strength as you set a goal to reach a heart's desire in the coming year – however daunting this may initially seem.

Cassiel, Saturn's ruler, connects to my sign, bolstering your stamina to rise above any challenges, for we angels believe that you can achieve all this and more. The part of the body with which I assist is your knees, and they are linked to acceptance of change. Work with me to increase your confidence and balance as you move steadily towards your new, chosen heart's desire.

DAILY AFFIRMATION WITH NADIEL UNTIL YOUR GOAL IS ACHIEVED:
Nadiel, Nadiel, Nadiel, my goal is to face and conquer any challenges that prevent me from changing my life in the way that I desire. I ask for your loving energy to ground, heal and strengthen me, allowing me to face up to all I need to address. Please help me to strengthen my strengths and overcome my weaknesses until my goal is achieved, in Love and Light, Love and Light, Love and Light.

Aquarius: Cambiel

IF YOUR ZODIAC SIGN IS AQUARIUS: your zodiac guardian angel is Cambiel. Cambiel offers support for your ideals and guides your deep desire to identify true aspirations and ambitions while maintaining integrity and principles. Cambiel's links to the human body are the bones and blood vessels.

Cambiel says:

As the Water Carrier, I also bring with me Ariel and Air, Breath of Life, as well as Uriel, ruler of Uranus and fire. Together, we combine these three vital elements in support of your ideals and aspirations. Masculine Fire of Life cleanses, purifies and empowers you, while feminine Water of Life calms, clarifies and builds your intuition. Both aid you to find the right level in life. Breath of Life lifts your consciousness skywards, bringing spiritual vision so, if you so choose, together we can truly transform many aspects of your life.

As the Age of Aquarius dawns for mankind, I urge you to review your own aspirations for this and the coming years, for as one of your guardians it is I who can assist you to achieve your potential. Be sure you consider the future with the integrity that makes you the person you are, and that you are true to your principles, the anchors of your existence, else your ambition will not result in the inner peace you seek.

The parts of the body with which I assist are your bones and blood vessels. Call on me for bodily strength to drive forward your ambition and help your blood to flow freely, while Breath of Life lifts your thoughts and inspires your imagination in brand new ways for future promise.

DAILY AFFIRMATION WITH CAMBIEL UNTIL YOUR GOAL IS ACHIEVED: *Cambiel, Cambiel, Cambiel, my goal is to grow my vision at this time in all possible ways, resulting in a new, clear and achievable ambition that is true to my principles. Let it be worthy of me, and let me be worthy of this ambition. Please help me to strengthen my strengths and overcome my weaknesses until my goal is achieved, in Love and Light, Love and Light, Love and Light.*

Pisces: Barakiel

IF YOUR ZODIAC SIGN IS PISCES: your zodiac guardian angel is Barakiel (ruler also of Scorpio). Barakiel's loving energy protects your intelligent, compassionate and thoughtful approach to others, yet also brings discernment. Barakiel's link (in Pisces) to the body is the feet.

Barakiel says:

As one of your guardians I observe and commend your loving nature and your depth of emotion, for you have many fine qualities and are capable of great acts of thoughtfulness and sensitivity. Yet your very kindness sometimes means you lack the firmness and necessary discernment when involving yourself in causes or situations. I try to protect you when this may be to your own detriment, such as when the result is extremes of emotion that drain your energy. I counsel you to be careful in your commitments so you do not make these to people who are unworthy of them.

With me I bring Phuel, Lord of the Waters, and he soothes and calms you, even as he helps to clarify what you should do next. He also rules Neptune, the planet in my sign of Pisces. Again, this heals emotional turbulence, bringing greater balance to your life. Phuel's colours of green and aquamarine (for thymus and personal heart chakras) are also the first link between mankind and the angels.

You can cultivate this special angelic link by working with us every day, for your deep compassion resonates with our vibration, and we magnify this with pure Love, returning it to you to aid you to determine and win your heart's desire. The part of the body with which I assist is the feet; surely you wish to walk strongly, yet calmly towards your goals? If so, we are here for you.

DAILY AFFIRMATION WITH BARAKIEL UNTIL YOUR GOAL IS ACHIEVED:
Barakiel, Barakiel, Barakiel, I have set a goal to build the emotional and physical strength necessary to achieve a desire that comes deep from my heart. Your loving protection aids me to form a plan to work calmly but steadfastly towards this desire. Please help me strengthen my strengths and overcome my weaknesses until my goal is achieved, in Love and Light, Love and Light, Love and Light.

VEHUIAH · IELAEL · SITAEL · ELEMIAH · MAHASIAH · LELAHEL · ACHAIAH · CAHETHEL ·
ANIEL · HAAMIAH · REHAEL · IHIAZEL · HAHAEL · MICHAEL · VEVALIAH · IELAHIAH ·

HAZIEL · ALADIAH · LAUVIAH · HAHAIAH · IEIAZEL · MEBAHEL · HARIEL · HAKAMIAH · LEVIAH · CALIEL ·
MIKIEL · ARIEL · ASALIAH · MIHAEL · VEHUEL · GEDAEL · ATAPHIEL · IMRIEL · NANAEL · NILAIHAH ·

TERATHEL · SEEHIAH · REYIEL · ORIEL · LECABEL · VASARIAH · IEHUIAH · LEHACHEL · CHAVAKIAH · MONADIEL
ANNAUEL · MEHEKIEL · DAMABIAH · MENIEL · EIAEL · HABUIAH · ROCHEL · IBAMIAH · HAIAIEL · MUMIAH

MEBAHIAH · POIEL · NEMEMIAH · KELIEL · HARAHEL · MIZRAEL · UMABIEL · IAHHEL ·
KEVEQEL · PAHALIAH · NEITHEL · ISIAEL · MELAHEL · HEHUIAH · NITHAIAH · HAAIAH ·

Identifying your star guardian angel

The Quinary Star Angels' message:

We are the 72 angels governing the firmament, called by some the Quinary Star Angels. We were appointed to this task by the Creator, who gave one of his 72 sacred attributes to each of us, so that no matter what quality or qualities you need to achieve your destiny, it resides in the stars. From the limitless well of the night sky, one or more of our number will come to aid you specifically towards your earthly (heart) and heavenly (soul) aspirations and, if your heart's desire is true, the paths will flow as one. It is for you to identify which of us will aid your quests.

There are several ways to find your star guardian angel. You should also bear in mind that there might be more than one who wishes to guide you, or that the star guardian might change according to your life path and where you are with regard to your Heart Quest or Soul Quest. On the following two pages you will find a list of the 72 Quinary Star Angels of Light. Here are three ways you could identify your personal star guardian angel:

- Read through the names, say twelve at a time, and if you immediately feel something on hearing a name, this will be the angel to invoke. If this happens several times, try to move on to the next step, for verification.
- Ask a friend to read the names slowly to you. To prepare, close your eyes, take some deep breaths of pure, crystalline energy (the energy of the Seraphim) and go into your heart. You will feel the resonance in your heart when you hear the right name (or names).
- Dowse over the list, asking from your heart to be shown your star guardian angel – remember, your heart already knows the answer to this question.

1. *Vehuiah:* angel of the rising sun – a new dawn
2. *Ielael:* angel aiding greater spiritual harmony
3. *Sitael:* angel to help overcome obstacles
4. *Elemiah:* angel of exploration, inner or outer
5. *Mahasiah:* angel aiding heart and spiritual development
6. *Lelahel:* angel of love, art, science and fortune
7. *Achaiah:* angel of patience, calmness and nature's secrets
8. *Cahethel:* angel of abundance for growth
9. *Haziel:* angel aiding spiritual vision
10. *Aladiah:* angel of higher self spiritual development
11. *Lauviah:* angel to retrieve knowledge and learning
12. *Hahaiah:* angel to reveal hidden mysteries
13. *Ieiazel:* angel for guidance on the future
14. *Mebahel:* angel to protect the innocent
15. *Hariel:* angel of animals, arts and sciences
16. *Hakamiah:* angel of general protection (also of France)
17. *Leviah:* angel to help raise spiritual awareness
18. *Caliel:* angel to overcome misfortune
19. *Keveqel:* angel of expanding spiritual consciousness
20. *Pahaliah:* angel guiding universal and unconditional love
21. *Neithel:* angel of mind, body and spirit balance
22. *Isiaiel:* angel of prophecy
23. *Melahel:* angel to show routes to spiritual pathways
24. *Hehuiah:* angel to guide spiritual opportunity
25. *Nithaiah:* angel of poetry and mysticism
26. *Haaiah:* angel of diplomacy and tact
27. *Terathel:* angel of civilisation with liberty
28. *Seehiah:* angel of health and long life
29. *Reyiel:* angel of spiritual truth
30. *Oriel:* angel of true destiny
31. *Lecabel:* angel of the abundance of nature
32. *Vasariah:* angel of divine justice
33. *Iiehuiah:* angel protector of princes and leadership
34. *Lehachel:* angel of gentleness and kindness
35. *Chavakiah:* angel of lower self spiritual development
36. *Monadiel:* angel of spiritual and physical harmony

37. *Aniel*: angel of non-judgemental love
38. *Haamiah*: angel for those who seek truth
39. *Rehael*: angel over health, long life and parental respect
40. *Ihiazel*: angel of spiritual abundance
41. *Hahael*: angel protector of Christianity
42. *Michael*: angel of strength, protection and truth
43. *Vevaliah*: angel of spiritual peace and calmness
44. *Ielahiah*: angel of wise and just decisions
45. *Mikiel*: angel guiding abundant spiritual development
46. *Ariel*: angel of psychic awakening, mystery and magic
47. *Asaliah*: angel of justice and life balance
48. *Mihael*: angel of fidelity and fertility
49. *Vehuel*: angel of spiritual and physical harmony
50. *Gedael*: angel of good fortune
51. *Ataphiel*: angel who helps to hold up the heavens
52. *Imriel*: angel of spiritual eloquence
53. *Nanael*: angel of science and mysticism
54. *Nilaihah*: angel of poetry, peace and solitude
55. *Mebahiah*: angel of love and conception of children
56. *Poiel*: angel of fortune and philosophy
57. *Nememiah*: angel of just causes
58. *Keliel*: angel of spiritual stamina
59. *Harahel*: angel of literary inspiration
60. *Mizrael*: angel of obedience and respect for elders
61. *Umabiel*: angel of astronomy and star guidance
62. *Iahhel*: angel of peace and protection from traumas
63. *Annauel*: angel of spiritual wellbeing
64. *Mehekiel*: angel guiding higher self soul path
65. *Damabiah*: angel over ships and water craft
66. *Meniel*: angel of greater physical and spiritual harmony
67. *Eiael*: angel over energy sciences and long life
68. *Habuiah*: angel of abundance of all growing things
69. *Rochel*: angel of lost things, including divine self
70. *Ibamiah*: angel of gaining a new level of spiritual wisdom
71. *Haiaiel*: angel aiding new spiritual direction
72. *Mumiah*: angel of physical health and wellbeing

Part Three: Angelic Healing for Heart and Soul

Part Three of the Almanac is intended to provide a wealth of useful material, giving intensive guidance on working with angels as effectively as possible to heal and transform life, whether for self (Heart Quest) or for others (Soul Quest). There are nine groups in the angel hierarchy, but remember there is no group with whom you cannot connect (even Seraphim) if you approach this from your heart. The purpose of this section is to aid you to pinpoint what you need to find wholeness in life with rainbows and Love, geometry and Light. Then, if possible, to guide others to find the Way of Love and Light.

Essene angelology is about finding harmony with angels. Invoking angels to help you heal can actually change your body's chemistry, raising your own level of vibration, and this is ongoing. As you complete a level of the Heart Quest, your own higher heart flower opens and fills with compassion and non-judgemental love, allowing the Soul Quest to begin. After working at this you may return to the Heart Quest at a new, higher vibration level, and so the harmony of your heart and soul journey continues towards the Abyss of Light.

COLOUR/ELEMENTAL HEALING

The first priority addressed through Heart Quest is the Love Factor: to self-heal and take the key step to open the flower of unconditional love within your higher heart. This means working with your guardians (and other angels) on self/life, and using colour healing to help clear and balance your chakras so that you can move towards achieving true heart's desires. There are healing colours of creation to aid with this. The four elements: earth, water, air and fire are also vital healing tools. Working with colour and elemental angels is paramount to physical healing and Heart Quest, and also offers alchemy for spiritual growth to aid your Soul Quest. In my book *The Angel Quest of the Heart*, I tell my own autobiographical story of this process, and of how you, too, can find true self at the heart of Melchisadec's Seven-Turn Labyrinth.

LIGHT FACTOR AND SOUL QUEST: SACRED GEOMETRY AND ASCENSION

The Light Factor starts with the fifth element: cosmic spirit, the ray of Seraphiel, Ruler of the Seraphim Creation Angels. At the vibration beyond the Star Gate this is white diamond Angelic (or Metatronic) Light, and you need to understand its relationship to sacred geometry and how and why it is accessed for All. Sacred geometry is the form that Angelic Light takes in this universe and by 'plugging' ourselves back into the geometry we can attain (or regain) Unity Consciousness. In turn this can lead us to Personal Heart Ascension, which then aids Planetary Ascension. Personal Heart Ascension is the start of transforming back to gem (Divine) self. Through these and other Seraphim secrets you can fast track your own Soul Quest to Oneness with All, and you will then realise that the true Quest (and remit of all of us) is to serve by helping others to find the Way of Love and Light.

You may be following both quests at once, or majoring on one or the other, the choice is yours. Wherever you start, the object of the Heart Quest is to open the higher heart flower (although there are many levels after this) while that of the Soul Quest is to achieve Personal Heart Ascension. This enables you to work with the Seraphim towards aiding Mother Earth and Planetary Ascension.

The Heart and Soul Quests

Seraphiel, Ruler of Seraphim Creation Angels, says:
*At this important time in your and Mother Earth's destiny, and as
the focus of many moves towards Ascension, I invite you to join me
on the next stage of the Way of Love and Light. You will have
reached this way station after guidance from Raphael, Gabriel,
Melchisadec and Pistis Sophia and, if you absorbed their wisdom,
you will be working with angels every day. Next, we explore the Love
Factor, as it relates to your Heart Quest to self-heal and open the
higher heart flower of unconditional Love. For truly this is the key to
the Light Factor and Soul Quest. When you grasp that it is Light
that empowers, while Love nourishes the spirit, together we shall
encompass the crystalline stars.*

The Heart Quest is a process of self-healing and opening the heart
flower. When calling on angels and focusing on their special remits, you
will begin to sense their presence more easily. I stress that angels cannot
overcome our challenges for us, but they can support us to overcome
them, and they share our joy when we move on, with a view to self-
healing and reaching a new level of vibration, opening the higher heart
flower – magenta – with unconditional Love.

The purpose of Soul Quest is to reach through the 44:44 Angel Star
Gate and draw back Angelic Light, to turn the higher heart flower to
crystalline form. This is how we start to transform into gem or Divine
self, by pledging to aid others to find the Way, and filling Mother Earth
with Love and Light. Again, the act of doing this raises our own
spiritual consciousness to higher and higher levels, because when we
use our skills to help All we receive manifold Love and Light in return.

How the Way of Love and Light leads to harmony and balance

THE LOVE FACTOR: OPENING THE HIGHER HEART FLOWER

The future ascended reality of earth is where she returns to her former vibration, that she held before the various falls. However, we can live this reality now, working towards Unity Consciousness by opening crown and higher heart. This is only attained through unconditional love, hence the Love Factor. First we must self-heal with Seraphiel's twelve colours of Creation, starting with traditional rainbow colours of red, orange, yellow, green, blue, indigo-purple, violet. The next two are turquoise (thymus) and magenta (higher heart flower), deeper angelic links that need to be seen and sensed through heart and crown. Then Raphael's gold and Gabriel's silver energies which, as you know from the Caduceus (see page 28), bring third-eye balance. Finally, when we truly understand unconditional (non-judgemental) Love from crown and heart, Metatron and Shekinah offer white-silver and white-gold, until with Seraphiel we access the white-diamond Angelic Light. Then we reach the point where duality no longer exists, only Unity, going through the 44:44 Angel Star Gate (called by Hermes Trismegistos 'the eye of the needle').

This is a rainbow journey about what you personally need to self-heal lower self, heart and higher self, and move through gold and silver towards diamond. There are many levels of healing; each new level raises new issues to deal with. Using the wisdom of angelology you can identify and remove chakra blocks with a host of angels who help you to bring in all the healing potential of colours plus Breath of Life, Fire of Life and Water of Life. The key step is to open the deep pink/magenta higher heart flower, completing a level of Heart Quest and commencing Soul Quest, the diamond path to your Personal Heart Ascension.

Fire of Life: red, orange, yellow

MEDITATION FOR HEALING AND INTEGRATING LOWER SELF

Determine any specific healing need(s) for lower self. Choose to work either with the chakra flowers, or the three Sacred Symbols (see page 221), or both. If you have crystals hold them in your left hand to programme during this meditation.

Invoke Camael, Uriel and Raphael to assist you for your highest good. Then close your eyes and take deep breaths of pure white energy, breathing out all frustrations until you start to feel relaxed.

Within you are three lower self flowers in bud: root – rose; sacral – tiger lily; solar – sunflower. Imagine that the three angels are pouring a stream of radiant red, orange and yellow Fire of Life, interwoven and sparkling, into your crown.

Now with every in-breath, Light flows down and into the flowers; each one unfolds; their colour rays travel to your heart, deepening your angelic link.

From your heart make these colour affirmations:

With power of red I am empowered (or other Camael qualities)

With power of orange I am transformed (or other Uriel qualities)

With power of yellow I ignite sun within (or other Raphael qualities).

With power of your will send Fire of Life throughout lower self, releasing blocks, purifying and bringing strength and vitality.

Visualise the three sacred symbols within your lower self and ask the combined energy to flow to heal your heart.

As you breathe out Fire of Life, it creates an aura of red, orange and yellow in the shape of wings, surrounding you with powerful new resolve.

Ask all three angels to help you lock in this resolve, remembering to thank them for their loving assistance.

ENERGY CENTRE HEALING FOCUS

BASE	RED Ruby, garnet, carnelian	Camael: Courage, justice, energy, empowerment, forgiveness, balancing and linking root chakra with heart.
SACRAL	ORANGE Amber, sunstone, carnelian	Uriel: Creativity, sexuality, innovation, transformation, balancing and linking sacral chakra with heart.
SOLAR	YELLOW GOLD Citrine, diamond, quartz	Raphael: Will and intent, decision and action. Heal/integrate lower self to move focus to personal heart.

Water of Life: green, turquoise, pink

MEDITATION FOR HEALING AND INTEGRATING HEART AND THYMUS
Optionally determine any specific healing need(s) for heart/thymus.
If you have crystals hold them in your left (universal taking) hand to programme during this meditation.

Invoke Haniel, Phuel and Gabriel to assist for your highest good.
Close your eyes and take deep breaths of pure white energy, breathing out all your frustrations until you start to feel relaxed.

Within you is the heart flower (it starts as a bud): a water lily flower on an emerald green lily leaf.

The three angels start pouring a stream of cool green, silver and turquoise Water of Life, interwoven and shimmering, into your crown. Now with every in-breath, Light flows down and into your heart chakra. As this starts to heal your angelic links will deepen.

From your heart make the colour affirmations you need:
With power of green I heal my heart (or other Haniel qualities)
With power of turquoise and silver I find emotional balance
(or other Phuel/Gabriel qualities)
With power of magenta I open my higher heart flower (Haniel).

With power of your will send Water of Life through heart and thymus, cleansing away blocks in these chakras, bringing calmness and balance.

Try to visualise the lily bud opening and the deep pink lily flower beginning to open in your higher heart (this is between solar and thymus chakras).

You may have to work at this but you will achieve it if you try!

As you breathe out Water of Life it creates an aura of silvery turquoise and green, with pink, in the shape of wings, surrounding you with calm resolve.

Ask all three angels to help you lock-in this resolve, remembering to thank them for their loving assistance.

Energy centre healing focus

PERSONAL HEART	GREEN AND SILVER Rose quartz, emerald, moonstone, selenite	Haniel: love, beauty, compassion (including for self). Gabriel: hopes, dreams, aspirations, intuition. Healing personal heart, linking heart to will and mind.
THYMUS	GREEN AND TURQUOISE Malachite, aquamarine	Phuel: emotional tranquillity and balance. Later: Creating heart grail filled with Water of Life.
HIGHER HEART	PINK-MAGENTA Alexandrite, tourmaline	After personal heart is healed, Water of Life opens higher heart flower: heart bridge to higher self and All.

Breath of Life: blue, indigo, violet

MEDITATION FOR HEALING AND INTEGRATING HIGHER SELF

- Optionally determine any specific healing need(s) for higher self.
- If you have crystals hold them in your left (universal taking) hand to programme during this meditation.
- Invoke Michael, Zadkiel, Ariel and Melchisadec to aid with this.
- Close your eyes and take deep breaths of pure white energy, breathing out all your frustrations until you start to feel relaxed.
- Within you are three higher self flowers (in bud): throat – blue pansy, third eye – indigo-blue iris, crown – violet crocus.
- The four angels start pouring a magical stream of Breath of Life, comprised of shades of blue, purple and violet, into your crown.
- Now with every in-breath, Light flows down and into the flowers; each one unfolds; their colour rays flow to your heart, deepening your angelic links.
- From your heart make the colour affirmations you need:
  With power of blue I find truth and freedom (or other appropriate Michael qualities)
  With power of indigo I retrieve my ancient wisdom (or Zadkiel qualities)
  With power of violet I transmute illusion from my life and grow spiritually (Melchisadec) or *I pierce the veils between worlds* (Ariel)
  As the Sacred Eden Tree I am One Heart with All (Metatron/Shekinah).
- With power of will and heart send Breath of Life throughout lower self, blowing away any residues of blocks and filling you with Light and air. (Optionally: visualise the Macrocosm star in your third eye, the Microcosm star on your crown.)
- As you breathe out Breath of Life it creates Light wings of beautiful shades of blue and violet, showing the universe your desire for spiritual growth.
- Ask all the angels to help you continue this path, remembering to thank them.

Energy Centre Healing Focus

THROAT	SKY BLUE AND INDIGO Sapphire, lapis lazuli, sodalite	After personal heart is healed. Michael: strength, protection and truth. Zadkiel: abundance, wisdom, kindness, integrity.
THIRD EYE	PURPLE AND VIOLET Amethyst, sugilite	Ariel: mystery, magic, psychic development. Melchisadec: spiritual fulfilment.
ABOVE CROWN/ BELOW ROOT	This is the step before white- gold and white-silver (see next pages)	Metatron and Shekinah, Twin Guardians of the Sacred Eden Tree: Portal to 44:44 Angel Star Gate after personal heart is healed.

Gold and white-gold solar balance

MEDITATION TO CHANNEL THE SUN: MASCULINE BALANCE IN CHAKRAS

- Invoke Raphael, Shekinah and Metatron to assist with their Love.
- Close your eyes and take deep breaths of pure white energy, breathing out any and all your frustrations until you are filled to the brim and you feel that you are also breathing out white energy.
- Within you, see the Caduceus, with just the solar snake of wisdom entwining it, as your focus is golden balance.
- Also see all the chakra flowers, fully opened and glowing after the colour healing you've done for each.
- Raphael pours a spiral stream of golden solar rays into your crown.
- With the next in-breath, see this solar energy flow down your spine.
- Tell Shekinah you pledge to ground and manifest this energy in Mother Earth's heart for earthly kingdom and All Below.
- Next bring the solar energy back through root chakra, and focus on taking it around the Caduceus within (anti-clockwise) balancing masculine aspects of each chakra to third eye, then return it to Raphael and sun. Each flower will be enclosed in a bright gold aura of healing and balance.
- From your heart, ask if you are ready to move towards crown, and Unity. If you are, Shekinah will send her white-gold energy from below through earthly kingdom to your heart, helping to open your higher heart flower.
- Empower and magnify the energy with unconditional Love and send it to your crown, where Metatron takes it through the Star Gate to Above. In gratitude, from Below and Above you will receive white-gold in crown.
- As you breathe out, sense rainbows and the energy of the Sacred Eden Tree around you.
- Thank all the angels for their loving assistance.

Energy centre healing focus

THIRD-EYE BALANCE	GOLDEN SOLAR RAYS	Raphael: masculine balance in all chakras to third eye.
MOVING TO CROWN CHAKRA	WHITE-GOLD RAYS	Shekinah: moving to white-gold below root, linking to higher heart, stepping out of duality into Unity Consciousness.

Silver and white-silver lunar balance

MEDITATION TO CHANNEL THE MOON: FEMININE BALANCE IN CHAKRAS

Invoke Gabriel, Metatron and Shekinah to assist you with their Love.

Close your eyes and take deep breaths of pure white energy, breathing out any and all your frustrations until you are filled with positive energy and you are also breathing out white energy.

Within you, see the Caduceus, with just the lunar snake of wisdom entwining it, as your focus is on silver balance.

Also see all the chakra flowers, fully opened and glowing after the colour healing you've done for each.

Gabriel pours a spiral stream of silver lunar rays into your crown.

With the next in-breath, see this lunar energy flow down your spine.

Tell Shekinah you pledge to ground and manifest this energy in Mother Earth's heart and earthly kingdom.

Next bring the lunar energy back through your root chakra, and focus on taking it around the Caduceus within (clockwise) balancing feminine aspects of each chakra to third eye, then return it to Gabriel and moon.

Each flower's heart will turn silvery, showing healing and balance.

From your heart, ask if you are ready to move towards crown, and Unity Consciousness.

If you are, Metatron will send white-silver energy from above, through the Star Gate down through your crown to your heart and heart flower.

Empower and magnify the energy with unconditional Love and send it to Shekinah below your root chakra, who returns it for you to send to Metatron.

In gratitude, from Below and Above you will receive white in crown.

As you breathe out, pastel silvery rainbows will form around you and you may sense the Sacred Eden Tree energy.

Thank all the angels for their loving assistance.

ENERGY CENTRE HEALING FOCUS

THIRD-EYE BALANCE	SILVER LUNAR RAYS	Gabriel: feminine balance in all chakras to third eye.
CROWN CHAKRA	WHITE-SILVER RAYS	Metatron: moving to white-silver at crown, linking to higher heart, stepping out of duality into Unity Consciousness.

Accessing diamond Angelic Light

MEDITATION TO CHANNEL THE DIAMOND RAY OF ANGELIC LIGHT INTO CROWN AND HIGHER HEART

- Invoke Seraphiel to assist you for your highest good.
- Close your eyes and take deep in-breaths of pure white energy, releasing all your frustrations until you feel you are breathing out white energy.
- Within you, see all the chakra flowers, fully opened, healed and balanced with gold and silver, including the green/magenta higher heart flower of unconditional Love.
- Now the diamond ray (highest vibration of Angelic Light) descends in spirals, like an oval DNA strand, from beyond the 44:44 Angel Star Gate. From your heart, tell Seraphiel your intention is to access this to help All.
- Seraphiel causes dazzling diamond energy to spiral into your crown.
- With the next in-breath, breathe the diamond ray down to your open higher heart flower, the angelic link is made between crown and heart.
- You may sense the flower becoming crystalline, this is the start of your own heart regaining the vibration of gem (Divine) self.
- Empower and magnify the energy with unconditional Love and return it to Seraphiel to be transmitted to All in this universe and even beyond.
- From your linked heart and crown make these affirmations:
  With power of the diamond ray I pursue my Soul Quest
  With power of the diamond ray I seek Unity Consciousness
  With power of the diamond ray I pledge to help others find the Way.
- As you breathe out, send diamond spiral wings around you – your link to the Seraphim Star Angels of Creation.
- You now have an Angelic Light wing print of your own.
- Thank Seraphiel for his loving assistance.

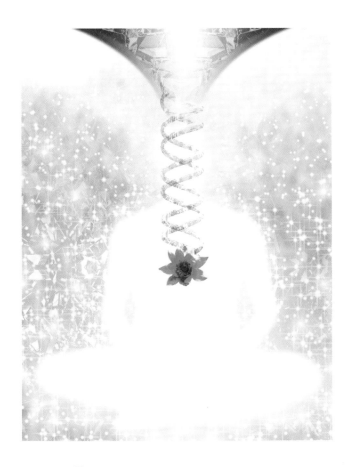

ENERGY CENTRE HEALING FOCUS

CROWN CHAKRA WHEN LINKED TO HIGHER HEART CHAKRA	DIAMOND RAY OF COSMIC SPIRIT/ ANGELIC LIGHT, CONTAINING ALL COLOURS OF CREATION	Seraphiel: Ruler of the Seraphim Creation Angels: Highest of all angelic spheres and the Ascension Angels. (Other Seraphim angels may also assist.)

213

How the Way of Love and Light leads to Ascension

THE LIGHT FACTOR: SACRED GEOMETRY AND ASCENSION:
First you must understand the two spectrums of Light. Angelic Light (Metatronic) is pure, unfallen and complete. It is the Divine harmonic of Light comprising all twelve colours of creation, a white diamond light vibration that we once had, and to which earth and all sentient life shall ultimately re-ascend. This is the Light vibration on the other side of the 44:44 Angel Star Gate, pictured opposite. The other spectrum is the Oritronic or fallen Light, creating a polarity world of Light and dark in which we currently find ourselves. This is the fear-driven reality with which we are surrounded on a daily basis. It is actually all happening, but we can choose not to focus on it too much or energise it.

One way to access the 44:44 Angel Star Gate and traverse it is via the Sacred Eden Tree of Metatron and Shekinah, but *only* through the open higher heart, as it is the flower of unconditional Love within it that allows this next step to happen. We pledge within our own higher heart to let go of the half-light (Oritronic) spectrum and work in the pure Angelic Light spectrum, to aid self-healing and to help heal All.

It is purely and simply a matter of choice and free will combined with a heart full of Love and Light. If we choose to work at this level and are capable of holding this vibration we can, and we can go on from there to achieve Personal Heart Ascension. If we do this, the higher heart flower will transform into the Flower of Life healing fractal, though once more this is only the start of moving to gem (Divine) self, and the angels assist us in this supremely important work. In fact they have said that the potential for us is always there, on our timelines, waiting for the time when we choose the Way.

Introduction to Ascension

What is Ascension? Many of us have heard of that ancient document, the Mayan calendar, which appears to end in 2012. What does this mean to us and our loved ones? As guided by Seraphiel, ruler of the Seraphim angels, I shall explain what I believe is the true meaning.

Let me start by saying that I do not feel it means that our world will end in 2012. Instead, we are being given a chance to try to help Mother Earth, to bring about a huge influx of positive Love and Light energy by 2012 to effect a change towards a more peaceful earth. So do not be fearful, as this constricts the soul and creates negative energy within. I believe we each have a Soul Quest that we are now being guided to undertake. If we do so we can potentially create a vast reservoir of Love and Light energy within our own hearts, and send it to Mother Earth's heart to restore her fallen spiritual vibration – a return to Eden. This is symbolised by the Sacred Eden Tree, the archetype of all trees on earth, that you saw and perhaps worked with in Part One of this book. The Sacred Eden Tree represents the Circle of Life and stores the Divine blueprint (Adam Kadmon: perfect man).

All is energy in vibration, and once earth's own vibration was much higher and more spiritual. Our true origins are lost in the mists of time – were we, as some suggest, seeded by extra-terrestrials as a slave race, symbolised by Adam and Eve and resulting in the first Fall from Eden? We can't be sure what happened 500,000 years ago. But we can be sure that once we existed in Unity Consciousness or Oneness – the Angelic Light connection from the heart through Love to All. And we also know that by mankind's own actions, much of this world is now in duality, polarised between peace and war, dark and light, masculine and feminine. For most of mankind the ancient spiritual wisdom, sense of harmony, balance, crown connection with All, has been lost.

How has this duality come about? We are led to believe that the first civilisation, recorded by glyphs on stone, was Mu (also known as Lemuria) in the Pacific. Colonel James Churchward pieced together Mu's story in India in 1868 after he became interested in a temple that had in its vaults many ancient stone tablets estimated at more than 25,000 years old. Churchward, an army intelligence officer, gradually deciphered their story; they tell of the motherland that perished through volcanic eruptions around 13,000 years ago with most of her 64 million inhabitants, leaving only a few remnants such as Hawaii, Easter Island and the Solomons. Lemuria was a civilisation in physical and spiritual harmony, with her inhabitants living and respecting the connection between earth, sky, and all sentient life forms.

The glyphs relate that before Mu went down, colonies and kingdoms were established in India, Egypt and South America. In fact Mayan glyphs in Yucatan, Mexico, are exactly the same as Lemurian ones. Atlantis flourished simultaneously, until mankind's greed encouraged manipulation of crystal power for personal gain instead of for the good of All. Then Atlantis and mankind fell again from grace. These falls meant that the original pure diamond Angelic Light vibration of Mother Earth and her sentient life forms descended, becoming denser, darker and polarised, becoming an incomplete form of half Light (Oritronic) in which much of what happens today in this world exists.

Ascension is the journey back. The angels have withheld certain secrets held in trust for 2,000 years, until we were ready to understand their meaning and importance. Now, they are saying that by coming back into Oneness, starting at a personal level, through opening the higher heart, we can begin this Ascension journey. Ascension means returning to the complete or white-diamond Angelic Light of Oneness that is still there, on the other side of the 44:44 Star Gate awaiting our connection, through heart and crown.

217

Sacred geometry

Seraphiel says:

Sacred geometry is the link between the universes within (Microcosm) and without (Macrocosm) – a tracery of crystalline Angelic Light from my celestial spheres directly into crown and heart. If your higher heart says you are worthy of it, I can encode you with this geometry. This opens the Way for Metatron and Shekinah to take you through the Star Gate to access pure Angelic Light, and so to share Seraphim secrets in Unity Consciousness, as we, the Creation Angels, fill your heart and soul with our diamond rays.

You could say that the universe is a pattern or matrix, a kind of celestial jigsaw constructed from sacred geometry shapes, from which we have become separated due to the falls in vibration. In fact everything in the universe, including us, is constructed in accordance with this sacred geometry. This is one of the reasons why certain music or art that has been created according to these laws is particularly pleasing to the eye and resonant to the ear, for in fact it communicates directly with heart and soul. Another way to look at attaining Unity Consciousness is to say that we need to 'plug ourselves back in to the sacred geometry'.

Apart from the supreme importance of the Love Factor, you need to understand sacred geometry of Angelic Light (the Light Factor) in order to realise how to reach through the Star Gate and then how Personal Ascension may perhaps be achieved. Geometry is the form behind all nature, including mankind, and also works in conjunction with angelic numerology (see pages 56 and 86). What happens when you work with the sacred geometry is rather dependent upon where you are on your Heart or Soul Quests. The more you have worked with angelic energy, the more you will be taken forward by the angels.

In Part Two, on page 167, I give the first of two important joining exercises that the angels have shown me. The simple but effective exercise with Pistis Sophia aids Heart Quest by linking your heart to All Above and All Below through Star Fire and Sacred Flame: a first step to inner peace. This is an exercise that I personally still do every day, and I follow this immediately with Seraphiel's Star Gate joining (below) which relates more to Soul Quest. It is as if these exercises re-pledge daily my desire to keep following both quests as well as to assist others to find the Way of Love and Light. You can choose to do one or both according to how they feel to you.

THE STAR GATE JOINING TO ALL
Seraphiel's stretch – to touch the 44:44 Angel Star Gate and draw Angelic Light through it and down into your heart.

If you worked with Metatron and Shekinah and the Sacred Eden Tree in Part One, now try Seraphiel's joining exercise to see if the Star Gate is calling you. Feel the pure tingling energy flowing down from the Seraphim Creation Angels into your heart.

* Stretch both your arms as high as possible above your head and make yourself into the five-point star of Microcosm (see page 222).
* Say: *Seraphiel, Seraphiel, Seraphiel, Metatron, Metatron, Metatron, Shekinah, Shekinah, Shekinah, as the Eden Tree I stand with my roots in the heart of Mother Earth and I reach with crown towards the Star Gate, drawing Angelic Light to my heart to heal and enfold Mother Earth. Let me be a pure channel for this energy in service of Love and Light.*
* Feel the energy flow down your arms and into your heart. Sense the heart flower and its power, for as it opens (usually with six petals), this is the beginning. As you move to higher levels of vibration the sacred geometry changes and the number of petals will increase.

FIBONACCI CURVES, SPIRALS AND RIGHT ANGLES

Spirals are all around us – even our galaxy is a spiral. Man is constructed in the phi ratio of 1.618 (the Golden Mean or Divine Proportion), as are many buildings that please the eye such as the Parthenon in Athens and the Great Pyramid of Giza. The equivalent in nature is the Fibonacci spiral. This is a numerical sequence starting with 1, 2, 3 and continuing by adding the previous two numbers together – so 5, 8, 13 and so on. When plotted in a graph (below left) this may be show as straight right angle lines (masculine) or curves (feminine). This spiral is found in shells, sunflowers and many other forms in nature. I have found Fibonacci spirals to be instruments of self-healing and balance, starting with those that entwine the Caduceus. We can learn to work directly with solar and lunar spirals with the aid of Raphael and Gabriel, and then move on to connect higher heart and crown with Seraphiel's diamond Angelic Light spirals.

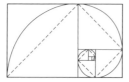 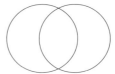

CIRCLES, SPHERES AND VESICA PISCIS

The first geometric form to consider is the sphere. This represents God/Goddess/the Creator and also the void. The Creator came out of the void to create the first sphere or cell, and from this the miracle of all life unfolded. It also symbolises the sun and the full moon – the solar and lunar (masculine and feminine) balance within us. Two overlapping spheres create Vesica Piscis (above right), the (third) area of exact and perfect balance between the two – important in Light Factor geometry.

The five Platonic solids

The five primal shapes shown below, left to right, are the tetrahedron (fire), cube (earth), octahedron (air), icosahedron (water) and dodecahedron (Spirit). Plato identified these five primal shapes as the key to Life and the universe. As the following pages will show, each shape has a direct relevance to healing.

The three original sacred symbols

The sphere, pyramid and cube are known as the original sacred symbols, and can be used for healing lower self. The mandala shown below can also be used in this way, with the meditation on page 202.

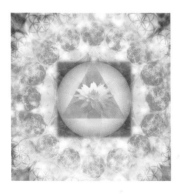

Microcosm and Macrocosm: key healing symbols

Below you can see the traditional representation of the five-pointed (penta) star of Microcosm (man's search for God and raising of spiritual consciousness) and the six-pointed (hexa) star of Macrocosm (All That Is) in perfection.

Microcosm is the universe within, while Macrocosm is the universe without. Everything that is Macrocosm exists in the heart, and vice versa. We can view a five-pointed star (Microcosm) also as a five-petal flower or a six-pointed star (Macrocosm) as a six-petal flower (heart of Seed of Life and Flower of Life). Straight lines are broadly equated with the masculine and curves with the feminine.

When the symbols are in the feminine petal form we can view them in special ways. The five-petal flower can be seen as representing the raising of spiritual consciousness through the Alchemy angels of the elements, an opportunity offered to you through working with these angels in Part One of this book. On the five-petal flower, clockwise, the top petal is Spirit, next petal water, bottom right is earth, bottom left is fire, upper left is air. On the six-petal flower, the petals link to the Sacred Seven Angels. They symbolise, from the top and clockwise: hope, courage, truth, wisdom, beauty and harmony. When a circle is drawn around the flower to use it in the heart (see page 227) then this circle itself denotes healing and Oneness.

I feel that straight-line geometry equates with Light and the curved geometry with Love. Certainly, both options must be built into our Light work, as only by doing this are we reconciling the two and bringing them into balance, masculine/feminine, gold/silver, physical and spiritual. This is when Light starts to flow out from the heart open to Love and we move from third-eye balance as our higher heart links to crown.

These symbols can be used to empower healing and are probably the most important geometric shapes to understand and to use with regard to attainment of both Heart and Soul Quests.

SELF HEALING
* Microcosm (expansion to next level) and Macrocosm (completion of a level) feature in all healing.
* At every healing level (a six vibration) you will be presented with karmic challenges.
* Each challenge you face and surmount offers an opportunity to:
  Demonstrate that you trust and surrender in your unfolding life path
  Gain certain wisdom that enables spiritual development.
* Thus reach the next level of self-mastery (a five vibration).

THE DANCE OF SIX AND FIVE
We need healing on many levels, to remove blocks incurred in this and perhaps hundreds of other lifetimes. Each time we complete a level, when we are ready, new levels of vibration will be offered to us, always moving us onwards and upwards. The equation continues in the same way each time. In other words the six of self-healing is needed at every level you reach, before you move on with five to further expand spiritual consciousness. The relationship between five and six is like an eternal dance between the two numbers that takes place along the Way of Love and Light.

STAR TETRAHEDRON:
THE BASIC GEOMETRY OF ASCENSION

Whether you are working on Heart or Soul Quest, this is an important geometry to understand. The first Platonic solid is the tetrahedron (fire), the element that can connect us to Spirit. If you add a second tetrahedron, pointing downwards, join the two and pivot the centre around, it becomes a star tetrahedron. This is the 3D version of the 2D six-point star of Macrocosm (geometric shape of perfection and completion). As you can see below, in 3D it has eight points plus a ninth, invisible central point. The nine points represent nine chakras – three sets of three: lower self (root, sacral and solar), heart (personal heart, higher heart and thymus) and higher self (throat, third eye and crown). Thus this equates to three times Hermes Trismegistos' sacred Law of Three.

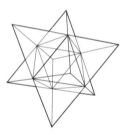

To heal these nine chakras (Heart Quest work) see earlier in this section, starting on page 202. The nine-chakra system and star tetrahedron together form the basic geometry of healing and also form the healing geometry from which the Angelic Light body (also known as the Merkaba), tool of Personal Heart Ascension, can be created. This is the first part of the Soul Quest, and with the help of the angels I teach how this can be constructed and filled with Love and Light.

In ancient Greece, as previously mentioned, the tetra form was fire and the next Platonic form, the cube, was earth. Both the tetrahedron and the star tetrahedron fit exactly into the cube (six faces), therefore the two are interrelated. Earth is of course our foundation, while the upward tetrahedron of Fire of Life (masculine) takes matter (us) up to meet Spirit. The downward tetrahedron to me associates with Water of Life (feminine), and is Spirit connecting down to matter (us).

In my view the star tetrahedron is the predominantly masculine form of the geometry of eight in 3D. Below (left) is the 2D form which is, of course, Macrocosm. The 2D Macrocosm form (six straight lines) is balanced by the six circles of the feminine geometric form of Seed of Life (below right). Both are geometries that we can use for healing. On the next pages we examine the Flower of Life and its potential as a healing fractal that we can send out to benefit All.

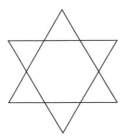 

FLOWER OF LIFE, A GEOMETRY SYMBOL OF HIGHER HEART

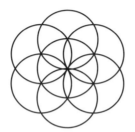 

Six overlapping circles form the Seed of Life (above left), heart of Flower of Life (above right), though in reality they are spheres. Broadly speaking, curves are a more feminine form of the geometry, while the straight lines are masculine (though each still has to balance with the other). As we plug ourselves back into the universal sacred geometry matrix, we need both forms of the sacred geometry in balance within us. You must also understand that the Flower of Life is not just a pattern, nor even just a fractal. It is the first complete, healing harmonic of pure energy that can generate and spin out infinite versions of itself at any size without ever diminishing its power in any way. This means that when we hold it within our higher heart we can even send it to our cells.

We can send the Flower of Life out to heal Mother Earth, universe – in fact we can will and intend it to heal All. It is the very act of being ready and willing to do this that returns magnified healing to our own hearts, so that if we continue our Soul Quest until we achieve heart Ascension with angels, the flower can become crystalline.

We are greatly aided on our Soul Quest by choosing to become part of the Sacred Eden Tree, and channelling energy from beyond the 44:44

Angel Star Gate into our heart flower. Because we are One with the tree, through our heart we can also manifest pure unfallen energy continuously to aid Mother Earth's Ascension and aid all her sentient life forms.

HEALING HEART WITH A FLOWER SYMBOL

When working on heart healing, you may find it easier to start by using a sphere of Phuel's healing Water of Life containing a flower such as a lily or rose. If you visualise this in geometric terms it becomes the six-petal flower of Macrocosm. As I said previously the six petals and circle symbolise hope, courage, truth, wisdom, beauty, harmony and healing, taking the essence of the Sacred Seven Angels right into your heart to support your own healing needs. Then you can aim to transform this simple geometry into the Seed of Life, willing and intending it next to grow into the Flower of Life itself, as this is the first powerful, healing fractal we can really use to benefit self and others.

Remember that what is within you (Microcosm) is also outside of you (Macrocosm) and vice versa. Therefore you can send this healing fractal to your own cells, as well as viewing it as Macrocosm and sending it out to help heal All That Is. The mandala on page 221 (for healing lower self) also shows the open higher heart flower and Flower of Life fractals emanating from the heart, as when lower self is healed the next step and focus moves directly to healing heart.

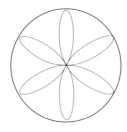

Cabbala Tree of Life connection

The Cabbala Tree of Life grew out of the Merkaba mysticism of Judaism and is said to show the secret laws of God the unknowable. A single ray of Light burst from the Creator, travelling down in a zig-zag, like a lightning bolt, and from this came nine other lights. Thus were formed the ten spheres or Sephiroth, and, where appropriate, corresponding planets. This was the order: Kether (God/God in man), Chokmah (Divine wisdom), Binah (Saturn), Chesed (Jupiter), Geburah (Mars), Tiphareth (the sun), Netzach (Venus), Hod (Mercury), Yesod (the moon) and Malkuth (Earthly Kingdom and God in woman). There are 22 paths connecting the ten Sephiroth together, one for each of the Hebrew alphabet letters (see Malachim on page 236). The Tree of Life is also the Sacred Eden Tree, sometimes being depicted as an actual tree, upside down or right way up, as in the end 'as Above so Below and as Below so Above'. As you will have seen, the Sacred Eden Tree image in the end becomes a circle or sphere – the Circle of Life or All That Is.

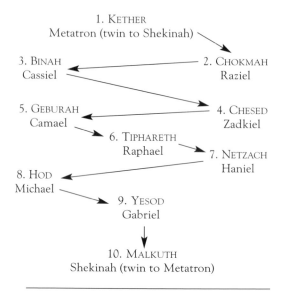

The Cabbala can also be shown in a three-column format and this can be fitted into the Flower of Life fractal, showing its connection to the healing wisdom. In this format, reading downwards, the left column (Binah, Geburah and Hod) is equated with masculine balance (initially to third eye). The right hand column (Chokmah, Chesed, Netzach) is feminine balance (to third eye), and the middle column Kether (Creator/Oneness), Tiphareth (healing/sun balance), Yesod (healing/moon balance), Malkuth (Earthly Kingdom) symbolises Oneness as higher heart links to crown and All.

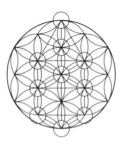

THE SOUL JOURNEY AND ANGELS LINKED TO THE TEN SEPHIROTH

The top and bottom Sephiroth/spheres, respectively, are Metatron: Crown/Kether/the Creator, our soul journey goal, and Metatron's twin: Shekinah: Root/Malkuth or Earthly Kingdom, i.e. our starting point. The Creator's route travelled downwards, as shown on the previous page. According to Cabbala wisdom our own soul journey starts from earthly kingdom with Shekinah and follows the route back through the spheres to Metatron (Light) at crown. I believe we can move far on this journey if we have achieved the opening of our higher heart through Love. Our soul's progress in this lifetime depends on how we live our life and the knowledge and wisdom gained; in other words our ascent is through enlightenment.

Of the other eight Sephiroth/spheres in this Sephiroth Tree, the seven equated with planets are therefore ruled by the Sacred Seven Angels with whom you have already become familiar in Part Two of this book.

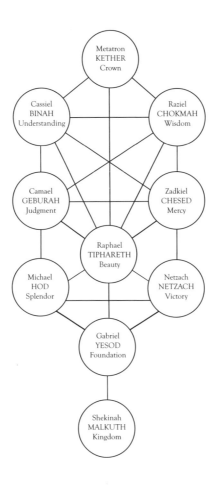

The angel usually shown for Chokmah is Raziel (though in ancient documents this sphere is sometimes given to other angels). Raziel (whose name means 'secret of God') is termed the chief of Supreme Mysteries. He is credited with writing *The Book of the Angel Raziel* in which all celestial and earthly knowledge is set down for mankind. Other angels such as Jophiel and Sandalphon are sometimes shown for this Sephiroth. Jophiel is the guardian angel of finding our true role in life and Sandalphon is the guardian angel of prayer. All these angels (and others) are enabling us to retrieve high vibration energies right now to aid Ascension. In my view, however, as this is Divine wisdom, perhaps the sphere should now be that of Pistis Sophia.

Another way of looking at the ten spheres and three columns is as a representation of the Adam Kadmon – our Divine self in perfect form and balance. According to Drunvalo Melchezedek, the three columns are also connected with the Platonic solids: the left column of masculine balance would be linked to earth (cube) and fire (tetrahedron including its form as star tetrahedron); the middle column is energy in balance – the one containing the sphere (Creator and void) and the octahedron (air) connected with Michael and Divine Truth. The right-hand column of the Cabbala in this format is feminine energy linked to water (icosahedron) and Spirit (dodecahedron). The dodecahedron, when star points are added to each face, is the Platonic solid linked to Seraphiel. The Platonic solids have always been, and (especially now) are being taught in Mystery Schools, including my own Blue Star Angels Mystery School Courses. In my view this is extremely important wisdom (particularly the dodecahedron of Spirit). It relates directly to our ability to send out healing holograms or fractals to All, even along timelines. Understanding and working with this ancient wisdom must be the ultimate aim of the Soul Quest.

HEALING WITH THE OCTAHEDRON (AIR)

As our Light work advances we may be involved in soul retrieval work (something I teach in my Blue Star Angels Mystery School). This means working with the octahedron, air and Michael to heal soul fragments (sending trapped souls back to the Light or retrieving our own lost fragments). To do this we should place ourselves inside an octahedron of crystal. The bottom of the octahedron is the entry point and the uppermost point the exit to Light. If we invoke Michael and ask for his protection, we can use the power of the higher heart to free trapped earthly souls/soul fragments and use Breath of Life to send them through the uppermost point through the void and back to the Light. Using sacred breathing we can also take the important spiritual step of retrieving our own lost fragments to aid us to reach wholeness within soul.

HEALING WITH THE ICOSAHEDRON (WATER)

Again linked to more advanced Light work and Mystery School teachings, is the icosahedron and its connection with water and Water of Life. We can work with this solid in various ways. We can visualise ourselves within an icosahedron of crystal and then ask Gabriel, Phuel and Haniel to help us create the grail within our own higher heart, surrounding and nurturing the flower within it. Love causes Water of Life to flow into the grail, and we can heal this water through the power of our own higher heart (us as Microcosm) and then send it out to all the waters of Mother Earth and sentient life (Microcosm to Macrocosm). As this returns to us (Macrocosm to Microcosm) it heals us, for we are 80% water). Then we can will and intend to aid Water of Life and heart healing on a Macrocosmic universal scale.

HEALING WITH THE DODECAHEDRON OF SPIRIT

The most advanced solid of all is the dodecahedron: Platonic solid of Spirit. This is Seraphiel's own geometry, and if you pursue your Soul Quest you may well reach the point where you wish to work with this ultimate sacred geometry shape. If you add star points to each of the twelve faces (one for each colour of Creation), it becomes a stellated dodecahedron – Seraphiel's 12-point diamond star. This has an invisible 13th central point (blue star sapphire/saf-fire) connected with earth's origins and the restoration of the Adam Kadmon perfect (divine) human form; this is key to the Seraphim Light redemption programme towards earth Ascension.

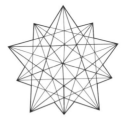

The Malachim Angel Alphabet

Haniel, Ruler of Friday and Venus, says:

Within the Wheel of Divine Connection is my rose Mirror of Grace; this offers you my unconditional Love to further your Heart and Soul quests. Learn to look in this mirror to see and appreciate your own true beauty, for when you can do this you will be less judgemental and more compassionate towards self as well as others – a key step in opening your higher heart chakra and attaining grace.

According to ancient wisdom certain ancient alphabets in their original format contained letters formed from the power of Light itself; thus they were food for the soul, deepening Divine Connection. Angelic alphabets also hold unconditional Love to heal and nourish the heart. I am guided that true Light languages come from Source via Seraphiel's diamond ray, through the 44:44 Angel Star Gate to the Sacred Eden Tree of Metatron and Shekinah, where if we can access them they aid both Heart and Soul quests as they lift us towards Oneness with All.

The Malachim Alphabet is associated with the Virtues order of angels (whose chief is Haniel), who confer grace on deserving people, as well as aiding healing and balance within heart and soul. Apart from learning to see the beauty of self and to be fully comfortable with this Divine Truth, Haniel's mirror offers an angelic focus on your priority to progress on your Heart and Soul quests. Whilst meditating on your message you can ask the mirror to reflect back to you the best way of acting on this message to self-heal, and/or find harmony and balance.

The angels invite you to look at the chart of Angelic Light letters opposite. To identify your message you can dowse over each of the 22 Light letters in turn or, alternatively, intuitively choose the letter that seems to draw you most. Focus on your Light letter for 30 seconds, then turn to the next pages to find your angelic message.

The 22 Light letters of the Wheel of Divine Connection

Below you will find the message relating to your chosen letter; this indicates what the angels feel is your priority to enable you to reach the next level of harmony and balance in self and/or life. Read the message three times, then close your eyes, and with the eye of the heart try to visualise your Light letter within the rosy radiance of Haniel's mirror. Ask to be guided on how to follow your message, ensuring you allow enough time to fully absorb and process its implications. Remember, you can work with Haniel for as long as necessary, until you feel ready for your next Angelic Light message.

Aleph: key words: guidance, learn, begin, multiply.

It is time for both an ending and a beginning. Seek a counsellor whom you trust; there is something new you must learn in order to advise others. The angels say you need gentle and wise counsel to find this out and work with it, but when you do it will multiply and benefit many people.

Beth: key words: home, prison, temple, respect.

The angels guide your focus towards home and family, asking you to ensure that this is a sacred and loving space, not somewhere that confines your talents such as a prison of your own making. As with home, so also with your own body – the angels tell you to make a temple of both body and home.

Gamel: key words: action, correction, balance, meditation.

Consider carefully your life vis-à-vis the Eight Roads to Heaven: rightness of beliefs, thoughts, speech, lifestyle, exertions, actions, meditations, Divine Connection, taking any necessary corrective action. If you feel comfortable and balanced with all eight, ask the angels to guide you further in meditation.

Daleth: key words: two halves, wholeness, gateway.

You have attained a degree of physical/spiritual balance; now you swim freely in the river of time. Seek balance, for soon you will be able to traverse the Star Gate to the unfallen Light, itself leading to the thirteenth zodiac sign (Delphinus, the Cetaceans), another gateway. Will you choose to go through the gates?

He: key words: exist, transform, become greater.

The angels say you are on a cliff edge of existence; you can either become less or infinitely more than you have ever been before. It is a time of huge potential for spiritual transformation that will inspire others if you take your next steps with angelic guidance, and remember – Love is the Key.

Vau: key words: hook, connection, positive focus.

You have already made excellent progress, but now you may feel that something is holding back your quest(s). The angels suggest you view things another way; turn negative into positive by seeing the hook as a connection to next steps instead of as an obstacle. With positive focus, all will come right.

Zayn: key words: fertility, re-birth, nurture, release.

The angels advise that the cycle of life you are in now holds all the potential you need for re-birth, either for physical self, life, spiritually or all three. Of course you cannot do this alone, nor without ability to focus, so make a choice, releasing what is necessary to enable your decisions and actions to start the new cycle.

Cheth: key words: Tree of Life, balance, Oneness with All.

The angels inform that this Light letter connects to the Tree of Life image, both in the Cabbala and as manifested in the Caduceus and Sacred Eden Tree. Work initially as guided with one or more of these systems to attain solar and lunar balance, as this is the first key to progressing your Heart and Soul Quests.

Theth: key words: foundation, Light, Below, Above.

As with the letter Cheth, this Light letter links you from All Below to All Above, suggesting that part of your path is to learn to work with the Sacred Eden Tree and 44:44 Star Gate, and to be able to channel the unfallen Light for the benefit of Mother Earth and all her sentient life forms.

Jod: key words: openness, power, true direction.

Look up, for your direction curves towards the sky, and the angels tell you the way is open for your Light empowerment to begin. Courage is needed to step into your personal power. When you use this with integrity and generosity to aid All, you will become a force to be reckoned with and a guide for many others.

Kaph: key words: bowl, abundance, surrender.

The angels liken you to a bowl that is tilted so not yet filled, but is almost ready for that step. Work on your beliefs and sense of security, for if you can only trust and surrender, when you choose to become the person you were designed to be the bowl will pivot and overflow with angelic blessings.

Lamed: key words: teacher, ancient wisdom, instruction.

You have been (in other lives) and will be again a spiritual teacher whom many will follow. The angels advise you to take immediate steps to retrieve your own ancient wisdom (choosing an energy healing skill that beckons), for many followers are out there awaiting your wise, firm and clear instruction.

Mem: key words: living water, inspiration, healing power of six.

The angels say that you are one who was 'borne upon the living waters'. This means that you can use water's healing ability to bring emotional calmness and balance. Work first on self-healing and then inspire others to develop their own healing skills, using the angelic numerology of six (linked to water).

Nun: key words: ankh of eternal life, Way of Love and Light.

The angels remind you of the ankh and its link with the Way of Love and Light. Love is infinite, Light is eternal; you hold both in heart and soul and are gifted to aid others towards this understanding. This will comfort and start many on their own journey of discovery towards physical and spiritual harmony.

Tau: key words: grief, desire, compassion, peace.

You have faced challenges involving desire and/or grief that you are still overcoming. The angels offer infinite compassion and advise that a new dawn is approaching, whereupon you can let go of sadness and move back from darkness into Light; this will herald a new peaceful phase in your life.

Schin: key words: summit, goal, discern, attain.

The angels advise discernment in your dealings with others, right now, for soon you can reach the summit of your aspirations. This represents something you have sought to attain for a long time. Verify your goal carefully, involving both head and heart, however, for in reality it is but one step ahead on the Way.

Samech: key words: hold firm, steadfast, sustain.

The angels praise your ability to stand fast and be a rock for others. This is one of your roles in this life path and you do it very well. They also ask you to make time to ensure that you also nourish and sustain your own need for spiritual development; your foundations are secure, so keep building up from there.

Ayn: key words: eye of wisdom, testify, pay heed.

In the heart of your heart you have much knowledge, but you feel daunted by taking the step of testifying to others about ancient wisdom. Seek angelic help to build up confidence in your own considerable ability, and make plans to start to pass on your knowledge in some way to others, for many need it.

Peh: key words: four corners, direction, oratory.

Tsadey: key words: loving intention, design, truth.

The angels tell you that when you speak others will listen, for you hold the important power of oratory that benefits others. It is time to develop this power further, so you should seek training in presentation and be prepared to travel, for you may be needed to take this message to the four corners of the earth.

The angels advise that in your heart resides the potential for power and truth, but that first you need healing. Work with green and then pink rays to heal and open the higher heart flower. It is time for you to move and progress on Soul Quest and for your loving intention to guide others to find the Way of Love and Light.

Qoph: key words: laws, right action, balance, harmony.

Resh: key words: foundation stone, build, retrieve.

Whatever you are considering at this time, the angels request you to pause and ensure that you weigh cause and effect, the consequences upon others. Act only in accordance with the spiritual laws – do as you would be done by – and only if your heart says the result of your action will be greater harmony and balance.

The foundation stone is the key to progress. The angels confirm that you have all in place to build something new and wonderful in your life. Do not be deterred in your dream; if it feels right in your heart then it is right, and you should go for it. There may be setbacks along the way, but stay focused to realise your dream.

A-Z of angels and their guardianships

This A-Z lists key life-assisting attributes/issues with their designated ruling angels, as well as the rulers of weekdays, seasons, elements, zodiac signs and Quinary star divisions. Following many requests, although not a Hebrew speaker I have included (in brackets) a general guide to pronunciation.

A

Abundance: Zadkiel (Zad-kee-el)

Abundance of nature: Lecabel (Leck-ah-bel)

Abundance of summer, Breath of Life: Tubiel (Too-bee-el)

Abundance with growing crops/plants: Cahethel (Ka-heth-el), Habuiah (Hab-oo-yah)

Acceptance, graceful: Ananchel (An-an-kel)

Air element (Breath of Life): Ariel (A-ree-el)

Ambition/aspirations, new: Gabriel (Gab-ree-el)

Animals (tame): Hariel (Har-ee-el)

Animals (wild): Thuriel (Thoo-ree-el)

Anger management: Phaleg (Far-leg)

Aquarius zodiac sign: Cambiel (Kam-bee-el)

Aries zodiac sign: Machidiel (Mak-id-ee-el)

Artistic inspiration, general: Radueriel (Rad-oo-airy-el)

Autumn: Torquaret (Tork-ah-rett)

Awareness, general and/or spiritual: Zephon (Zeff-on)

B

Beauty, within self and general appre-ciation of: Haniel (Han-ee-el)

Beauty, general, awareness/appreciation of: Zephon (Zeff-on)

Birds (tame): Tubiel (Too-bee-el)

Birds (wild): Anpiel (An-pee-el)

Blue Star, Angel of the: Sanusemi (San-oo-sem-ee)

Broken heart, healing of: Mupiel (Moo-pee-el)

C

Calculating, managing risks: Barakiel (Bar-ak-ee-el)

Calming, soothing emotions: Phuel (Foo-el)

Cancer zodiac sign: Muriel (Moo-ree-el)

Capricorn zodiac sign: Nadiel (Nad-ee-el)

Celestial secrets, studying/retrieval of: Raziel (Raz-ee-el)

Central Sun of All Central Suns (Sacred Heart of The Creator): Mazuriel (Maz-oo-ree-el)

Change of direction, job, house etc:
Nadiel (Nad-ee-el)

Choices, finding door to Light: Tabris
(Tab-reez)

Clarifying issues/life/goals: Ramiel
(Ram-ee-el)

Cleansing life to start over in autumn:
Torquaret (Tork-ah-rett)

Climax of a matter/project, to reach:
Amnediel (Am-ned-ee-el)

Closure on a matter/project, to
obtain: Geliel (Gel-ee-el)

Colours: Hahlii (Hah-lee-eye)

Comfort and compassion: Rachmiel
(Rak-mee-el) or Cassiel (Kass-ee-el)

Communication (written): Dabriel
(Dab-ree-el)

Communication (verbal): Michael
(Mik-ay-el)

Compassionate love and care (of less
fortunate): Rachmiel (Rak-mee-el),

Creativity, artistic: Radueriel
(Rad-oo-airy-el)

Creativity, general and innovative:
Uriel (Oor-ee-el)

Crystal power and alchemy: Och (Ok)

Confidence in leadership: Verchiel
(Ver-kee-el)

Cosmic Spirit/Angelic Light:
Seraphiel (Ser-af-ee-el)

Courage and self-confidence: Camael
(Kam-ay-el)

D

Decisions, making timely: Zuriel
(Zoo-ree-el) and Raphael (Raf-ay-el)

De-cluttering, simplifying your life:
Tual (Too-al)

Deliverance from a certain situation:
Pedael (Ped-ay-el)

Destiny, true, seeking guidance: Oriel
(Oo-ree-el)

Diplomacy/tact: Haaiah (Hah-eye-ah)

Divine Connection: Metatron
(Met-at-ron)/Shekinah (Shek-ee-nah)

Divine justice: Camael (Kam-ay-el),
Asaliah (As-ali-yah) and Vasariah
(Vass-ah-ree-ah)

Door to Light, finding/choosing:
Tabris (Tab-reez)

Dreams, ambitions and hopes:
Gabriel (Gab-ree-el)

E

Earth element: Ariel (A-ree-el)

Emotional calm: Phuel (Foo-el)

Empowerment from security within:
Camael (Kam-ay-el)

Energy and wellbeing: Mumiah
(Moo-mee-ah)

Energy science, health, long life:
Raphael (Raf-ay-el) and Eiael
(Ee-ay-el)

Expansion of personal horizons,
inner/outer: Adnachiel
(Ad-nak-ee-el)

Exploration, inner and/or outer:
Elemiah (El-em-eye-ah)

F

Faith in self: Pistis Sophia
(Pis-tis Sof-ee-ah)

Faithfulness/fidelity/loyalty: Icabel
(Ik-ah-bel) and Mihael (Mih-ay-el)

Feminine balance in chakras: Gabriel
(Gab-ree-el)

Fertility (conception): Yusamin (Yoo-sam-een), Mebahiah (Meb-ah-yah)

Fertility of mind (new ideas): Yusamin (Yoo-sam-een) and Mihael (Mih-ay-el)

Financial affairs, managing: Vasariah (Vass-ah-ree-ah)

Finding lost things including divine self: Rochel (Rosh-el)

Fire element (Fire of Life): Uriel (Oo-ree-el)

Flower secrets: Achaiah (Ak-eye-ah) and Anahita (Ana-hee-tah)

Food/nourishment, physical/spiritual: Isda (Iz-dah)

Forgiving/atoning for something in the past: Phanuel (Fan-oo-el)

Free will/choices, seeking right ones: Tabris (Tab-reez)

Friday and Venus: Haniel (Han-ee-el)

Future harmony: Isiaiel (Iz-ay-el)

Future, guidance on: Ieiazel (Eye-az-el)

G

Gemini zodiac sign: Ambriel (Am-bree-el)

Gentleness/kindness: Lehachel (Leh-ack-el)

Goals in life, new and true: Machidiel (Mak-id-ee-el) or Gabriel (Gab-ree-el)

Going with the flow, finding right level: Haurvatat (Hoor-vat-at)

Good fortune: Gedael (Ged-ay-el)

Good luck (golden): Diniel (Din-ee-el) and Kadmiel (Kad-mee-el)

Good luck (silver): Aniel (An-ee-el) and Padiel (Pad-ee-el)

Golden healing protection: Diniel (Din-ee-el) and Kadmiel (Kad-mee-el)

Graceful acceptance in life, patience: Ananchel (An-an-kel)

H

Harmony and balance: Cassiel (Kass-ee-el), plus Raphael (Raf-ay-el): masculine balance. Gabriel (Gab-ree-el): feminine balance

Harmony and balance, mind/body/ spirit: Neithel (Neye-thel)

Healing, general: Raphael (Raf-ay-el)

Healing, sun for depression: Raphael (Raf-ay-el) and Savatri (Sav-at-ree)

Healing of plants/herbs: Anahita (Ana-hee-tah)

Healing the past, moving on: Phanuel (Fan-oo-el), and Camael (Kam-ay-el)

Health and wholeness, nutrition: Sofiel (Sof-ee-el), Isda (Iz-dah)

Health and longevity: Rehael (Reh-ay-el) Seehiah (See-hee-ah)

Heartbreak, overcoming: Mupiel (Moo-pee-el)

Heart's desire, true, pursuing: Pagiel (Pagg-ee-el)

Heavenly peace: Anafiel (Ana-fee-el)

Heavenly Mother of zodiac angels: Pistis Sophia (Pis-tis-Sof-ee-ah)

Hidden talents within self: Parasiel (Para-see-el)

Holding up, maintaining Heaven: Ataphiel (Ata-fee-el)

Home/work balance, correcting: Dokiel (Dok-ee-el)

Home/work relationships, improving: Hamaliel (Hama-lee-el)

Hopes/aspirations/ambition/dreams:
Gabriel (Gab-ree-el)
Hurts, washing away, cleansing:
Matriel (Mat-ree-el)

I
Ideas, new: Yusamin (Yoo-sam-een)
Inner feelings, voicing: Muriel
(Moo-ree-el)
Innovation and change: Uriel
(Oor-ee-el)
Insight, flash of: Zikiel (Zik-ee-el)
Inspiration, artistic: Radueriel
(Rad-oo-airy-e)l.
Inspiration, flash of: Zikiel (Zik-ee-el)
Inspiration, literary: Harahel
(Har-ah-el)
Inspiration, music: Tagas (Tag-az)
Inspiration, poetry: Israfel (Iz-raf-el)
Integrity: Zadkiel (Zad-kee-el)
Intuitive problem-solving: Ambriel
(Am-bree-el)
Intuitive skills, building: Cambiel
(Kam-bee-el) and Ofaniel
(Off-an-ee-el)
Invisibility, temporary: Gabriel
(Gab-ree-el)

J
Jobs/roles in life, finding right one:
Jofiel (Joff-ee-el)
Joy: Haniel (Han-ee-el) and Zadkiel
(Zad-kee-el)
Just causes: Camael (Kam-ay-el) and
Nememiah (Nem-emy-ah)

K
Key to Heavenly Peace, finding:
Anafiel (Ana-fee-el)

L
Leadership skills development:
Verchiel (Ver-kee-el)
Leo zodiac sign: Verchiel (Ver-kee-el)
Liberty and Light in civilisation:
Terathel (Ter-ath-el)
Libra zodiac sign: Zuriel (Zoo-ree-el)
Life partners, true, finding/keeping:
Shekinah (Shek-ee-nah)
Living your truth: Michael
(Mik-ay-el)
Lost things: Rochel (Rosh-el)
Love/self-confidence: Haniel
(Han-ee-el)
Love, power of, to solve problems:
Rikbiel (Rik-bee-el)
Love, sexuality: Rachiel (Rak-ee-el)
and Nathaniel (Nath-an-ee-el)
Loving kindness: Amabiel
(Amah-bee-el)
Loving relationships: Haniel
(Han-ee-el), Shekinah (Shek-ee-nah)
and Amabiel (Amah-bee-el)
Love, sending out unconditionally to
All: Amabiel (Amah-bee-el)
Loyalty/faithfulness: Icabel (Ik-ah-bel)

M
Magic of nature: Aratron (Ar-at-ron)
Managing/expanding time: Eth (Eth)
Masculine chakra balance: Raphael
(Raff-ay-el)
Metals, healing power of: Hagith
(Hag-ith)
Monday and moon: Gabriel
(Gab-ree-el)
Moon power: Gabriel (Gab-ree-el),
Cambiel (Kam-bee-el), Ofaniel

(Off-an-ee-el), Geniel (Gen-ee-el), Amnediel (Am-ned-ee-el), Adiel (Ad-ee-el), Geliel (Gel-ee-el)

Moons, two, earth's original Eyes of Heaven: Mirabiel (Mee-rah-bee-el)

Mountains, purity, majesty and peace: Rampel (Ram-pel)

Moving job/house/country: Nadiel (Nad-ee-el)

Music and harmony with All: Tagas (Tag-az)

N

Nature's bounty, appreciation of: Sofiel (Sof-ee-el)

Nature's secrets, flowers and oils: Achaiah (Ak-eye-ah)

Nature's magic/Circle of Life: Aratron (Ar-at-ron)

Nature's plants, aiding: Sachluph (Sak-luff)

New plans, birthing and growing in spring: Spugliguel (Spug-ligg-oo-el)

New projects (calculation of risks involved): Barakiel (Bar-ak-ee-el)

New projects commencement: Geniel (Gen-ee-el)

Non-judgemental love: Aniel (Ann-ee-el)

Nutrition: Isda (Iz-dah), Sofiel (Sof-ee-el)

O

Obedience, respect for elders: Mizrael (Miz-ray-el)

Opportunity for (summer) abundance: Tubiel (Too-bee-el)

Opportunity for recognising abundance, e.g. love, health, wealth,

success, self-development: Zadkiel (Zad-kee-el)

Opportunity for (spring) change: Spugliguel (Spug-ligg-oo-el)

Order: Sadriel (Sad-ree-el)

Overcoming trouble/obstacles/ misfortunes: Sitael (Sit-ay-el), Pistis Sophia (Pis-tis-Sof-ee-ah), Caliel (Ka-lee-el)

P

Passion, life and/or sexual: Nathaniel (Nath-an-ee-el)

Patience: Achaiah (Ak-ay-ah), Michael (Mik-ay-el), Rampel (Ram-pel)

Peace and protection from traumas: Iahhel (Ee-ah-hel)

Peace with nature: Sachluph (Sak-luff) and Zuphlas (Zoof-laz)

Personal beliefs, strengthening, upholding: Arad (Ar-ad)

Personal vision and expansion: Adnachiel (Ad-nak-ee-el)

Philosophy and wisdom: Hermes Trismegistos (Her-meez Triz-mej-istos) and Poiel (Po-yel)

Pisces zodiac sign: Barakiel (Bar-ak-ee-el)

Pitfalls, awareness of: Zephon (Zef-on)

Poetry, inspiration in: Israfel (Iz-raf-el)

Poetry, peace and solitude: Nilaihah (Nil-ay-hah)

Poetry, mystic: Nithaiah (Neeth-eye-ah)

Power of will and mind: Gazardiel (Gaz-ahd-ee-el)

Prayer, guidance from and power of: Sandalphon (San-dal-fon)

Problem-solving ability: Ambriel (Am-bree-el)

Problem-solving with power of love: Rikbiel (Rik-bee-el)

Prophecy: Isaiel (Iz-eye-el)

Protection, general: Michael (Mik-ay-el), or Hakamiah (Hak-am-eye-ah)

Protection of innocence: Mebahel (Meb-ah-el)

Protection of princes, world leaders: Iiehuiah (Eye-hu-yah)

Protector of Christianity: Hahael (Hah-ay-el)

Psychic awareness: Barakiel (Bar-ak-ee-el)

Psychic/spiritual development: Aratron (Ar-at-ron) or Ariel (A-ree-el)

Q
Quiet reflection/finding inner still point: Duma (Doo-mah)

R
Rainbows, power of colours: Hahlii (Hah-lee-eye)

Rainbows, healing with: Melchisadec (Mel-kee-zad-ek) or Raphael (Raf-ay-el)

Reaching for the sky physically or spiritually: Sahaqiel (Sah-hak-ee-el)

Re-birth, recuperation and winter preparation for: Farlas (Far-laz)

Re-launching your future: Spugliguel (Spug-ligg-oo-el)

Reprogramming life template: Pistis Sophia (Pis-tis-Sof-ee-ah)

Rest and re-birth preparation in winter: Farlas (Far-laz)

Retrieving spiritual knowledge/ learning: Lauviah (La-oo-vee-ah)

Revealing hidden mysteries: Hahaiah (Hah-eye-ah)

Right job or role in life, recognising: Jofiel (Jof-fee-el)

Rising sun, a new dawn: Vehuiah (Vehoo-yah)

Rivers, clarity, going with the flow: Haurvatat (Hoor-vat-at)

S
Sagittarius zodiac sign: Adnachiel (Ad-nak-ee-el)

Saturday/Saturn: Cassiel (Kass-ee-el)

Science and mysticism: Nanael (Nan-ay-el)

Scorpio zodiac sign: Barakiel (Bar-ak-ee-el)

Sea mammals, dolphins and whales (also ancient Lemurian wisdom-keepers): Manakel (Man-ak-el)

Secret wisdom and alchemy: Raziel (Raz-ee-el) and Hermes Trismegistos (Her-meez Triz-mej-istos)

Seeking self, freeing heart within: Salathiel (Sal-ath-ee-el)

Seeking truth: Haamiah (Hah-mee-yah)

Self-belief: Arad (Ar-ad), Haniel (Han-ee-el), Pistis Sophia (Pis-tis-Sof-ee-ah)

Sensitivity, protection: Barakiel (Bar-ak-ee-el)

Serenity, re-finding: Cassiel (Kass-ee-el)

Sexuality: Nathaniel (Nath-an-ee-el) and Rachiel (Rak-ee-el)

Ships/water craft: Damabiah (Dam-ah-byah)

Silent reflection: Duma (Doo-mah)

Silver protection, invisibility: Aniel (An-ee-el) and Padiel (Pad-ee-el)

Simplifying, de-cluttering life: Tual (Too-al)

Sky is not the limit spiritually: Sahaqiel (Sa-hak-ee-el)

Sky, secrets of seasons and nature's geometry: Sahaqiel (Sah-hak-ee-el)

Soul path of higher self: Mehekiel (Meh-ecky-el)

Source (healing with crystalline diamond ray): Seraphiel (Ser-af-ee-el)

Speaking your truth: Michael (Mik-ay-el)

Spiritual abundance: Ihiazel (Ih-yah-zel)

Spiritual awareness, raising: Leviah (Lev-ee-ah)

Spiritual connection: Metatron (Met-at-ron) and Shekinah (Shek-ee-nah)

Spiritual development: Chavakiah (Kav-ack-yah), Mahasiah (Ma-ha-see-ah)

Spiritual development, higher self: Aladiah (Al-ad-ee-ah)

Spiritual direction: Haiaiel (Hah-ee-eye-el)

Spiritual eloquence: Imriel (Im-ree-el)

Spiritual fulfilment: Melchisadec (Mel-kee-zad-ek)

Spiritual growth, abundance of: Keveqel (Kev-eck-el), Mikiel (Mik-ee-el)

Spiritual harmony: Ielael (Eye-lay-el)

Spiritual opportunity: Hahuiah (Hah-oo-yah)

Spiritual pathways: Melahel (Mel-ah-hel)

Spiritual peace/calmness: Vevaliah (Vev-aly-ah)

Spiritual perception: Raguel (Rag-oo-el)

Spiritual and physical harmony: Monadiel (Moe-nad-yel), Meniel (Many-el) and Vehuel (Veh-oo-el)

Spiritual/psychic development: Ariel (A-ree-el), and Melchisadec (Mel-kee-zad-ek)

Spiritual stamina: Keliel (Kell-ee-el)

Spiritual truth: Reyiel (Ray-ee-el), Raguel (Rag-oo-el)

Spiritual vision: Haziel (Haz-ee-el)

Spiritual wellbeing: Annauel (Ann-ow-el)

Spiritual wisdom: Ibamiah (Ib-am-yah), Zadkiel (Zad-kee-el), Hermes Trismegistos (Her-meez Triz-mej-istos)

Spring: Spugliguel (Spug-ligg-oo-el)

Star Angels of Creation, Ruler: Seraphiel (Ser-af-ee-el)

Stars, astronomy/astrology: Umabiel (Oo-mahby-el)

Strength: Michael (Mik-ay-el) or Zeruch (Zer-ook)

Summer: Tubiel (Too-bee-el)

Sun/Sunday: Raphael (Raf-ay-el)

Sun, power of for healing: Raphael (Raf-ay-el)

T

Taking stock, reckoning, in autumn:
  Torquaret (Tork-ah-rett)
Taurus zodiac sign: Tual (Too-al)
Thursday/Jupiter: Zadkiel (Zad-kee-el)
Time: Eth (Eth)
Tranquillity and calmness within:
  Phuel (Foo-el)
Transformation of self or life: Uriel
  (Oor-ee-el)
Treasure, hidden within self: Parasiel
  (Para-see-el)
Trees, peacefulness and wisdom:
  Zuphlas (Zoof-laz)
True loving kindness: Amabiel
  (Am-ah-bee-el)
True self, finding: Ithuriel
  (Ith-oo-ree-el)
Truth, personal and absolute:
  Michael (Mik-ay-el)
Tuesday/Mars: Camael (Kam-ay-el)

U

Universal unconditional love,
  guiding: Pahaliah (Pah-ahl-ee-ah)

V

Virgo zodiac sign: Hamaliel
  (Hama-lee-el)
Vision, developing and realising:
  Adnachiel (Ad-nak-ee-el)
Voicing inner feelings: Muriel
  (Moo-ree-el)

W

Washing away hurts, cleansing:
  Matriel (Mat-ree-el), Phuel (Foo-el)
Water element (Water of Life):
  (Foo-el)

Wednesday/Mercury: Michael
  (Mik-ay-el)
Wellbeing/energy: Mumiah
  (Moo-mee-ah)
Wholeness/health/nutrition: Sofiel
  (Sof-ee-el)
Wild animals and birds, messages
  from: Thuriel (Thoo-ree-el) and
  Anpiel (An-pee-el)
Willpower, strengthening: Gazardiel
  (Gaz-ah-dee-el), or Raphael
  (Raf-ay-el)
Winds of change and healing: Ruhiel
  (Roo-hee-el)
Winding down situations: Adiel
  (Ad-ee-el)
Winter: Farlas (Far-laz)
Wisdom, just decisions: Ielahiah
  (Eye-lah-yah)
Wisdom, retrieval of: Zadkiel
  (Zad-kee-el), and Hermes
    Trismegistos (Her-meez
    Triz-mej-istos)
Wisdom, Lemurian: Manakel
  (Man-ak-el)
Work/home balance, improving:
  Dokiel (Dok-ee-el)
Work/home relationships, improving:
  Hamaliel (Hama-lee-el)
Worries, letting go of: Iadiel
  (Ee-ah-dee-el)

Index

Author's acknowledgements

A huge debt of thanks is owed, as ever, to many. To my wonderful family, as well as some dear friends, who always give sterling support during these deep and consuming book and card projects. Also, sincere thanks to my publishers; I'd particularly like to mention my editor Anne Furniss and my artist Richard Rockwood, the other two invaluable components of our very own Rule of Three, who help me make it all unfold as it should. Thanks also to Claire Peters and Nicola Davidson for taking a collection of such diverse subject matter and making it into a beautiful book. My gratitude to Chas Cronk for his inspiring music on the CD. And finally, most of all, heartfelt appreciation to the angels who are always there for me – indeed, if we can but know it, for all of us!

This paperback edition first published in 2010 by
Quadrille Publishing Limited
Alhambra House
27–31 Charing Cross Road
London WC2H OLS
www.quadrille.co.uk

Project editor: Anne Furniss
Design: Claire Peters, Nicola Davidson
Production: Marina Asenjo, Vincent Smith

British Library Cataloguing Publication Data
A catalogue record for this book is available from the British Library.

ISBN: 978 184400 830 8

Printed and bound in China
10 9 8 7 6 5 4 3 2 1